THE ESSENTIAL ~ TO

Fly-Fishing

Clive Schaupmeyer

Blue Ribbon Books

JOHNSON GORMAN PUBLISHERS

The Publishers
Johnson Gorman Publishers
Red Deer Alberta Canada

Credits
Cover design by Boldface Technologies.
Text design by Full Court Press.
Arctic grayling photo, color insert, by Bruce Masterman.
Mountain whitefish photo, color insert, by Vic Bergman.
Northern Pike photo, color insert and back cover, by Kiyoshi Kimura.
Printed and bound in Canada by Friesens for Johnson Gorman
    Publishers.

Acknowledgments
Financial support provided by the Alberta Foundation for the Arts, a beneficiary of the Lottery Fund of the Government of Alberta.

COMMITTED TO THE DEVELOPMENT OF CULTURE AND THE ARTS

Canadian Cataloguing in Publication
Schaupmeyer, Clive, 1947–
The essential guide to fly-fishing
ISBN 0-921835-36-1
1. Fly fishing. I. Title. II. Series.
SH456.S38   1997   799.1'24   C97-910754-7

5 4 3 2

For Willie, Evan and Mike

Special thanks to Dad for my first fishing outfit when I was ten; to my brother, Gary, for showing me how to fly cast and how to fly-fish effectively; and to John for being a great fly-fishing partner and friend.

Author's Acknowledgments

Thanks to the many people who helped with this book. Kiyoshi Kimura developed and printed the black and white photographs. Kiyoshi also took the pictures of me holding pike. Thanks, KK, you were a huge help.

Art Kruger allowed me to take his picture many times. That's Art on the front cover. He also read an early manuscript, as did Shelley Barkley and Nigel Seymour. Shelley also proofread a late-edition manuscript. The Russell boys—Reg, Lorne and Kent—all pitched in. Reg reviewed an early manuscript; Kent and Lorne allowed me to take their photos and tied at least one fly for pictures.

Troy Folk, my brother, Gary, Mike Materi, Cal and Lee Murphy, Ron Secretan, John Tunstall, Greg Walton, Scott Woods and Ken Zorn all allowed me to take photographs of them, which sometimes interfered with their fishing.

Bruce Masterman urged me to "get on with it." I bothered Vic Bergman countless times. Bruce and Vic each lent me pictures of fish.

My wife, Willie, read everything twice and remained patient while I let household chores slide. Thanks, Will.

Dennis Johnson of Johnson Gorman Publishers believed this book would help new fly anglers. He spent many sleepless nights completing the final stages of the book.

Thanks to all of you, and if I missed anyone I apologize.

–Clive Schaupmeyer
June, 1997

Contents

Foreword

Award-winning and fellow Outdoor Writer of Canada member Clive Schaupmeyer has penned an attractive, compelling and practical guide for fly-fishers.

Best summarized as a full creel of clear and sensible ideas, supported by excellent line drawings and photographs, *The Essential Guide to Fly-Fishing* is one of the more functional guides for the freshwater fly-fisher to be published in some time. Destined to be one of the classics of in freshwater fly-fishing literature, it is full of practical tips for both the beginner and the experienced fly-angler.

Throughout the book it is obvious that Clive Schaupmeyer loves fly-fishing, the skills of fly-fishing and the freshwater environments that fish inhabit. He is quick to point out that "Fly-fishing will provide enjoyment for the rest of your life whether you are seven or seventy. Novice or expert, you are fortunate to be looking toward years of discovery and fascination. Get on with it and have some fun."

Those of us who are experienced fly-fishers fully agree with him. *The Essential Guide to Fly-Fishing* is a practical manual which details clearly what is needed to be a successful freshwater fly-fisher. Without doubt this functional and attractive book is a must for every fly-angler's library.

–BARRY M. THORNTON, fly-fishing columnist and author of *Saltwater Fly Fishing for Pacific Salmon; Steelhead: The Supreme Trophy Trout; Steelhead;* and *Salgair: A Steelhead Odyssey*

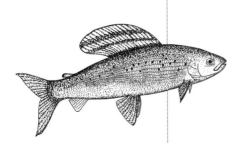

Chapter 1

An Introduction to Fly-Fishing

You are going to start fly-fishing.

For a while now you've daydreamed about standing in a clear stream, holding a willowy rod and casting a colorful flowing line to rising trout. The line gracefully waves back and forth in the fading spring daylight. . . .

In your dream you are not sure why the trout are rising and what they are rising for. You imagine tying on a fly. You are not sure what the fly is supposed to represent, but you've casually noticed all of those bins of colorful flies down at the local sports store when you've gone in to buy sneakers or spinnerbaits.

You are not certain exactly why you are becoming a fly-angler, but it seems neat. Maybe you saw *the* movie a few years ago—*A River Runs Through It.* Again last week you saw a fly-fishing show on television, and by God it is pretty to watch.

Perhaps some of your friends or colleagues fly-fish and you've heard them talk about it. Or they've asked you to come along next summer.

It's fishing. It looks enticing. And it's in the great outdoors.

Fly-fishing also has a faint sparkle of mysticism about it—mildly eccentric folks in funny hats and vests wading in pristine mountain streams performing fly-fishing rituals.

A typical western trout stream. Scenes like this are part of what fly-fishing is all about.

And if you've overheard some of them, well, they speak a different language. But you've also watched folks from town in T-shirts and ball caps fly-fishing at a local pond. They often catch trout with more regularity than the lawn chair crowd and they are anything but eccentric. You think there must be some middle ground in the sport of fly-fishing that fits you—a conservative person mildly interested in being just off-center and doing something not everyone else does. Fly-fishing.

You are embarking on a most interesting learning process. A process that with the right start, with the right equipment and the right instruction will provide enjoyment for the rest of your life—whether you're seven or seventy.

Our objectives

Whatever your motives you want to take up the sport with a maximum of pleasure and a minimum of frustration, and without wasting time and money.

The objectives of this book are to help you do this by telling you about what equipment you'll need and how to get started, and by helping you develop the basic skills needed by a fly-angler.

As someone developing your fly-fishing skills you will:

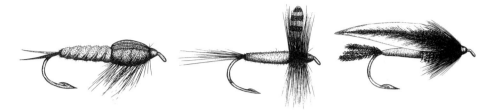

1. Learn about what you'll need to buy;
2. Assemble a fly-fishing outfit and necessary supplies;
3. Learn the basic overhead cast;
4. Learn about line control;
5. Learn what fish eat and how to imitate fish food with flies;
6. Learn about fish, where they live and about their senses;
7. Learn how to fish with dry flies, nymphs and streamers.

These are not so much distinct steps as they are interwoven parts of a never-ending process. The first three items are simply not well separated. And, although the phases are listed in an order, there is lots of shifting back and forth—you learn a bit here, buy new equipment there, learn and develop more. And so on, all the while having fun.

Left: A wet fly, like this nymph, imitates aquatic insects that spend part of their lives in the water.

Center: A dry fly imitates insects on the water's surface.

Right: A streamer imitates minnows and other aquatic creatures eaten by fish.

What is fly-fishing?

Fly-fishing is the use of a fly rod, fly line and fly reel to cast artificial flies that float (dry flies) or flies that sink (wet flies). These flies imitate things trout and other fish eat including aquatic and terrestrial insects, minnows, leeches and other critters that live in or around water.

We could argue the definition of fly-fishing forever. Some do. Clearly, casting dry flies to rising trout is fly-fishing. But casting gaudy 6-inch streamers with a heavy fly rod to catch powerful pike is also fly-fishing. And it counts if you cast showy popper flies to bass lurking in the weedy shallows of a man-made pond late at night when normal people have gone home. Using a spinning rod with flies is not fly-fishing. As long as you're using a fly rod loaded with a fly line and some type of artificial fly then you're fly-fishing.

There are records of ancient people catching fish with lures made with feathers and fur. However, in official circles fly-fishing is considered to have started over 400 years ago in England—at least that's when and where people started writing about fly-fishing and describing flies. Back then, and through to the mid-1800s, the flies used were usually wet flies; that is, they sank.

Dry-fly fishing became popular in England in the 1800s, where it became so fashionable with some dry-fly purists that they considered any other form of fishing to be barbaric. But common sense prevailed, and today effective fly-anglers use both dry flies and wet flies to catch trout and many other freshwater and saltwater gamefish. There are still a few anglers in England and North America who insist that anything other than dry-fly fishing is a perversion. Perhaps they fish alone and they deserve it. Sure, most of us love to cast dry flies to rising trout during the choice insect hatches throughout North America. Watching a trout come up for a dry fly—perhaps one you tied yourself—is pure delight. But on many flowing waters in North America, and especially where I live in Alberta, sticking to dry flies is simply not practical all the time. We fish a variety of flies in a variety of waters and have a hell of a lot more fun for it.

Experts estimate that at least 90 percent of a trout's diet consists of subsurface aquatic insect larvae and pupae. This makes sense. An individual mayfly, for example, is available as underwater trout food for several months before it emerges on the water's surface, where it can be eaten.

So, often when we're fly-fishing, the trout are eating insects below the surface, and we use subsurface wet flies like nymphs and streamers. Other freshwater gamefish like pike also eat the vast majority of their food under the surface. So that's where we fish.

Our quarry

This book is primarily about fly-fishing for trout in freshwater streams and rivers—the ultimate fly-fishing experience. But since many of us also fish in natural and man-made lakes for trout and other freshwater species, we won't neglect techniques for stillwater fly-fishing. Gamefish other than trout are fun to catch, and the places they inhabit are often closer to home than trout streams.

Among the freshwater gamefish we chase with fly rods are coldwater fish like the several species of trout, grayling, mountain whitefish, pike and yellow perch, the northern version of panfish. Fly-anglers also pursue warmwater species such as largemouth bass, smallmouth bass and other members of the sunfish family including bluegills, crappies and small sunfish.

Why fly-fish?

No doubt there are times and places where other fishing techniques are more productive than fly-fishing, but it is perhaps the most effective way to catch trout and other fish under a wide range of conditions. The handmade or store-bought flies we use are effective imitations of fish food, or they are gaudy enough to induce fish to strike. What makes fly-fishing so effective, and what makes it stand out from "hardware" fishing, is its versatility. On a stream or pond you can start the day by casting large streamers, which imitate baitfish, through deep fish-holding pools. If fish start eating insects on the surface—rising—you can tie on floating dry-fly imitations of whatever insect is making the fish look up.

It's this wide variety of opportunities that attracts many of us to fly-fishing and keeps us at it. I caught an Atlantic Salmon on the Miramichi River on a Bomber fly in 1992. Also in 1992, and again in 1993, my brother, Gary, and I waded in rough-and-tumble narrows between lakes in the Northwest Territories and landed one grayling after another while watching hundreds of barren

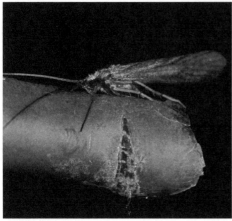 

Left: An adult caddisfly.

Right: A dry fly used to imitate it.

ground caribou cross 100 yards away. Several local fly-anglers and I fly-fish for pike 15 minutes from our small-town prairie homes.

One June afternoon in 1996 in northern Alberta, Don Lamont from Winnipeg and I caught line-hauling 5- to 10-pound pike on big streamers for three hours—nonstop. My right wrist ached. I've fly-fished in the River Tuul in Mongolia for lenok, an Asian member of the trout family. Didn't catch any, but I wouldn't have tried if I wasn't a possessed fly-fisherman who hauled a four-piece fly rod, a reel and one small box of flies halfway around the world. The encyclopedia said there were troutlike fish in northern Mongolia. Who could blame me?

Mostly, I fly-fish for trout in many streams and rivers throughout my home province of Alberta. I've caught 5-inch cutthroats and brookies in creeks and beaver ponds, 4- to 5-pound rainbows in big water like the Bow River and 4-plus-pound browns in one of Alberta's spring creeks. And, of course, I sometimes fish nearby trout ponds for rainbows and local reservoirs for northern pike.

And you should see my wish list. I've been at the sport for over two decades and my enthusiasm is still growing. That's variety for you. I'm hooked.

Many of us tie our own flies, an added dimension to this already varied sport. Fly tying is entertaining, and for those of us

afflicted with a condition called winter, it's a great way to spend cold Saturday nights. It's an aspect the beginner may want to pursue after developing some fly-fishing skills, although the economics of fly tying are highly questionable. You can start tying flies for, say, $200, and that seems to offer the prospect of saving you a lot of cash at one or two bucks each for commercial flies. But the cost of supplies and neat doodads that accumulate over the years adds up to more than the few dozen flies you're likely to use each season.

The best part of fly tying is the added satisfaction of catching fish on your own flies, especially those of your own design. The most satisfying flies are those tied late at night in camp to imitate an insect that the fish were eating today and that you weren't prepared for. There's no similar pattern in your fly books or in your fly boxes, but you paid close attention to the size and color of this unfamiliar insect. Perhaps you collected a specimen or two. So you whip up a few imitations, and the next evening the

Trout are a favorite quarry of fly-anglers throughout North America.

insects hatch again. And you catch fish on these imitations that you created to look like one of God's own creatures. Cool.

If your interest develops, the best advice I can offer is take an introductory course on fly tying. Of the many aspects of fly-fishing it's the one for which you must have some personal instruction. The instructional tying books are great after you have learned a few basic skills. And fly-tying videos are a boon to the novice but still don't replace personal instruction to get you started.

If all of these great dimensions of fly-fishing still aren't enough to provoke your interest, then consider the many memorable moments spent with young fly-anglers. Perhaps you are a parent with a couple of kids who want to learn to fish. Fly-fishing is the perfect parent–child recreation because it involves more that putting a worm on a hook and sitting in a lawn chair. It requires an understanding of water and insects and feeding habits of fish. With a little help kids who can barely cast a fly line will somehow manage to catch a few rainbow trout in a lake, cutthroats in a high-mountain stream or panfish in a local pond. You both will learn, catch some fish and have some great fun.

Fly-fishing is also a wonderful lifelong learning experience. I don't know about you, but I get more pleasure out of learning about water ecology, fish and aquatic insects than, say, baseball or basketball statistics.

Getting Started

A novice starts fly-fishing by learning about casting, about trout and other fish, about rivers, insects and water ecology, and, of course, by acquiring fly-fishing equipment. I've been at the sport for years and I'm still doing all of these—including buying stuff—so I guess that makes me a novice. If you're just starting, you are fortunate to be looking toward years of discovery and fascination. The buying part is up to you. You don't have to accumulate a mountain of gear.

Don't be in a rush to buy your first fly-fishing outfit. It's a

Join a club or take fly-fishing lessons to learn about the many aspects of fly-fishing.

good idea to know what you need before spending a pile on the "wrong" stuff. Read this book, talk to the folks at a local fly shop and take an introductory course on fly-fishing before blowing a few dozen or a few hundred dollars on gear. But don't delay buying equipment for too long, as you might as well get some on-water practice while you're picking up the basics. I read somewhere that beginners should master casting before buying their own equipment. Yes, you need to learn some basics of casting and fly-fishing before you spend the big bucks. But really, mastering casting first? Get on with it and have some fun.

No amount of reading will turn the novice into an expert fly-angler. You will need the help of others, and you will need experience on the water. Most specialty fly-fishing stores offer courses

Staff at specialty fly shops offer professional advice on equipment, flies and local fly-fishing. Many offer casting and fly-tying classes, on-stream instruction and guiding services. Fly shops are the best source of information about fly selection for local waters.

on fly casting and fly-fishing. Some local further education councils or college extension departments offer courses by experienced fly-anglers. Introductory courses usually cover equipment, casting techniques, line control, understanding feeding habits of trout and other fish, and reading water.

Beginners may find the help of experienced fly-fishers to be useful, but ask for help from more than one person. A second opinion is always useful.

Fly-fishing equipment

Fly-fishing equipment can be cheap. It can also be very expensive. Both can cost you in different ways. Inexpensive fly gear can cost you a lifetime of fishing enjoyment. Cheap gear is not easy to cast and may break or wear out sooner than you'd expect. Don't miss out on a full life of fly-fishing because of poor equipment that frustrates you enough to quit after a few trips. Expensive gear can also cost you. I heard secondhand about a fellow who walked into a sports store and came out with an excellent $800 fly rig. Unfortunately, it was a heavy steelhead outfit, and he was going fishing for rainbow trout in a small river. Make your needs clearly known to the sales staff of a good specialty fly shop.

Select a fly-fishing rig that is right for you, your budget and for the principal type of fishing you plan to do at the start. As you expand your fishing interests, you'll likely want another outfit or two. The novice should buy the best equipment he or she can afford, but the first fly-fishing outfit doesn't have to cost a small fortune. And even if you have the money, don't spend a fortune on the wrong gear.

Fly casting

Casting a fly line is easy. But without basic instruction many novices fail to overcome common mistakes and quit. After you read this book I would hope that you could pick up a fly rod and make a basic overhead cast. But casting is too involved to be learned from a book, and the novice is again urged to sign up for a fly-casting course from a reputable fly-fishing speciality shop, a local fly-fishing club or further education group.

Whatever you do, don't go fly-fishing before you can cast 30 feet or so with some accuracy. Of course, on-stream practice is essential, but you'll find other things to distract you when you're on the water—like should you use a 3x or 4x tippet? And would it be better to cast upstream, across stream or downstream? It might be frustrating for you to see a 16-inch rainbow rising 20 feet in front and not be able to cast to it. This experience will urge you to improve your basic skills in a hurry.

Fly-fishing lingo

Like most recreations, fly-fishing is teeming with jargon. Can you decipher the following? *After tying on a #18 midge emerger to a 5x tippet with a clinch knot, cast it to the head of the riffle and mend the line as necessary to prevent drag.* For the novice, fishing jargon like this can be bewildering.

Many years ago, when I started to get serious about fly-fishing, I read an article in which the author said something about "mending" the line. I had no idea what mending the line was. I didn't know it was broken. (Later I learned that when the fly is in or on the water, the line between the rod tip and fly is tossed upstream to prevent a bow from forming and the fly from dragging. That's mending.) You can catch fish without knowing all of the lingo and technical terms, but some knowledge will help you understand what you see, hear and read.

I've tried to write with as little jargon as possible, and where it's needed I've explained it. The glossary has been added at the back to define or describe many of the words and phrases you may not be familiar with.

More than just casting

A beginner can learn the basic overhead cast with a fly rig in about 30 minutes. Sure, there's lots more to casting and line management than the basic cast—line control, mending and casting in wind—but you have to start somewhere. After a lesson or two, some coaching and some basic instruction, you'll be ready to head out, start fly-fishing and catch fish.

It's another big step—and a rewarding step—to becoming a fly-angler who, to a small degree, partially understands what's going on in the water. Someone who can take this partial understanding of insects, water and trout and convert it into a successful day of fly-fishing. And success is not measured in the catching of large numbers of fish. Sure, fish are the goal, but success also is having fun and perhaps learning a little along the way.

The impact of the difference between knowing how to cast and knowing how to fly-fish became clear to me one spring day two years ago on the Crowsnest River in southwestern Alberta. Apparently, I had never given the subject a lot of thought before this day.

My fishing partner, John Tunstall, and I had been enjoying a particularly popular and known-to-be-good spot since early morning. We were hoping for a blue-winged olive hatch that we doubted would happen because the water was so cold.

When the olive hatch did start in the early afternoon, the fishing was just fine for a couple of hours. This made the wait all the more worthwhile, especially since it was the first dry-fly day of the year. After months of not fishing at all, or occasionally nymph fishing when a brief Chinook would allow, casting to rising rainbows and catching them during the solid blue-winged olive hatch was very satisfying.

To get to the spot we were fishing, you have to walk quite a ways along a railroad track high above the river. If you arrive to look down and find other anglers fishing the pool and the runs and riffles upstream, it's depressing. But if you're the one in the water, and chance to look up and see others approaching along the tracks, you feel like a hotshot for planning it like you did— for getting up before the alarm and not stopping for coffee on the drive down. If you're the one on top looking down, you may out of envy unfairly classify the guys below as buffoons who likely don't know how to fish the runs, glides and riffles properly. On this day two pairs of anglers approached our spot.

The first duo came along the tracks about two hours after we arrived, so we didn't feel guilty about being there. It wasn't like we had raced them there. On this trip we had driven down the night before and stayed at the Falls Inn Hotel in Lundbreck only three miles from this hole. We had planned to arrive early and spend a long day on the river. And we especially wanted to fish this popular spot. The first pair watched us casting without results for a few minutes and then continued along the tracks to fish farther upstream—likely calling *us* clowns because we weren't catching fish. Then, and for some time after, we couldn't buy a trout even though we knew they were there. Quite often before a blue-winged olive hatch, trout can be caught on small nymphs, the wet flies we use to imitate underwater stages of insects. But not that day.

Later in the day, when the olives were coming off and we were catching rainbows with some regularity, a couple of guys arrived at about the same time from downstream. Turns out that one was a bit of a grump. He passed behind me and started complaining because he had driven such a long way to get there. Apparently, he wasn't catching fish and was miffed because he had watched me land two or three rainbows in the spot I was fishing. (He hadn't been there to witness me *not* catching fish for three hours before.) I'm a nice guy and all, but he didn't get a lot of sympathy, since we had an hour longer drive home and had paid to stay overnight on this trip. More importantly, we had waited out the fish and the bugs.

The grump was a fair caster. The decent guy was a good caster. He could really shoot the line out with tight loops and a pretty good landing. Although both could cast well enough, it was quickly apparent they were fishing blindly. Just sort of casting at random with heaven knows what flies. This random technique works on a lot of water, but not in this spot. These trout all have post-doctoral training in entomology, artificial-fly design and fly construction.

The "revelation" that struck me is now so obvious I am embarrassed to tell it. But in an instant it hit me: fly-fishing is more than just casting. That afternoon the difference between simply fly casting and fly-fishing became so obvious. Here were two fair-to-good casters, but neither seemed to have a clue what he was doing. They had the gear and could cast well, but they thought this coupled with a prime location would naturally result in catching fish. They didn't take the time to watch the water and see what was happening. If either had asked John or me what flies we were using we'd have been pleased to show them and would have given them a fly to try. It was clear they would benefit from some on-stream instruction.

I remember being there and doing the same thing. We all start somewhere and there's no shame in that. There are still times today when I fish at random, hoping that something will connect because my senses haven't been able to figure out the pea-sized brain of the trout. But I usually know where the high probability spots are and how to approach the water and place the

fly. I don't always catch fish—as my friends will confirm—and I still mess up a pool and put fish down.

You can buy good equipment and quality flies that will catch fish where you plan to go, and you can learn how to cast well. But you still may not know how to fly-fish or at least not know how to fly-fish effectively. To do that you will need to advance your skills and learn more about dry-fly, nymph and streamer fishing. Then you'll catch more and more fish.

There will be no end to the learning. But at some point you will have evolved into an accomplished fly-angler—as accomplished as you want to be. You'll watch the water, maybe screen the surface for bugs, rig up with a fly or flies that should work and present the flies in such a way that gives you as good a chance as anyone to catch trout.

Stephen Hawking, the British theoretical physicist, said in his book *A Brief History of Time* something like "Time is what

Fly-fishing is more than just casting. On-stream instruction will help new fly anglers how to read water, identify insects, select flies and approach fish.

prevents everything from happening at once." It is not possible to arrive at a river the first time and be able to cast, read water and know everything there is to know about the sport. And in that little piece of philosophy lies the best part about fly-fishing. Expertise comes with time and practice on the water. Damn fine excuse to go fishing, right?

Catch-and-release fly-fishing

The one technique you should learn before catching fish is how to release them without harm. If you are fishing wild stocks of trout, the law may require you to release them. Other regulations in many provinces and states require the release of certain species of fish under a certain length. If you mess up a few casts, so what? Just don't mess up the fish.

The regulations are necessary because all types of fishing, including fly-fishing, are becoming increasingly popular and there is more pressure on the fish, especially trout in coldwater streams.

In order to maintain trout and other fish populations for the future, we have to practice some level of self-imposed fish release. Politicians have typically been slow to recognize the need for stricter creel and size limits to maintain healthy breeding populations of many species of fish.

I'm not getting into a whole mess of philosophical and political debate about catch-and-release fishing. If you want to eat fish that's up to you, but please limit your catch to one or two trout or whatever species you're after. Or fish for fun, release everything and buy farm-raised fish at a store. If you want to keep more than a few fish, catch them in a put-and-take pond, where they will be replaced. (There are some types of fish, like brook trout and panfish, that tend to overpopulate and can tolerate heavier harvest, but they are the exception.)

Catch-and-release fishing is here to stay, but don't just "throw 'em back." Handle and release fish carefully so they are not injured or stressed. They can then grow, breed and be caught again.

The survival of fish is affected by the type of hooks and lures used, hooking injuries, handling, exhaustion and the method of release.

Releasing fish helps conserve fish stocks for future generations.

Very few trout die when caught on lures or artificial flies with either barbed or barbless hooks. However, barbless hooks reduce the handling time, which increases long-term survival. Debarb your fly hooks by pinching the barb down with needle-nose pliers or forceps. Properly played fish are not usually lost from barbless hooks as long as constant, light tension is applied. And if a fish gets off, so what? You were going to release it anyway.

Bring fish to the net or hand as soon as possible without playing them out because exhaustion contributes to fish stress and mortality. Use leaders that are strong enough to allow you to bring fish in quite fast. Using ultralight lines—for macho reasons—is not recommended because it results in playing fish for too long. When river or stream fishing, keep fish out of fast water because they may tire excessively if they have to battle both the

PLEASE DO NOT DISTURB THE LIVESTOCK OR FENCES. PARK TO THE SIDE OF GATE HAPPY FISHING THANKS

Respect private property, obey trespass laws and respect the rights of other anglers on streams.

current and the line. Fast water also puts a lot of stress on mouth parts. Never drag fish over sand or gravel shorelines that may cause fatal damage to their delicate mucus and skin.

Trout are difficult to grasp because they usually struggle when they come near. Grayling and whitefish wriggle so much they are almost impossible to hold. A soft cotton net helps gather them in, reduces retrieval time and reduces stress.

Excessive squeezing pressure around the body may cause unseen internal injury or may damage to the gills, which often results in slow death. Gently hold smaller fish around the body behind the gills when removing the hook.

Fish should be returned to the water immediately and released. Most often fish will dash away the moment they are released. If a fish seems tired, cradle it in your hands, and when it is able to swim upright let it move away. If a fish is exhausted and floats on its side after release, hold it upright in slow water and gently move it back and forth. Oxygen-rich water will flow through the gills and help it regain strength. Usually after a few seconds it will splash away. Release river and stream fish into slow flowing water only.

We should all practice proven catch-and-release techniques to ensure that the fish we return to the water survive for fishing in the future. Our guidelines should be to:

1 Use flies with barbless hooks.
2 Reduce exhaustion by bringing the fish to net or hand as soon as possible.
3 Use tackle that allows you to control fish quickly.
4 Never drag fish to shore or place them on dry soil.
5 Use a net carefully to quickly and safely control trout.
6 Keep fish in the water or hold them in the air for the shortest possible time.
7 Grip fish gently behind the gills when removing the hook.
8 Never touch or damage the gills of fish.
9 Allow exhausted stream fish to recover in slow-moving water before letting them swim to fast water.
10 Cradle fish carefully and let them swim away when ready.
11 *Never just throw fish back!*

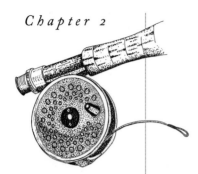

Chapter 2

Fly-Fishing Equipment

It's not unusual for beginning fly-anglers to be baffled about fly tackle, and who can blame them? In some minds the sport has taken on the qualities of a mysterious cult.

Well, fly-fishing and fly-fishing gear are not mysterious and complicated. There's no more gear to select than for a spinning rig. But new fly-anglers do need to be familiar with fly-fishing equipment before spending a lot of money—perhaps on the wrong gear. It's important to select an outfit that is easy to cast and suited to your specific needs and the type of fly-fishing you'll be doing.

Selecting the right weight of fly rig

A fly-fishing rig includes a line, reel and rod. Yes, there's more stuff, but we'll start here with the essentials. Fly lines, reels and rods come in various weights, and all three must be matched so casting will be easy and effective. Only then will early fly-fishing experiences be enjoyable and productive. The weight of your first fly-fishing outfit will depend on the type of fish you'll be chasing, so the decision will be yours.

Line weights—and matching weights of rods and

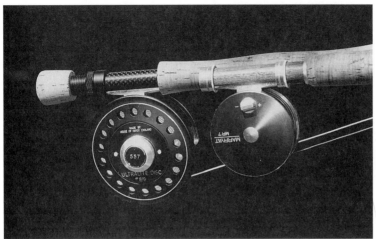

There is a wide range of fly-fishing rig sizes. The large 8-weight rod and reel is used for pike and steelhead. The small 4-weight reel is ideal for small streams and small fish. A midrange 6-weight outfit is suitable for many types of fly-fishing that most beginners will encounter.

reels—range from 1 to 13 (and higher) based on the weight of the first 30 feet of the fly line. The higher the number, the heavier the line. Heavier lines and rods are better suited to larger flies; they cast better in wind, cast farther and are used for larger fish. Lighter outfits are ideal for small fish in small water.

Ultralight 2- and 3-weight rigs are used to present small dry flies accurately and delicately, but you can't "put the wood" to larger fish with this featherweight gear. They are of little use where the wind blows and are not well suited to lake fishing because these light lines do not cast as far. Light 4- and 5-weight outfits are ideal for trout, panfish or small bass in small- to medium-sized streams or ponds. They, too, are difficult to cast in the wind and are not well suited to big streamers and bass bugs. At the heavy end of the scale, 8-, 9- and 10-weights are for big pike, lunker bass in tough cover, steelhead and salmon.

A midrange 6-weight outfit is a good starting weight for beginners because it casts easily and can be used to cast a wide range of fly sizes and weights. A 6-weight is delicate enough for casting to fussy trout, yet stout enough to handle any size of river or pond trout you're likely to hook. So if your target is trout or average-sized bass in streams, rivers and ponds, then you simply can't go wrong with a 6-weight rig. I own and use 4-, 5-, 6-, 7-

and 8-weight fly-fishing outfits, yet the 6-weight gets used more than any other. A 6-weight outfit equipped with the right leader and light tippet will delicately present a small #22 dry fly. Re-rigged with a heavy leader it will also chuck a large #2 weighted streamer. If your target is a wider range of fishing—small and big rivers and ponds, and perhaps casting for medium-sized pike and bass in heavy cover—a 7-weight might be a better choice for the beginning fly-angler. If you'll only be fishing small streams and ponds for small trout and panfish, perhaps start with a 5-weight.

As a novice you might become frustrated when selecting your first fly-fishing outfit. If you ask several friends and sales staff you'll likely get several different opinions on what is the "best" starting weight. Two things come to mind. First, it's important that you explain to your friends or the sales staff what type of fishing you think you'll be doing most often. If you mistakenly ask them what they would buy, they may tell you what they use for the type of fly-fishing they do and where they do it. Or they might tell you the next rig they're buying will *definitely* be a 4-weight while neglecting to tell you they started with a 6-weight and have been happily using it for ten years.

Second, I said that lightweight outfits are for small flies and the heavier rigs are for big flies. Well, sort of. Fly rigs of different weights have a range of uses. It is, in fact, not quite correct to say that a 5-weight is only for small stream fishing and small flies. And that an 8-weight is for pike, big bass and steelhead. Yes, both are better suited to these specific uses, but I've used my 8-weight to fish in the 100-yard-wide Bow River, where I needed distance and when the wind was howling. It was the 8-weight or go home. I've also used a 4-weight in the same place to catch the same fish when the wind was down. Just because I felt like doing it and was casting small dry flies. I've caught small trout in small creeks with my 7-weight rig and once caught a 13-pound pike on the same rod. So don't be bamboozled by someone who tells you that a beginner needs three outfits to cover a wide range of fly sizes and fishing conditions.

Selecting a fly rod

There is a huge difference in price between a cheap, poor-casting $20 fiber glass rod and a top-drawer $600 graphite rod. Don't despair, there are many good rods in between.

A cheap fiber glass rod is castable, but it will tend to wobble and cause the fly line to do funny things, making accurate casting and fly presentation difficult. Graphite rods, on the other hand, are easier to cast, are light and less tiring, and are "sweeter" to cast. A reasonably good starter graphite rod will cost from $80 to $150. High-end graphite fly rods cost between $150 and $600.

Before deciding on golf as your recreation because of these prices, consider that most manufacturers of quality rods offer lifetime guarantees—no questions asked. If you're going to spend big bucks on a good rod make sure there is a replacement guarantee. In mid-1995 my fishing partner, John Tunstall, and I were wade fishing on the Bow River. I had just landed and released a decent rainbow and was getting organized to start fishing again. John waded to shore, and unknown to me, set his rod on the gravel bar, then walked away to drain his lunchtime coffee. I wandered over to the gravel bar and proceeded to step on the top section of his rod. Of course, it shattered. It cost a few dollars to ship to the manufacturer to be fitted with the free replacement top section. After a few weeks John was fishing again with his favorite fly rod—and he was still talking to me. So quality counts.

Popular 4- to 8-weight fly rods are usually between 7½ and 9 feet in length. Most people I know use 8½- or 9-foot rods. These lengths help reach farther over and around obstructions, and they cast well. Shorter rods don't have enough reach for me even on mountain creeks, but they're popular with some anglers who fish small streams for small fish. If you'll be fishing from a float tube you'll need at least a 9-foot rod because you sit low in the water. A 9½- or 10-foot rod would be even better. This is not an issue when casting from pontoon or kick boats because you are at least a foot higher out of the water.

Most top-end graphite fly rods are classed as having a certain "action." This refers to the flexibility or stiffness of the rod. Rod actions are described as extra-fast, fast, medium-fast, medium or slow. Fast rods are somewhat stiff, and slow rods are quite flexible or willowy. Medium-fast and medium rod actions are good for most fly-fishing. Before spending big bucks on a soft rod or stiff rod ask to test one at a fly shop. You might like the different action, but you might not.

Fly rods should have at least ten line guides. If there are too few guides the line sags between them and reduces casting distance. Many cheap and even midrange rods have only seven or eight line guides.

A medium-fast or medium-action 8½- or 9-foot graphite rod with at least ten line guides is a good beginner's rod for most types of fly-fishing. The weight will depend on what types of fishing you'll be doing, but, again, you really can't go wrong with a 6-weight for a wide range of fish and water types.

Selecting a fly line

Fly lines are described by their weight, floatability and taper. We've already discussed line weights in relation to rig weights.

Some fly lines float (F), some sink (S) and some have sinking tips (F/S). A floating line is versatile and can be used with both dry flies and wet flies on many types of water. It's also easier to cast and manage than a sinking line. You won't find much difference practicing on your lawn, but you will on the water. Floating lines are suitable for fishing nymphs and streamers in most rivers. For shallow-pond fishing a floating line with about 10 to 12 feet of leader and tippet and a split shot or two are usually adequate to get the fly down a few feet.

If most of your fishing will be on lakes and ponds where you'll be fishing quite deep, say, below 10 or 15 feet, you will need either a sinking-tip line or a full-sinking line. Sinking lines come in different densities and therefore sink at different rates. If you

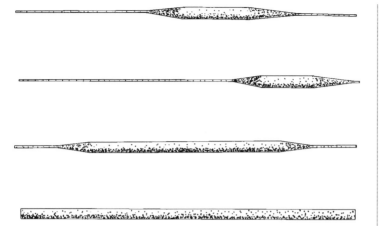

are uncertain, purchase a medium density line for lake fishing. If you think you'll need to get down fast and stay down as you cruise along in your float tube or kick boat, then you'll need a high-density fast-sinking line. Fast-sinking lines are also used to get streamers down fast when fishing rivers from boats. Seek the advice of experienced anglers who have fly-fished where you'll be heading or check at the local fly shop.

Fly lines are tapered—or not. As a fly line moves forward during the cast, the amount of energy available to throw the line forward decreases because of air resistance. Lines tapered near the end have less resistance, require less energy and straighten properly at the end of the cast.

Tapered fly lines are available in several different types. Double-tapered (DT) lines are fatter in the middle and symmetrically tapered toward each end. They are easy to cast and you theoretically get two lines for the price of one. The theory is that after the front portion cracks and gets worn, the line can be turned around, but I honestly don't know anyone who has ever done it. Weight-forward (WF) lines have the fattest part of the line nearer the front than the middle. They cast a bit farther than double-tapered lines and are preferred for casting bigger flies. I prefer WF lines, as do most people I fish with. If you'll only be bass or pike fishing, and will always be using large flies, buy a bass-taper or bug-taper line. It's a special weight-forward line with the bulk of the line concentrated closer to the front.

Level lines (L) are not suitable for most types of fly-fishing. You might be tempted to buy one because it costs so little compared to a tapered line. Bad move. I can't think of anything that will end a fly-fishing hobby quicker than buying a cheap level line since they are difficult to cast.

A good starting line for beginners is a weight-forward floating fly line in a weight to match your new rod, most likely a 6-weight. The code on the package will read "WF–6–F." Fly shops sell good quality fly lines for $30 to $50.

Selecting a reel

Someone once said, "A fly reel is simply a place to store fly line." The implication being that any cheap reel is okay. Fish innards! Sure, a $20 reel holds line; however, it will probably vibrate when a fast-running rainbow is hooked, and your new expensive line may get jammed and damaged in the wide gap between the spool and frame. The drag will be poor to nonexistent, and it will likely break after a few outings. A $40 to $80 reel will stand up well and last a few years. As expensive as they may seem, perhaps the cheapest reels in the long run are the top-end models. A $150 to $300 reel will last a lifetime, will be reliable, have a smooth drag and won't vibrate. Your grandchildren will be using your top-quality reel decades from now. As with the rod, buy the best reel you feel you can afford.

There are two main parts to fly reels: the round-shaped frame and gearing, and the line spool and handle. The spool fits inside the frame and turns on a spindle. It's not rocket science. Select a reel in which the outer rim of the spool is outside of the frame. Then, when a big fish screams out line, you can apply braking pressure to the spool with your hand or fingers. Most quality reels—and some cheaper models—have exposed spools, sometimes referred to as palming rims or palming spools. This is an

A floating line and a sinking-tip line are stored on two spools and used with one reel. The dark section of line on the spare spool is the sinking portion.

important feature, especially on cheaper reels that often have poor to nonexistent drags. The spool on some reels, however, fits inside the frame, making it impossible to use your hand to apply braking pressure to the spool. Avoid these.

You can buy extra spools for most makes of fly reels. This can save you lots of money. Say you'll be fishing a wide range of conditions and will need a floating line, a sinking-tip line and a sinking line for your 6-weight rod—something beyond the immediate needs of the novice. You don't want to buy three reels, and you certainly don't want to unspool lines to change. You can buy three spools for the one reel and load the different lines on each spool. They snap in and out in seconds.

Quality fly-fishing reels have drag mechanisms that control the ease with which the line unwinds from the reel. By adjusting the drag tension, the line can either free spool from the reel or be difficult to pull out. When the drag is set "just so," a fish can haul out line and make a sudden stop, and even if the reel spool is not palmed (braked with the hand), the spool stops without spinning and creating a rat's nest of line.

Reels have two types of drag systems. Click systems use a spring-loaded pawl (or arm) to apply braking pressure to a gear. Disk-drag mechanisms have a pressure plate and pad and work on the same principle as disk brakes in a vehicle. Whatever drag

The drag and click mechanisms inside a fly reel. The disk drag plate is at the bottom. The audible click is created by the triangular pawl striking the gear. This reel needs cleaning.

system you select make sure that there is a wide range of drag tensions and that the drag allows line to run from the reel smoothly. Generally, the more you pay, the better the drag system.

Pawl drags and most disk drags have audible clicks that squeal when a hard-running rainbow peels off line. (The sound can be turned off on some reels.) I like the feature for two reasons. The first is . . . well, I guess it's a guy thing. The reel sounds cool when a fish is peeling out line. But more practically, I know without looking that the fish is peeling line and how fast. I know if I have to manually increase the tension by palming the reel. On smooth reels with the drag clicker turned off, you don't always know how hard and fast a large fish is running. And neither do your friends. If you're into the backing with a great fish you might as well let your friends enjoy the truly great sound of a fish peeling line, right?

A fly reel should match the weight of line and rod it will be used with. Moderately priced to expensive reels are designed for one or two specific line weights only. They have model numbers, like 5/6, that indicate the line weights they are designed for. Not only must the reel match the weight of your new rod, it must fit in the reel seat on the rod.

Most fly reels can be set for either left-hand or right-hand winding by changing a couple of doodads inside. Check the instruction sheet that comes with the reel to see how it's done. More than half of the right-handed fly rodders I know crank with the left hand. I cast with my right hand and feel that rod control is better with that hand—so I wind with my left. This eliminates the need to switch the rod from hand to hand to wind line in. You have to make the decision to crank with the left or right hand.

All new reels come from the factory set for right-hand cranking. But be aware that there are still a few models of fly reels that cannot be changed to left-hand winding. Before making a purchase check the information sheet in the box to see if the reel can be changed. A reversible reel is recommended so you can field test both left- and right-hand winding.

If you decide to reverse cranking hands after the line has been put on the reel, you will have to unwind the line and rewind it onto the reel. You can't just reverse the reel on the rod.

Single-action reels have no internal gearing mechanisms that speed up the spool rotation. For every turn of the handle, the spool rotates once. Sounds fairly inefficient, but single-action reels work well and are used by the majority of fly-anglers. Multiplier reels have internal gears that turn the spool more than once for each turn of the handle, which makes for faster retrieves. Automatic reels have internal spring mechanisms— like windup toys—that are wound tighter as the fly line is pulled from the reel. When a brake handle is released, the line comes zipping in and you don't have all that hand cranking to do. In all fairness I have never used an automatic reel, but there are two diverse opinions about them: people who swear by them and people who swear at them. Stick to the single-action hand crank reel for starters.

So, to recap, purchase a single-action fly reel with an exposed line spool for palming. Make sure the drag has a wide range of tensions and that it lets out line smoothly. Buy the best reel you can comfortably afford.

Assembling the fly rig

In addition to a line, rod and reel, a few more supplies are required before attending casting and fly-fishing classes or heading to the stream or pond. Necessities include line backing, leaders, tippet lines and flies. Various knots are used to connect all this stuff together.

Here's the sequence of how everything is connected: reel > backing > fly line > tapered leader > tippet or tippets > fly or flies.

About 100 to 150 feet of braided Dacron backing line are wound on the reel spool before the fly line. Backing serves two purposes. It bulks up the reel spool so the fly line is wound in a larger diameter. This makes for faster line retrieval, and the fly line is less likely to form bothersome coils. But most importantly, backing is simply extra line that is needed from time to time when a large fish makes a long run and hauls out more than the 90-foot fly line—one of the best moments in fly-fishing! (Now you know why you have the click on your new disk-drag reel: *zzzzzzing.*)

Tie the backing to the reel with a reel-to-backing knot, something we'll discuss in a moment. Then attach the fly line to the backing with a nail knot. The brochure that came with your new reel should tell you how much backing you can expect to fit on the spool and still have room for the fly line. If you wind on the two lines and the fly line rubs against the reel frame before it is fully on, you will have to unwind the lines and remove some of the backing to make room for the fly line. There should be at least ¼ inch of free space between the fly line and reel frame. Any less and you'll find that the line will still rub and sometimes bind because you won't always wind in the line as neatly and tightly on the water as you do in your workshop.

A fly is not tied directly to a fly line, but at the end of a tapered leader and tippet(s) tied to the end of the fly line. Tie a 7½- to 9-foot knotless tapered monofilament leader to the end of the fly line with a nail knot or loop-to-loop connection. (A tapered leader gets progressively thinner toward the fly end.)

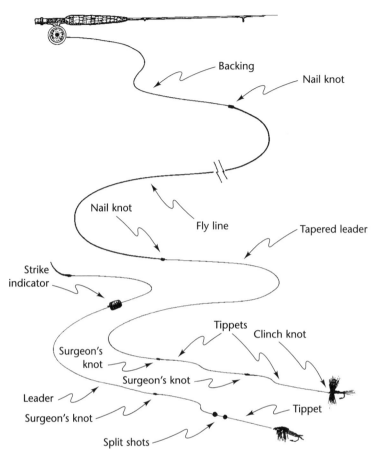

Backing

Nail knot

Nail knot

Fly line

Tapered leader

Strike indicator

Tippets

Clinch knot

Surgeon's knot

Surgeon's knot

Leader

Surgeon's knot

Split shots

Tippet

The dry-fly setup on the right includes reel, backing, fly line, tapered leader, two sections of tippet and a dry fly. The wet fly assembly on the left includes a strike indicator attached to the leader, two split shots attached to the tippet and a nymph.

Usually, one or two short lengths of monofilament "tippet" leaders are attached to the end of the tapered leader.

Leaders cost $2 to $4 each and a novice is quick to question the sanity of paying that kind of money for a few feet of tapered line when you can buy perhaps 100 yards of plain old monofilament spinning line for the same price and make dozens of leaders. But tapered leaders serve a very real and important function in fly-fishing: it has to do with physics—laws of diminishing energy or something. Tapered leaders are required so that the leader, tippet and fly turn over properly. That is, the end of the leader and fly lay out in a nice straight line at the end of the cast

Reel-to-backing knot. The lead end of the backing is threaded around the reel spool. An overhand knot is tied around the backing at A and another at B. The backing is then pulled taut. The knot at B prevents the first knot from slipping.

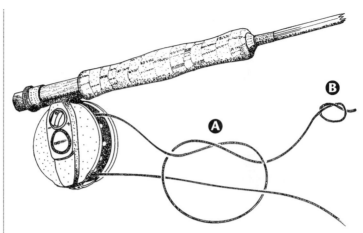

instead of piling up. Leaders made with straight monofilament line will not turn over properly and pile up when casting small flies. You can, however, use straight monofilament leaders when fishing big heavy flies like pike streamers and even large nymphs and trout streamers. But for most types of fly-fishing, you must use tapered leaders.

Tapered leaders can be made by knotting together progressively thinner sections of tippet monofilament. But commercial knotless tapered leaders are recommended when you are starting out. You'll only use three or four tapered leaders a year, and you have enough other things to be concerned with when you're getting started. For me, store-bought knotless tapered leaders work well, but in all fairness I've never fished with hand-tied tapered leaders, which many anglers claim are superior. Apparently, there are special combinations of tippet thicknesses that turn over better than store-bought leaders. Could be, but frankly I couldn't be bothered because I'm happy with the ones I buy. Tying instructions for tapered leaders are found in many fly-fishing books. Study them and try them if you wish.

Flies can be tied directly to the tapered leader, but there are some advantages to tying one or two sections of tippet leader to the end of the tapered leader before tying on a fly. First, as I said, leaders cost a few dollars and are usually only 7½ or 9 feet long.

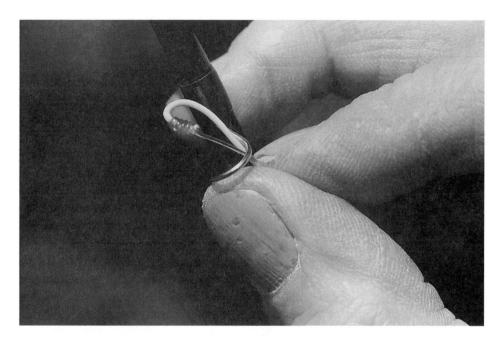

It's not uncommon to tie on, say, ten or twenty different flies in the course of one day. And every time a fly is cut off and another added, you lose 2 or 3 inches of leader. Pretty soon the new leader is too short and fat. By tying a 2- or 3-foot section of tippet to your new leader you will lengthen its usable life many fold. The tippet will last for perhaps ten flies before it needs changing. Second, during the course of a day on the river or lake you not only will use many different types of flies, you will use many different sizes of flies. And as we'll see below, different thicknesses of tippets are used for different sizes of flies.

The fly line and leader are easy to thread through the rod guides if the fly line is doubled over near the leader.

The ends of tapered leaders and tippets come in different thicknesses and therefore different strengths. Their thickness is described by an "x" code—3x and 5x, for example. The thicker the line, the *lower* the x number. Different thicknesses of tippets are tied to the end of the tapered leader depending on the size of the flies used. Small flies require thin tippets, such as 5x. Thicker 3x tippets are used for larger nymphs and streamers. Tippets sized 3x are around 8-pound test, and 5x tippets are around 5-pound test.

Hook sizes

Fly-anglers constantly talk about hook sizes and use hook sizes to describe insects. "Yup, there were swarms of #12 caddisflies flitting around and we hammered 'em on tan Elk Hairs." Before going further we need to cover the size of hooks because much of the following discussion about leaders and tippets is closely related.

At the risk of being criticized for oversimplifying hook sizes, here goes. Hook-size codes are based on the width of the bent part of the hook. The smaller this gap (also known as "gape" in some literature), the smaller the overall size of the hook and vise versa. Ninety-five percent of your trout fishing will likely be with hooks between, and including, size #20 and size #4. With perhaps 90 percent on flies from #6 to #18. Two #20 flies will easily fit across the width of a dime. They are small. A #4 hook will more than cover the width of a Canadian dollar coin.

To put hook sizes in perspective, of the couple thousand trout I've caught in the past few years, perhaps four were taken on #22s. I recall one in Montana and two rainbows on the Crowsnest for sure. I can't remember what I ate for breakfast some days, but catching a trout on a really small fly is quite memorable if you don't do it often. A #22 is quite big for some anglers who get into the microflies. They tie really small flies down to #26 and #28. I have tied #26 flies but never used them.

The other main hook-size variable is the hook length, which increases with gap width. Hooks of any one gap size come in standard lengths, short lengths and long lengths. The short and long business is also described by an x code. (The same engineers as the leader and tippet companies?) Hooks designated as 2x-short are really squat, and 2x-long hooks are quite long.

If you get into fly tying, you'll soon realize that hook size is a hugely complicated subject. There's up eyes, straight eyes, down eyes; thick and thin wire; curved and straight shanks; and ones with different types of curves in the bend of the hook. All of this results in a #12, 2x-long hook with a particular bend style looking a whole lot like another company's #10. And to make things

Three hook sizes, top to bottom: #8, #12 and #16.

totally unbearable, those devilish but fun-loving engineers or marketers at the different hook companies have all devised their own nomenclatures and coding systems.

Leaders, tippets and hooks

The chart following shows how thicker tippets are used for larger flies and vice versa. Similar charts in other books show only two or three fly sizes as suited to each tippet size. But such recommendations are more theoretical than practical. (I hate to be a critic, but when I see recommendations for using a 3x tippet for #14 flies, I have to wonder. A #14 dry fly does not float well on such a thick tippet and 3x is far too thick for smooth water and spooky fish.)

If your knots are good, you can tie on several hook sizes to one size of tippet. Once in a while you may have to tie a #16 fly— even a #14—to a 6x tippet for spooky fish in flat water. And it works the other way, too. If you tie good knots, a #2 streamer is quite safe on a 3x tippet.

One serious problem with trying to tie a #4 streamer on, say, a 5x tippet is that the diameters of the line and hook wire are so different that the thin line does not grab the hook eye wire very

Leader and Tippet Thickness, Strength and Uses			
Thickness code	Diameter (inches)	Approximate strength (lbs)	Fly sizes and types
1X	0.010	12±	*For big streamers and nymphs from 0/2 to #4 hooks.*
2X	0.009	10±	*For big streamers and nymphs from 0/2 to #4 hooks.*
3X	0.008	8±	*A basic tippet for nymphs and dry flies from #4 to #10 or even #12. It's not common to use this thickness for dry-fly trout fishing.*
4X	0.007	6±	*For nymphs and dry flies from #8 to #14.*
5X	0.006	5±	*For dry flies from #14 to #18.*
6X	0.005	3±	*For dry flies from #20 to #22. Used maybe a few times a year with larger flies for fussy fish.*
7X	0.004	2±	*For very tiny dry flies.*

well and will likely slip. In any case, if you're fishing a fly that big, especially in a river, you're presumably after bigger fish and are likely to break the fine line. And even if you don't, the poor fish will be exhausted by the time you are able to land it.

Small flies tied to thick tippets tend to float unnaturally and may cause fish to shy away. And, of course, there's a limit to the line thickness that will actually fit through the eye of the hook. You just can't thread a 3x tippet through a #18 hook eye—a function of physical limits and the age of the angler.

If all of this is starting to sound a little too complicated, don't get too hung up with ultraspecific recommendations. As with many things in life, the KISS principle applies here: Keep It Simple, Silly. When I'm trout fishing, 95 percent of the time my flies are attached to 3x, 4x and 5x tippets—and I fish big rivers, like the Bow River in Alberta, small creeks and everything in between. I usually use a leader with a 2x end (sometimes 3x) and attach 2 feet or so of 3x tippet to it. If fishing big flies, I tie them directly to the 3x tippet. If I change to smaller flies, I'll tie a 1½- to 2-foot section of 4x or 5x tippet to the 3x tippet. Simple and functional.

Occasionally, I'll use a 2x tippet for really big (#2) streamers in heavy water where there is some chance of hooking a 4-pound rainbow. Or I'll use a 2x leader or tippet if I think there is a 7-pound brown in a deep hole, though I've never caught one. But most often I use 3x for the larger flies. Once or twice a year, when conditions are just so and I'm after fussy leader-shy fish feeding in smooth water, I'll tie small dry flies to a 6x tippet. I bought a spool of 7x tippet once, but don't recall ever using it, and it got tossed out after about three years. (Tippet material does have a limited life and weakens after a year or two.)

There is an advantage to using a heavier leader, like 2x, compared to, say, a 4x leader. You can add one or two sections of progressively thinner tippets so you can fish large flies and small flies with the one leader. But it doesn't work the other way. If you use thinner leaders, like 4x, they are too fine for larger flies in heavy water, and you should not add a thicker section of tippet to a fine leader. In other words, if you tied a 4x leader to your fly line, you should not tie a 2x tippet to it if you are switching to large streamers. You'll have to change leaders. That's too much messing around for me, so I stick to the 2x or 3x leaders and add thinner tippets as required.

Tippet strength and stiffness vary from manufacturer to manufacturer. Ask the sales staff at a specialty fly shop for some

A packaged leader with 2x tip section and spools of 3x, 4x and 5x tippet. These three tippet sizes suit a wide range of fly sizes and fly-fishing situations.

advice. Make sure you are buying fresh stock that hasn't been sitting in the back warehouse of the for a year or two. At least one manufacturer uses "best before" dates on their leader and tippet packages. A good idea.

Tying basic knots

Now you need to know how to connect lines, leaders and tippets. First, the thick end of the 2x leader is attached to the fly line with either a nail knot or loop-to-loop connection. Then a 2- or 3-foot piece of 3x tippet is tied to the thin end of the leader with a surgeon's knot. A large nymph or streamer can be tied right to the end of the 3x tippet with a clinch knot. If small wet flies, nymphs or dry flies are to be used, a thinner piece of 4x or 5x tippet is tied to the end of the 3x tippet, again with a surgeon's knot. Clinch knots are used to tie flies to tippet leaders.

There are many other knots for connecting lines and tying on flies, but these will work well enough for starters. For that matter they work just fine for everyone. Expand your knot array and skills when and if you need.

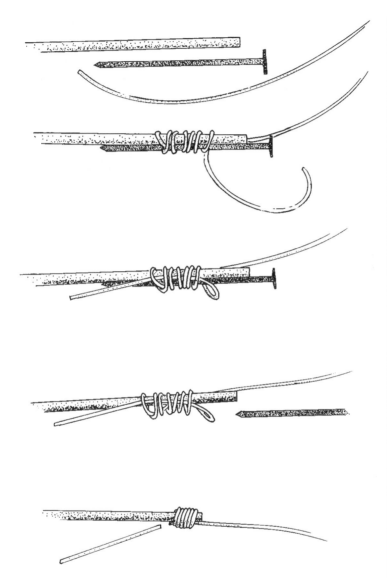

The nail knot is used to attach the backing to the fly line and the the fly line to the tapered leader. It is tied with a thin nail or round toothpick. There are other ways to tie nail knots and other knots can be used to connect these lines and leaders. In this illustration the thin line represents either the the backing or the tapered leader.

If you take a fly-fishing course make sure your instructor goes through the basic knots and lets you practice. He or she will likely have a different opinion about what knots you must know. Fine.

Braided loops come attached to some fly lines or can be purchased separately. The loop is threaded through a loop in the leader to create a loop-to-loop connection.

The nail knot is a tad tricky to finish so it's not too thick and so the tip of the fly line under the knot stays straight. You don't want the last ¼ inch of the fly line to have a kink in it, a common problem with poorly tied nail knots. The trick is keeping the coils together when the tag end is tightened. The coils want to wander and not all stay in neat progression like they should. After the nail is removed, pinch the coils so they have less chance of becoming mixed up. When they're all snug they should look neat and tidy like a hangman's noose. Make sure your leader is securely connected with a nail knot before you head fishing. It's not an easy knot to perfect and you are far better off practicing at home. Or use the simpler loop-to-loop connection to attach the fly line to the backing and the tapered leader to the fly line.

There are a couple of advantages to connecting fly lines and leaders with loop-to-loop connections. The connection is fast and simple and allows you to change leaders in a hurry. The disadvantage is that loop connections are a bit bulkier than nail knots, so you have to be careful when playing and landing a big fish. If you are using a 9-foot leader with, say, another 4 feet of tippet, that's a total of 13 feet of leader between the bulky line connection and the fish. Unless your rod arm is 4 feet long there is no way to net the fish unless you wind the line in far enough that the loop-to-loop connection (or nail knot) comes in past the

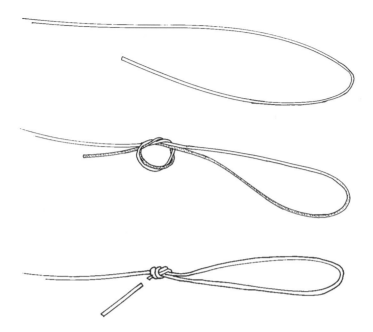

A loop can be tied at the thick end of a tapered leader by doubling over about 4 inches of leader and tying an overhand knot.

tip-top guide on the rod. For smaller fish that's fine, but here's the rub, especially if you have Walter on. (Remember the big trout in *On Golden Pond*? It was Walter.) If you have a bulky knot inside of the top guide, and ol' Walter wants to run away, the knot might get stuck or momentarily bind in a guide and you may execute the SDR (the short-distance release), not to be confused with the LDR (the long-distance release). The knot jams and the fish keeps going with your fly.

There are three ways to make a loop at the end of the fly line. One is to buy a fly line with the loop pre-formed. Another is to buy a braided-loop kit at a fly shop and follow the directions. Still another is to double over about 1½ inches of the fly line tip and wrap fly-tying thread around and around the double section, leaving about ½ inch of free loop at the tip. Finish the wrapping with several half-hitches and glue the thread with flexible head cement used for fly tying. It's easy to tie a loop in the butt end of a leader. Double over about 4 inches of the butt section and tie an overhand knot.

Top: A loop-to-loop connection. The fly line has a homemade loop tied at the end instead of a factory-braided loop. Both fly-line loops are suitable, although factory loops are less bulky.

Bottom: Thread the two loops to make a loop-to-loop connection.

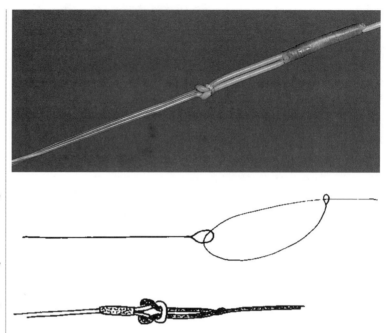

Surgeon's knots are used to connect leader to tippet or sections of tippet to tippet. It's a great knot because it's simple, it's stronger than the often-touted blood knot and it can connect sections of line that are quite different in thickness. It does not have the smooth symmetrical form of the blood knot, but who cares? Because it is so simple you can tie a surgeon's knot in fading light with the wind howling, and I defy any middle-aged angler with bifocals to tie a blood knot under similar conditions.

Two tips for the surgeon's knot. When the loop is being tightened make sure that two strands of line forming the loops stay close together. Before the loop is tightened, wet it with saliva so it closes easily and does not heat and stress the line.

The standard clinch knot works well for tying a wide range of hook types to tippets. There are many other knots you may want to learn, but the clinch knot is simple and strong. However, it does not hold well if you tie a fairly large fly, say #6, to a fine

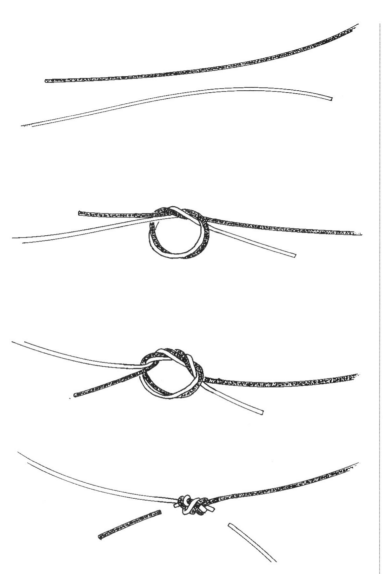

The surgeon's knot is used to connect leader to tippet and tippet to tippet. In this illustration the tippet is the top dark line. The two lines are overlapped about 4 to 5 inches and an overhand knot is tied where they overlap. Before closing the loop the tippet section and tag end of the leader are passed through the loop a second time.

tippet like 5x. Change tippets. To tie the knot properly, make seven wraps before tightening it. Any less and the knot may not hold. Any more and you increase the friction required to close the knot and run the risk of heating and weakening the line. Wet the clinch knot before closing.

To tie a standard clinch knot thread the tippet through the hook eye and wrap the tag end seven times around the main section of tippet. The tag end is then threaded through the open gap next to the eye. Moisten the wraps and pull evenly to close the knot. Trim the tag end. Other knots can also be used to attach flies to tippets.

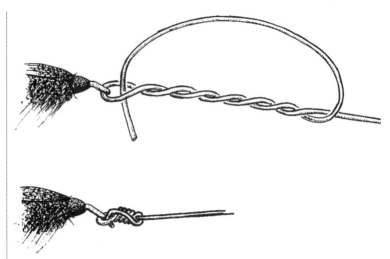

The essential fly vest

You're starting to accumulate a few supplies like extra leaders and tippets. There's more to come, and soon you'll need a way to pack your gear on the water. The most popular way to carry fly gear is in a fly vest. It has loads of pockets, and when full of essential gear you become a self-contained fly-fishing unit.

You can't go wrong by buying a good fly vest. Whereas fly-anglers follow trendy bandwagons as quick as any other flock of sports nuts, several decades of fly-vest use by thousands of anglers speaks well of their utility.

Good fly vests are quite expensive, running as high as $200 or more. But you can get a good quality one for around $50 to $100 that will last several years. Most are made of heavy cotton and are quite warm in the summer. You might consider buying a light-weight mesh vest for the heat of summer and a heavier vest for the rest of the year. If you'll be deep wading consider buying a short-cut vest.

I'm sitting here at my word processor with my vest on my lap and trying to decide what the salient components are. Here's what's in and on my current vest that you'll find handy:

A good fly vest has many pockets and pouches. The lower 6-inch portion of this vest can be removed to create a short vest for deep wading. The lower portion also doubles as a fanny pack.

Four large zippered pockets are needed to hold four or more fly boxes and other supplies.

A large number of Velcro and snap-button pockets are needed for holding other assorted items like extra leaders, bug dope and toilet paper. My fly vest has 17 pockets and pouches in addition to the four large pockets. The more pockets, the easier it is to lose things, or at least not be able to find them the moment they're needed. Does happen!

A dee ring on the back of the neck holds a net.

One or two dee rings on the front are handy for tying or clipping on various items. Mine holds the case for my polarized sunglasses and a bear whistle. (I've never used the bear whistle mainly because I tend to avoid beary fishing holes. Even if I needed to there's little chance I'd be able to blow it anyway.)

A roomy external zippered back pouch is handy for carrying lunch, water, raincoat or net.

Fly-fishing coats and packs

Fly vests are great. But there are other options you need to consider before dropping a hundred bucks or more on a good-quality vest. Some fly-anglers prefer fishing coats, chest packs or fanny packs. You'll have to decide which is best for you.

Fishing coats are Windbreaker-type jackets but have more pockets and pouches. I have one but use it as a casual coat and for holding camera lenses, not for fishing. Mine has five external pockets up front and a large back pouch. These don't provide enough nooks for all the fly-fishing paraphernalia I usually haul around, but enough so I can never find my truck keys. The sleeves are held on with zippers and can be removed during warm weather. There's an advantage to a fishing coat if you're flying into a remote lodge and have a baggage weight restriction. It doubles as a coat and a fly vest. And if you buy an expensive waterproof fishing coat you save more weight yet, as you should never fly to a lodge without rain gear.

Because of its length a fishing coat is not suited to deep wading. And you're not likely to want to wear it for casual dress after a couple of trips to the water because it will be stained with fly dope and other grunge.

In the past few years chest packs have increased in popularity. Guides seem to like them because they hold oodles of fly boxes. They are squarish semihard packs with many compartments to hold flies and other gear. The advantage of chest packs is that flies are stored right up front for easy selection. And the pack doubles as a miniature table for putting things on—like eyeglasses—while tying on a fly.

I flirted with a fanny pack one summer when I was going to become a one-fly-box angler, but it didn't pan out. Probably you'll have more gear and supplies than will fit into a fanny pack, but you can carry your extra stuff in a large fly-fishing case—like a camera bag. Then each day you can select what you need for where you'll be fishing and the conditions. (I recall having to walk back to the truck once because I didn't have salmon fly dries

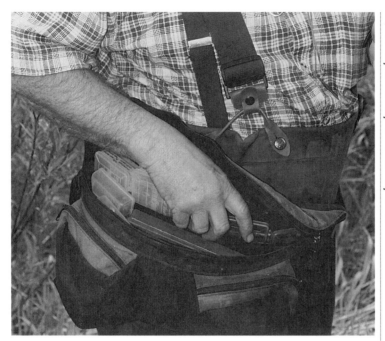

A well-organized fanny pack may have enough space for some anglers. It is recommended for anglers who have upper-neck problems.

in my fanny pack.) Like fishing coats, fanny packs are not suited to deep wading.

If you have upper-neck problems, a fanny pack might be a better choice for you because the weight of your gear is held by your hips and waist. A heavy fly vest exerts downward vertical pressure on the neck and can be quite uncomfortable during long days on the water. It's something to consider.

Essential gear for the fly vest

This is going to be fun. I'm about to empty the 21 pockets and pouches of my fly-fishing vest. Pocket by pocket here's what I found:

Seven (count 'em, *seven*) fly boxes in three zippered pockets. (You don't need seven full fly boxes to start. Nor do I. But honestly, all seven are rarely in my vest at one time. There are about

Nymphs and streamers that frequently hit bottom must be sharpened.

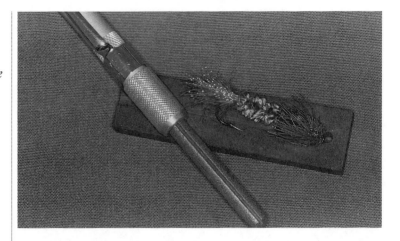

600 flies in these boxes. Two or three boxes containing perhaps 50 to 100 flies will do for starters depending on where, what and how you plan to fish.)

The fourth zippered pouch contains fly floatant, five tippet spools (one spool each of 3x, 4x and 6x, and two spools of 5x) and soft lead split shot. (Try 3x, 4x and 5x tippets to start.)

Bug spray, two more small packs of split shot and a spool of twist-on lead weight are in one small pouch. (Some types of bug dope have been reported to melt the outer casing of fly lines, so be careful where you carry it in your vest.)

Flexible-head flashlight in one pouch pocket for tying knots at night.

Two packs of pocket Kleenex, a.k.a. toilet paper (TP) in one outer pouch.

One partially flattened roll of toilet paper in another inside pouch. (Hey, you never want to run out of TP!)

A hook and knife sharpener, three 9-foot 2x tapered leaders and one pack of small hard strike indicators in one inside pouch.

One 3-inch square aquarium net for screening the water for bugs, and another bottle of bug spray in another pocket.

One vial of fly-line dressing in one top outside pouch. (You should have fly-line dressing, but it's not usually necessary to carry it with you. It's made an awful stain on the left side of my vest.)

Left to right: Strike indicators of poly yarn, closed-cell packing foam attached with a clove hitch knot, stick-on foam, slotted indicator of hard foam held with an elastic band, large slotted indicator of hard foam held with a piece of round tooth-pick, and a high-floating dry fly. At least one type of strike indicator should be carried in the fly vest.

One pipe-tobacco tin containing pieces of cut soft foam for strike indicators and brightly colored commercial hard-foam indicators, one 9-foot ox tapered leader and one pack of sticky foam indicators—this all in one large external pouch.

Nine small pouches, mostly hidden behind other pockets on the inside, are empty.

There's also a sheep's wool drying patch to which six small nymphs have been attached since God knows when.

Hanging on dee rings are the bear whistle, polarized sunglasses and a leader straightener. (These are leather or rubber devices used to take the kinks out of tapered leaders. You can carry a small patch of inner tubing to do the same thing.)

A combination scissors-forceps hangs on a retractable clip. (You can use plain forceps, but then you'll need a pair of line clippers as well.)

What's missing? I need more split shots. And one or two more leaders should be added before next season. In addition you may want to carry a small tape measure for accurately measuring

*A leader
straightener
removes coils
from tapered
leaders while
preventing
finger cuts.*

*Forceps are
useful for
removing hooks
and bending
down hook
barbs.*

those real wall hangers. A thermometer would be useful for taking water temperature, but determining it is often more of interest than practical use.

Pretty much everything in the vest is used. No one needs 600 flies, but they'll stay. In fact, a couple of dozen streamers have been drying in the sun-room all winter and have to be returned. I've tied several dozen nymphs and dries so far this winter, and they'll all find homes in the boxes. I will sort the boxes, and a few ragtag flies will either be discarded or given away. (Honest, I don't always carry all seven boxes.)

Nail clippers or speciality fly clippers are used to remove tag ends from knots and to cut knotted line from hooks.

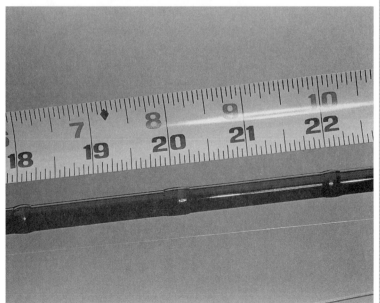

A tape measure can be carried to measure fish. This custom-made fly rod has bands of epoxy-covered thread wrapped every 2 inches, starting at 16 inches from the handle end of the rod.

Fly boxes

There are two questions about fly boxes that all fly-anglers wrestle with: What type do you buy, and how do you organize flies so you can find them? Do I have solutions to these questions? No. Just a few opinions. That's because I've yet to find the perfect fly box, and even if I did I'd never get totally organized. I prefer loose compartments for small dry flies and big flies. And boxes with flat dense foam for nymphs and rippled foam for medium-sized dry flies.

There must be as many types of fly boxes as there are flies. Some have worthwhile features to look for. Clear lids are a bonus. You can see immediately what's inside, which is handy if you have two or more identical fly boxes. Two-sided boxes (with two lids, top and bottom) are handy if space and fly selection is limited. One quite neat one I have has a compartment side for dry flies and a rippled dense foam side for nymphs. It's my favorite fly box. Two-sided boxes bring up another required feature: firm-holding closing devices. I had a little incident with a compartment-type two-sided box a few years ago. Yes, you guessed it. The underside lid opened. I was rummaging through the upright compartments when I noticed a bunch of flotsam out of the corner of my eye. I lost half a dozen flies or so. I still use this box (more carefully now) since it has large compartments for my largest nymphs on one side and streamers on the other.

Sooner or later you'll accumulate a few fly boxes and wrestle with how they should be organized. Figure out some way that reduces searching and allows you to safely leave some boxes at home. Perhaps put dry flies together, nymphs together and streamers together. You may want a caddisfly box if they are dominant where you fish. It could contain caddisfly dries on one side and pupae imitations on the reverse. If you really get into fishing green or brown drake mayflies for a few weeks each spring, keep them in one box. But why carry them the rest of the year?

You will find a day-use box useful. One in which you carry the majority of flies you'll potentially to need where you are fish-

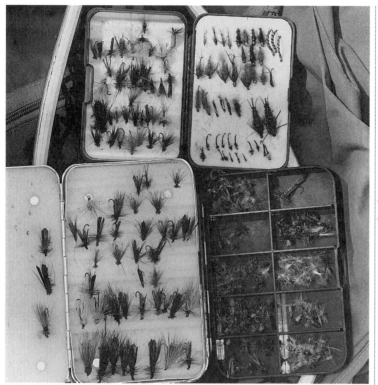

The upper fly box has flat foam in the lid and ridged foam bottom. The large metal box on the left has deep ridges in the foam which reduces flattening of fly hackles. Small dry flies are usually stored in compartments like those on the right.

ing that day. Mine started as a box mainly for one specific river that I fish more often than any other. It is a shirt-pocket-sized single-lid box with a rippled foam insert on the bottom and a flat foam sheet inside the lid. It contains what I am most likely to need on that river at any time of the year—except for the dry flies which I keep in another box—and it saves much searching. It's always in the same pouch and I know what's in it. If I'm fishing elsewhere for a few days, the contents of the day-use box evolve slightly to accommodate the needs of the new stream.

This concept of one box as your main, or day-use, fly box is something to consider. It saves a lot of time because it contains, say, three-quarters of the flies you'll use in one day or on one trip. The benefits of this main box are apparent when I start searching other boxes that don't have the same comfortable familiarity.

Waders

You need either hip waders or chest waders to fish in trout creeks or rivers. Trout are coldwater fish and you are warm-blooded. It is not uncommon to see people on small creeks without waders. It's a mystery how they'll spend $400 on a fly rig and won't bother to spend $50 on a pair of hippers. They tiptoe around the rocks and banks, scared to get wet and all the while not really fishing effectively. I don't know about where you live, but our mountain creeks are too cold for wet wading even in August. Perhaps you can get away with wet wading where you fish.

If you plan to restrict fishing to small creeks, you can get by with hip waders. A decent pair costs $30 to $50 or more. But for versatility on all types of water, you really need a pair of chest waders.

There are two general types of chest-wader materials: neoprene and lightweight rubberized cloth or synthetic material. Neoprene waders are the choice of most fly-anglers because they are comfortable and warm. They tend, however, to be too warm in the summer, especially if you are hiking along a stream or if it's a long walk to the river from the parking spot. Some anglers find that a reasonable compromise is to buy thin neoprene waders, which are quite warm in cool water, yet bearable in summer.

Although I own neoprene waders, I prefer lightweight waders for temperature comfort. In winter I wear warm sweat pants inside my lightweights and find them as warm as neoprene waders.

Neoprenes are especially recommended for float tubing. Because they tend to be cut higher and are usually tighter at the top, water doesn't splash down your backside. And in all but the warmest water they prevent you from getting cold when you're sitting for extended periods of time.

Waders have either boot feet or stocking feet. Stocking-foot waders are like stocking-foot pj's worn by kids. Special wading boots are worn over stocking-foot waders. Boot-foot waders have built in walking feet just like a pair of regular rubber boots.

Top: Felt-soled wading boots are worn over these light-weight waders. The neoprene bands are called gravel guards and prevent fine grit from getting inside the boots while wading. The grit can be uncomfortable and weakens the waders.

Bottom: Light-weight boot-foot waders.

I prefer boot-foot waders because they are easy and fast to get in and out of. They are reasonably priced and have fairly good traction. But they lack the ankle and sole support of sturdier boots made for stocking-foot waders. If you have ankle problems buy stocking-foot waders and a sturdy pair of wading boots.

If you buy both neoprene waders and lightweight waders, consider getting stocking feet in both (most neoprenes come with stocking feet anyway). That way you can buy one good pair of wading shoes and wear them with both sets.

Most wading boots have felt soles. These grip on slippery underwater rocks better than hard-sole boot-foot waders. If you buy boot-foot lightweights, consider buying a felt-sole kit and gluing on felt soles. But a word of caution. Felt soles improve underwater grip and prevent falling, but they become dangerously slippery in wet grass and on wet muddy banks when clogged with mud or river silt.

Wader repairs

Sooner or later your waders will rip or otherwise get a hole. It matters little if they cost $100 or $400. (Murphy bets on the more expensive ones.) Carry a repair kit for the type of waders you'll be using on any fishing trip.

Vinyl repair kits for vinyl/canvas waders seal well, and the glue dries in a few hours. For emergency repairs, duct tape (this is not a joke) also makes an instant waterproof seal on many types of lightweight waders with smooth surfaces. Test the bonding of duct tape to your lightweight waders and carry a roll in your fishing bag if it sticks. Cut a strip much larger than the tear and stick it on the inside. If your waders also are smooth on the outside, apply another strip there. Work the surfaces well with your fingernail or forceps handle to make a good bond. You'll probably want to replace the duct tape with something more permanent and better looking when you get home.

There are special neoprene repair kits that also patch well. The downside is that they require time to set, so your one-day fishing trip could be over if you tear your waders. Tears in neoprene waders can also be repaired with regular silicone bathtub caulking. Just work the sealer into and over the tear from both sides and squirt it under a torn flap. Let it dry for a day. To get a smooth finish, place a piece of plastic bread bag on the gooey surfaces and press the patch between two books. The plastic won't stick to the silicone sealer and will peel away, leaving a smooth surface.

Landing net

A soft cotton landing net helps bring medium and large trout under control quickly so they can be released with as little stress as possible. Clearly, you don't need to net small trout and panfish. Bass are usually lipped. It's not a good idea to net large pike you plan on releasing—they tangle like mad.

What kind of net should you buy? The only essential requirement is that the netting be made of soft cotton or other soft material. Some cheaper nets have raspy, stiff plastic webbing that surely damages fish scales or at least removes mucus.

Whether your net is made of wood or aluminum, or has a folding metal frame is up to you. I like the wood-frame nets because they look cool and they float. My current wooden net cost $20 and is quite adequate. I owned a fancy (read *expensive*) wooden net once, but on about the fourth trip it ended up in the river, and I never saw it again.

You'll need a way to carry a rigid-frame net while you're on the water or walking around. Most nets come with an elastic cord and snap that hooks onto the dee ring on the back of your vest up near the neck. While you're on the river it can hang loose. But when you are walking along the banks and through the bush, the net should be stored in the large external back pouch on your vest. Or you can buy a quick-connect net holder that snaps onto the dee ring at the back of your neck and holds the net up high. A low free-swinging net is forever getting caught on twigs. It can give you quite a smack in your back or head if it suddenly breaks free under tension.

Many anglers use a folding net stored in a carrying pouch usually worn on a belt around the waist. There are at least two types: those with hinged rigid frames and those with spring steel frames that coil up inside a pouch.

Once in a while you'll need a net to land a small feisty fish. Most nets are quite large, so the fish will tangle in the bottom of the loose netting. To prevent this, grasp the tail of the net and use the now-shallow net to scoop up the fish.

The fishing camera

Fishing pictures are an added dimension to the sport. I have a couple of thousand fishing slides of family, friends and a whole bunch of other folks. They are great. Not necessarily technically great (as in magazine-cover quality) but just great to have to look at now and then and to show at fly-fishing club meetings.

You're going to end up spending several hundred dollars on fly-fishing "capital equipment" before you're done—and you're never done. Then there are "operating costs" like gas, vehicle depreciation, meals, beer and scotch (should you be so inclined) flies, new lines and leaders.

A few years ago I gave a talk on fishing photography to the Edmonton Trout Fishing Club. At that time I calculated what it might cost to catch a 28-inch brown trout—assuming it would take considerable effort over five years. The total was something like $19 thousand! (Just figure the depreciation on a sports utility vehicle alone.)

So there you are, the happiest guy on earth—for the moment—holding the biggest trout you'll ever catch. The Big Kahuna of brown trout. It took you five, maybe ten, years to catch this fish. A fish, that if you got out a sharp pencil, cost you nearly twenty grand. And you don't have a camera. I know. I know. This is recreation and we shouldn't place value on it. We do it for the fresh air, exercise and memories. I'll buy that, but winter is long in parts of North America.

Two or three hundred bucks for a pretty good camera is a small price to pay for recording some fine memories. A medium- to good-quality fishing camera is something you should really consider as part of your core gear. How could you take a kid fishing and not take a camera along?

I carry a waterproof camera virtually all the time I'm on the water. It's either around my neck or in the vest. One day my partner, John, and I are going to catch a real wall-hanger brown trout—that's 28 inches in case you need to know where my catch-

and-release policy runs out—and by God we're going to take a whole roll of film while deciding whether it lives or goes on the wall. That day may never come.

In the meantime I'll keep taking lots of riverside pictures for my pleasure—and that of others. Right above my computer monitor are two nighttime pictures of me holding two different, fat 22½-inch 4-pound-plus brown trout caught in "Frenchman's Creek" on the evenings of July 15 and July 16, 1995. The big brown on the second night was caught on a huge compara-dun *Hexagenia* dry fly I whipped up earlier that day in response to what I saw the night before. Good memories. Good pictures.

What type of camera? Buy the best camera you feel you can afford. Good quality point-and-shoot cameras are ideal for fishing. They have good lenses, are lightweight, rugged and fit in a large pocket of a fly-fishing vest. For a few extra dollars you can buy a splashproof or even waterproof model. (The picture of the first big brown above my desk may never have been taken had it not been for my waterproof Nikon. As I handed the camera to another angler to take the picture, it fell in the water. . . .)

All point-and-shoot cameras come with built-in flashes, but look for one that has a force flash or fill flash that lets you choose flash, even when it's bright out, and still give the correct exposure. Fill flash on bright days removes unwanted facial shadows, especially under hats. On dull days flash adds color to you and the fish. A zoom lens is handy to compose pictures and move in close.

Other things to look for are autoexposure and autofocusing, DX coding, macro or closeup mode, and remote control or self-timer. Expect to pay $200 to $400 or more for a point-and-shoot with all the toys. Well worth it.

Line, rod and reel care

You've spent a fair amount of money on a new fly-fishing outfit, so you're going to look after it. Most cleaning and maintenance is straightforward and commonsense.

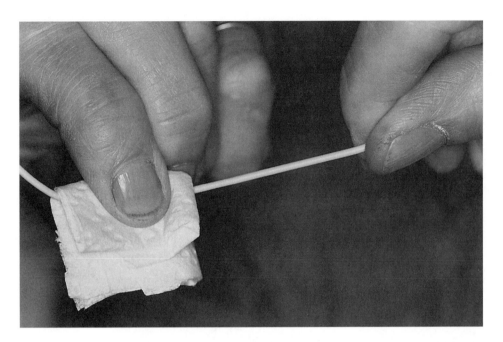

Fly lines are cleaned a few times a year and treated with line dressing to reduce cracking and friction with line guides during casting.

Once or twice each season unreel lines in the house or back-yard and clean them with fly-line dressing. The dressing cleans the line, coats it with a fine film of smooth dressing fluid and apparently lengthens line life. If the line is dirty wipe it with a damp cloth before applying the dressing. To apply the dressing put a small blob on a soft cloth and pull the line through the treated material.

One important but often neglected element of fly-line care is drying the line after each trip. If you transport your rods and reels in closed cases, open them when you get home and let them air. In warm weather this can be done in any dry spot outdoors or in. But in late fall and winter, when nighttime temperatures dip below freezing, dry your rigs in the house where it's warmer. It's not a great idea to dry wet reels and lines where they will freeze. Ice crystals could form in microcracks in the line and make them worse. A few times a year—some say every trip—unreel fly lines, strip out a few feet of backing, and let them dry thoroughly where the dog can't tangle them.

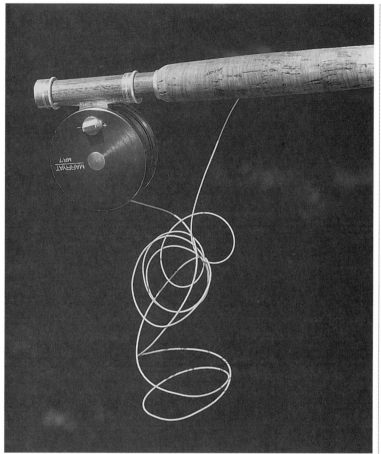

Memory coils form in some fly lines more than others and are reduced by stretching the line. In addition to creating tangles while fishing they cause floating fly lines to kink and coil while dry-fly fishing on lakes.

If your fly line becomes kinked, it's quite easy to limber it up and relax the memory coils. You'll need a buddy to help. Unreel the line in a straight line on a clean piece of lawn or pasture. Each of you grabs one end of the line and walks away from the other until there is fair tension on the line. Hold the line under this pressure for a few seconds. This is best done on a warm day when the line is quite pliable. You may find stretching and dressing your lines to be especially helpful first thing in the spring after they have been drying out and becoming smarter (acquiring memory) all winter long.

Stretching and dressing will enhance line performance dramatically. But sooner or later (it seems always sooner for me) the line will crack to a point that it interferes with casting, sinks or simply looks like hell. You'll then have to break down and buy a new line. If it's a double-taper line in fair shape you can reverse the line on the reel.

It seems no matter what I do I can't get more than two years from any fly line on any of my two or three frequently used rods. Last summer I replaced a $30, 6-weight line that gave me two long solid years—not too bad. Last fall I noticed that a new $50 4-weight line was nearly ruined, and I doubt if it was out more than twenty times. I certainly won't get another full summer out of it. I've tried many brands of fly lines over the years, and there doesn't honestly seem to be a clear pattern about which brands and which price ranges perform best and last longest. While I'm not buying the same model of 4-weight again, I've bought lines from the same company before and they've performed well.

Once or twice a year—or more often if there is obvious dirt in a reel—remove the spool from the reel frame and clean the moving parts. Cotton swabs and paper towels get most of the grime. You may have to use solvent to wash away persistent dirt, but remove the line and backing from the spool first. Lube the moving parts with reel oil or reel grease. That seems to keep them going. If you take a fall and get sand in your reel clean it immediately. A few rotations with grit inside are probably the equivalent of five year's cranking. If you are not near your truck and your replacement reel, take the reel apart on the stream and clean it as best you can. Water, your handy supply of toilet paper and perhaps a small twig will help clean the reel. Clean the reel properly and re-oil it the first chance you get.

There's not much to say about rod care. The greatest threats to your rod are car doors, tailgates and stompers like me. Other than these, rods are quite maintenance free.

After a few years two or three things may start to be less than ideal on your rod, and you may have to hire someone to repair it. Or repair it yourself. This is particularly true for the tip-top guide

Hard cases like this Reel Neet protect expensive rods. The great thing about them is that the reel does not have to be removed.

at the end of the rod. It takes a lot of stress and sometimes will wear through on a favorite rod. Occasionally, the tip-top guide may come loose. If you are uncomfortable replacing it yourself, ask at a local fly shop. They can arrange to have it repaired or will give you the name of a local rod builder.

When rods are put together, line guides are wrapped in place with thread and covered with an epoxy coating. If the epoxy cracks, or was not put on properly, the line guide wrappings may turn white, indicating that water is in the epoxy and thread. The wrappings could be okay for a while but keep an eye on them. Sooner or later they will need replacing.

Selecting a rod and reel case

High-end rods come with either plastic or metal rod cases. That's good because you don't want a $300 rod kicking loose around the basement. If your new rod doesn't have a rod case buy one or build one. You can build a case with the plastic pipe used for central vacuum systems. Buy a 4- to 5-foot section of pipe and two end caps for each case. Glue a cap on one end of the pipe. Secure a piece of chain or cord to the pipe and on the other cap to make a removable lid.

Unfortunately, standard rod cases have no compartment for the reel. When you're cruising around in your rig, fishing awhile here and then driving to another spot, it's a real pain to dismantle your rod and reel every time you move. And it's not a good idea to lay an expensive rod on the dash while you're bouncing along a logging road. Sooner or later you'll be using that lifetime rod warranty.

Thankfully, there are several types of cases that store the rod with reel attached. They have a reel compartment built right into the case. I'm not comfortable with endorsing products in books, but in this instance I have to make an exception for the Reel Neet case, a gem of a product, made by Grizzly Ridge Outdoor Products. (10542 Seaton Road, Lake Country, B.C. V4V 1K4. Canada. Phone: 250-766-3600.) Reel Neet cases are made of durable plastic including the reel compartment.

Fly-fishing trip checklist

For a while I would forget stuff when John and I made a mad unplanned dash to the Crowsnest River. So a few years ago I typed a checklist that I'd print before each trip. I don't use it all the time now because I seem more organized, but each spring, or after an extended time away from the water, I print a copy of it and go through it before we head out. Of course, not all items apply to each trip, and your trip list will be different than mine, but make one. Nothing is more frustrating than to be on the water, miles away from home, and find you've left essential gear behind.

Checklist		
Fishing Gear	Vest Gear	Clothes
❏ Chest waders	❏ Sun glasses	❏ Gloves
❏ Hip waders	❏ Fly floatant	❏ Extra socks
❏ Fly vest	❏ Clippers	❏ Feather vest
❏ Net	❏ Forceps	❏ Neck scarf
❏ Rod and reel #1	❏ Extra leaders	❏ Hat(s)
❏ Rod and reel #2	❏ Split shot	❏ Sweat shirt
❏ Extra reel(s)	❏ Foamies/ indicators	❏ Sweat pants
	❏ Bug dope	❏ Raincoat
	❏ Pocket Kleenex	❏ Coat(s)
	❏ Tippets	❏ Extra pants
	❏ Fly boxes	❏ Extra shirt
		❏ T-shirts

Chapter 3

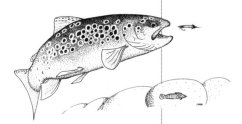

Fly Casting and Line Control

You cannot learn to cast from this or any other book. But you can grasp the essential concepts that will prepare you for casting classes sponsored by a speciality fly-fishing store or fly-fishing club. You also may be fortunate to have a friend skilled in the art of fly casting who can help.

Many good videos are available from speciality fly-fishing shops or from mail-order services provided by some fly-fishing magazines. They are good primers for the beginning fly caster. Seeing how others cast is better than reading. But you can only read so much and watch so much. At some point it's essential to take a class or get an experienced friend to help. I would be honored to be taught by many of my fly angling friends. They cast well and have the temperament to help others learn. But I've also seen groups of two or three fly-anglers on the stream, and I'm quite certain that you wouldn't want to learn from some of these "teachers." I'll leave it up to you to determine if your best buddy is really the one who you want to help you.

Learning to cast with a fly rod is easy, although it may not seem that way if you've already given it a try without some coaching. As time passes, the novice fly rodder will reflect and realize that learning basic casting was in fact the easy part.

Casting skills and techniques will develop with time, but trying to understand trout and other fish, reading water and learning about insects and other fish food are more complex, and there is simply no end to the learning.

My first real casting lesson came from my brother, Gary, a few years after I had purchased my first fly-fishing rig. The main reason for the delay was that my kids were growing up and fly-fishing was not a priority in my life, so I only tried it a few times.

As the kids grew, my interest renewed. When my veteran fly-fishing brother was visiting, I asked him to show me a few things since my fly casting was dreadful. I figured that with his years of experience he should know something. After about 30 minutes in the park, I learned the basics of fly casting—some straightforward stuff I simply had never known before and had never taken the time to learn. Don't make the same mistake as me! Don't miss out on years of fly-fishing fun just because you need a bit of help learning to cast. Take lessons as soon as you can.

Casting lessons are a great help to learn the basic cast and prevent casting problems from developing early.

With a few exceptions, I've noticed that some folks learn to cast much quicker than others. Geez, I hate to say this guys—especially you guys with years of fishing experience—but usually those with the least fishing experience learn the quickest. That's my judgment anyway, and for good reason. The "physics" of delivering a fly are entirely different than casting a heavy metal lure with a bait-casting or spinning outfit. And casting habits can be difficult to break. Could it be that boomer-aged and older men are a bit more narrow-minded about learning something new? Or perhaps they can't admit they don't know everything about fishing? I've seen it: some medium-to-old fart (over forty) who has been chucking hardware for 30 years, and by God he knows how to fish. This fly-fishing can't be that tough, eh? (Of course, fly-fishing is not tough, but techniques are different and a less-than-open attitude can interfere with progress.)

At a casting class I conducted several years ago, we went through some essentials, and I demonstrated the basic overhead cast and the common mistakes beginners make. After the demo and discussion the students had a chance to practice one at a time. The first one to show us his stuff was a fifty-something guy who had spin-fished for years. He damn near broke the tip of the practice rod on the first try because his experience encouraged him to totally ignore the things we carefully explained and demonstrated!

The next person to step forward was a lady who had fished little. She had an open mind, paid attention and didn't have preconceived ideas and locked-in habits. She picked up the rod, gently lifted the tip, raised the 30 feet of practice line up from the lawn, made a nifty textbook back cast, paused and laid the line smartly forward. Perfect. The point I'm trying to make here is that if you have fished a lot before, try to understand that fly casting is different. Pay attention and listen; then it will be easy.

The primary difference between hardware casting and fly casting is that a spinning lure is thrown with the spinning rod, and the line goes along for the ride. The heavy fly line, on the other hand, is propelled with the fly rod, and the near-weightless fly goes along for the ride. In one you cast a lure, in the other you cast a line.

The basic overhead cast

To cast a fly rod and line, the forearm travels back and forth, pivoting at the elbow and shoulder. The wrist stays more or less rigid. The position of the forearm at the back position and the end position form a neat V. Back, forth, cast.

The basic overhead cast involves five parts. Let's assume there are 30 feet of fly line lying straight ahead on the water with no slack line wiggling here and there. To start the cast the rod tip is gently lifted up to about the 10 o'clock position; then power is applied backward, and the line is carried up and over the head. The rod is stopped at about 1 o'clock (way sooner than you may be accustomed to if you're a spin caster) and paused while the line travels backward, parallel to the ground, until it is straight. This is the back cast. When the line is straight behind, and hopefully high in the air, forward power is applied, and the line is carried forward until the rod is again at about 10 o'clock. At the end of the forward cast, the rod is stopped, and the line moves ahead. It lays out straight while still a few feet over the water and then gently drops to the water. Easy up to 10 o'clock; power to 1 o'clock; pause; power to 10 o'clock; easy down. This is just one of many types of casts, but it's the first and most essential.

There are a couple of fairly important concepts that may help you cast better. Back to the spinning cast. There the back cast is simply a necessity to move the rod to the position where the forward cast is started. A decent spin cast can be made by starting with the rod held behind the back or off to the side. From a stopped position the lure is propelled forward with wrist and arm motion on the forward cast. The mass and accelerating speed of the lure loads the rod. All this speed and rod loading projects the lure forward. Sure, spin casts are a little more complicated than this, but you get the idea—it's not unlike a slingshot.

The Basic Overhead Cast

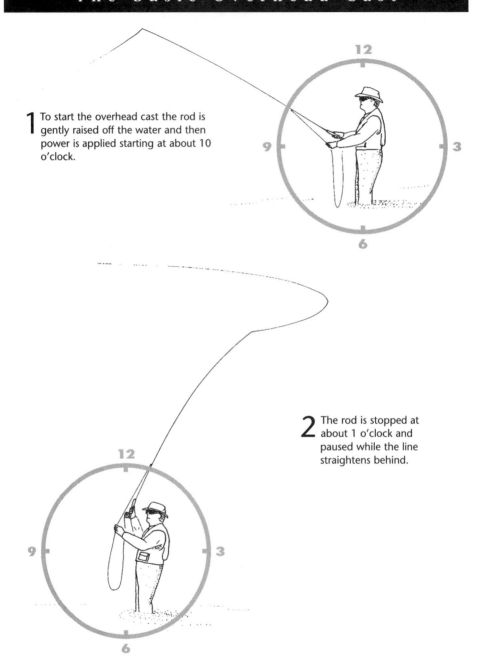

1 To start the overhead cast the rod is gently raised off the water and then power is applied starting at about 10 o'clock.

2 The rod is stopped at about 1 o'clock and paused while the line straightens behind.

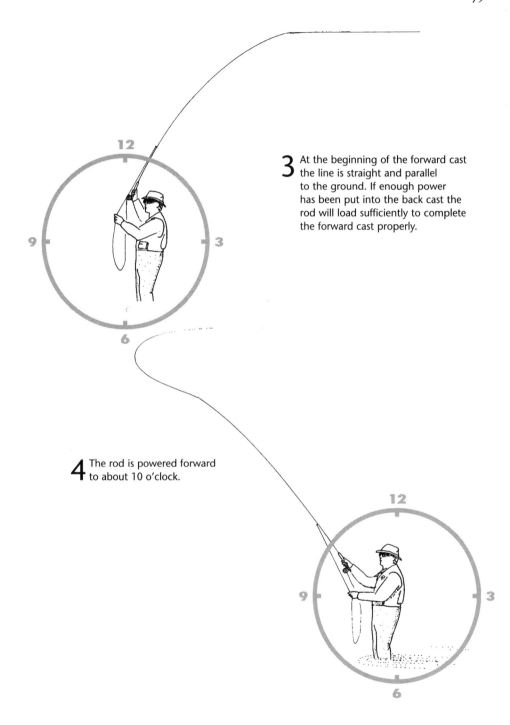

3 At the beginning of the forward cast the line is straight and parallel to the ground. If enough power has been put into the back cast the rod will load sufficiently to complete the forward cast properly.

4 The rod is powered forward to about 10 o'clock.

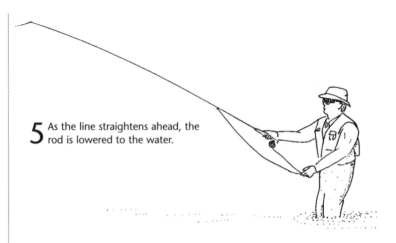

5 As the line straightens ahead, the rod is lowered to the water.

The back cast in fly casting is much more critical to the success of the forward cast. The inertia generated during the back cast helps load the rod. This loading, combined with the forward arm movement, creates the energy for the forward cast. This is fairly important: the back cast assists the forward cast. We'll return to the basic cast and go through it in more detail later.

Fly-casting practice

Rigging up for casting practice is straightforward. You've already connected a leader to the fly line and tied on 2 feet of, say, 3x tippet to the end. Thread the line, leader and tippet through all the lines guides. This is best done by folding the fly line where it connects to the leader and threading this thick folded section ahead of the leader and tippet.

For casting practice you need a hookless fly or piece of yarn tied to the tippet leader. I prefer a fly because yarn is too light and fluffy and doesn't fairly represent how an actual fly will behave. The hookless fly is a visual signal to let you know where you are actually casting. Without the fly attached you won't always be able to see the end of the line.

Holding the rod

Hold the rod in a way that feels comfortable. Usually, the thumb is placed on top of the rod handle and pointed straight ahead. The line guides should be straight below the thumb and not at an angle. You can also hold the rod with a baseball grip. It's nearly the same as the standard grip; however, the thumb is moved down over the index finger.

One way of holding a fly rod. A baseball grip can also be used in which the thumb is lowered to touch the index finger.

Practicing the basic overhead cast

Let's review the basic cast, but in more detail. Again, it's: easy up to 10 o'clock > power to 1 o'clock > pause > power to 10 o'clock > easy down.

Find a large unobstructed lawn so you have about 60 feet of clear space in front and behind you. Strip out about 30 feet of line

Casting practice stance. The feet are angled at about 45° to the direction of the cast. This allows the caster to look over his shoulder to see what the line is doing on the back cast. There is no slack line between the line hand and first line guide on the rod.

including the leader. Lay the rod down in the direction you want to cast and walk the line out. Pick the rod up with your right hand (if you are right-handed) and hold the handle firmly with your thumb pointing straight forward.

Angle your right foot at about 45° back of the direction that you will be casting. The angle is more than you will be comfortable with when actually fishing, but it will allow you to get a good view of what the line is doing behind you on the back cast. Grasp the line in your left hand about halfway to the first line guide. For the first few casts you will not let out any line, so just hold the line with your left hand and don't let go.

To start the cast, point the rod down the line toward the fly, and if necessary take up any slack with your left hand. Raise your right forearm with increasing speed while holding the line with the left hand. As the rod tip approaches 10 o'clock the line will rise in the air and then continue in an overhead direction during the back cast. At the end of the back cast, if all goes according to plan, the line will be straight out behind you, level with the ground or even angled upward. Take a look over your right shoulder. (If all has not gone to plan and the line is piled up on the ground behind you, abort the cast and start again.)

At about the same time as the line straightens out, commence the forward cast. Again, distinctly and evenly apply power to the rod from the 1 o'clock position until it reaches 10 o'clock, then stop. The line should move forward in a loop, straighten out well above the surface and then gently fall. As the line settles to the surface lower the rod tip.

The energy you put into the back and forward casts transfer

This is no way to start a practice cast. There is slack line between the line hand and rod guide and too much slack in front of the rod tip.

Rod and arm position at the end of the back cast and start of the forward cast.

into the fly line, so apply firm power. The presentation of a fly line has to be delicate, but the back and forward casts are not feeble—they are deliberate. Adequate power must be applied to both. Be firm and deliberate, but don't apply too much muscle either.

Practice the basic cast without attempting to increase the distance. If you have problems, lay the rod down and straighten the line by hand. Have a friend watch your back and forward casts. Even if your friend is not a fly-angler, he or she can coach you on the 1 o'clock, pause and 10 o'clock rules. Use a video camera to capture what you're actually doing. You'll likely be surprised how the rod and line are behaving.

Overcoming four common casting problems

When my brother first helped me, he showed me the things I was doing wrong that resulted in my lousy casts. Since then I've learned that almost every beginning fly caster makes a few of the same mistakes. Overcoming them is simple and will improve beginning casts immediately and immensely. Let's go through these problems and then look at some other features of the basic cast.

Problem one During the back cast—pulling the line up, over the head and behind—the rod tip is lowered too low to the ground behind. There are two causes. First, the entire rod arm is simply lowered too far to the ground. And second, even though the arm may have stopped at 1 o'clock, the wrist may have snapped back. (The arm stopped, but the wrist kept going, breaking the wrist.) This results in hooking ground vegetation or dragging the line in the water behind. A poor forward cast also results because too much energy is wasted recovering the line from its low position—if it can be recovered at all.

Solution one At the end of the back cast the backward motion of the rod is stopped at just past vertical. Assuming straight up is noon, the rod is stopped by the time it gets to 1 o'clock. The natural tendency of all casters—including seasoned pros—is to carry the rod past 1 o'clock. But 1 o'clock is where the rod is stopped. The energy of the back cast will naturally pull the rod tip and your arm slightly past the stop point, but powering the rod farther back results in the line falling too low. If the rod is stopped quite high, and if enough power has been put into the back cast, the line will stay elevated and travel backward until it is straight and parallel to the ground—or better yet, somewhat above parallel.

One way to overcome the problem of moving the rod too far back is to pick out a cloud (or whatever) that is at about a 45° angle above and behind. A target. When raising the rod up and behind, try to shoot the line in the direction of the cloud you selected. Not straight behind you, but up in the sky as if you were going to punch a hole in it. In reality the line will still end up

On-stream coaching while learning to cast can be a great help. It can also aid seasoned anglers in overcoming casting problems.

dropping lower than your cloud target, but this technique impresses the concept that the line must be maintained well above the ground or water behind.

A few years ago during a casting class, I saw a new and different back-cast problem. One student was having difficulty with his line forming an S wiggle near the rod tip on the back cast. His casts kept crashing, yet he seemed to be doing things right. Another helper and I watched closely. The caster had accepted the need to stop at 1 o'clock so much that he brought his arm and wrist to an *immediate* full stop at just past noon. But the stop was jerky, and his wrist snapped slightly forward momentarily—

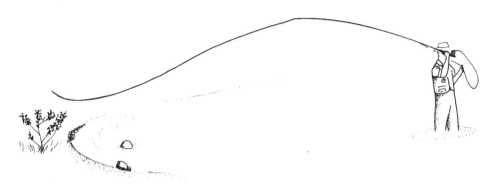

almost unnoticeably. This resulted in one or more small S wiggles in the fly line right above the rod tip. It was enough to disrupt the smooth backward flow of the fly line and caused improper line extension on the back cast and a poor forward cast. So, practice to make a smooth transition from the backward motion to the full stop at 1 o'clock.

Problem two The forward cast is started before the line has straightened out on the back cast. This may result in cracking the line or possibly snapping off the fly. Also, because the rod has not been fully loaded, the forward casting distance will be reduced or the line may pile up.

Solution two When the rod reaches the 1 o'clock position at the end of the back cast, it is held for a short time to allow the line to straighten out behind. Power the rod to just past vertical on the back cast and pause. This is critical, but it's success depends on there being enough power in the back cast to cause the line to travel straight back without falling out of the sky.

If you have put enough power into the back cast, the line will continue its backward travel during this pause until it is straight out behind. This whole pausing business only takes a fraction of a second or so. It's no time for a sandwich or cigar. It can be so subtle that it may not even be noticeable. What is readily noticeable is failing to pause and snapping the line.

Problem three At the end of the forward cast the rod tip is forced too low to the water, often resulting in line slap and splashy fly landings that can put fish down.

If too little power is put into the back cast the line will fall to the ground. Here the rod tip has traveled too far past 1 o'clock and is too low to the ground because the wrist is bent back. Too much energy is wasted trying to recover such a cast, and the forward cast will likely pile up.

The arm has stopped at about the right angle, but the wrist is broken (moved back), resulting in the rod tip and line being too close to the ground.

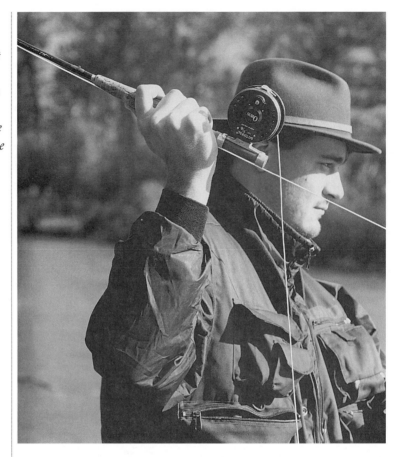

Solution three Apply power to the rod through the forward cast to the 10 o'clock position. When the line starts its gentle descent to the water, the rod can be lowered to follow the line down. A good way to remember to stop the forward motion of the rod is to imagine that you are casting onto a table about 3 feet above the actual level of the water. Attempt to get the line to settle on this imaginary platform.

Problem four During the forward and back casts, too little power is applied to the rod. Without enough power on the back cast, the line will start to fall to the ground instead of straightening out behind. Without enough power on the forward cast, the

line will pile up or the fly and leader will fail to straighten out properly.

Solution four Apply more power to both the back and forward casts. Fly casting is delicate, but deliberate power must be applied to both the forward and back casts. This solution is hard for people to grasp. It may be because fly-fishing is perceived as being gentle. It's gentle in that the fly and leader—when dry-fly fishing—normally must land gently on the surface. But firm power must be applied to the back and forward casts to give proper direction to the fly line.

At the start of the forward cast, the fly line is straight back and level with the ground.

Raising the line from the water quietly

When casting to rising fish, especially in quiet water, the line must be lifted from the water easily at the start of the back cast. The natural tendency is to jerk the line from the water in an effort

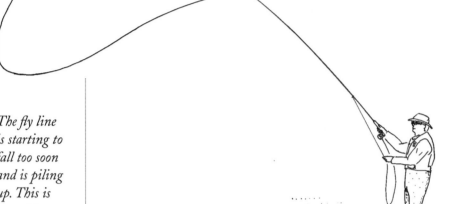

The fly line is starting to fall too soon and is piling up. This is caused by too little power during the forward cast or by the rod being too low on the back cast and too much energy being lost recovering the line.

to put lots of power into the back cast, assuming, of course, that you have learned that back and forward casts require some degree of power. This, however, may result in a noisy slurping of the line from the water. To overcome this problem the line is quietly lifted from the water by slowly lifting the rod toward 10 o'clock and at the same time gently hauling on the fly line with the line hand.

Controlling loop size

During the back and forward casts the line is always in a U-shape except at the end of the back cast and end of the forward cast. The rest of the time it's turning over somewhere along its length and is therefore formed in a U-shaped loop. The depth of the U-shaped loops is controlled by the speed of the back and forward casts and by the distance power is applied during the back and forward casts. A snappy short-action power stroke results in narrow loops. A slower wider-angled power stroke results in a wider loop.

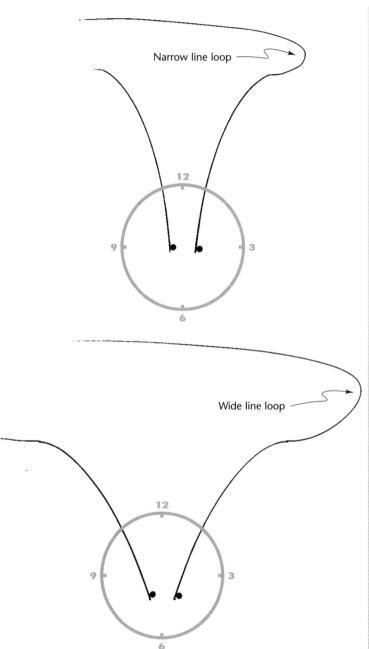

Narrow line loop

12

9

3

6

A narrow power angle and fast casting speed result in a narrow line loop. Because friction with the air is reduced, the line travels farther on the forward cast.

Wide line loop

12

9

3

6

A wide power angle results in a wide loop, which is desirable when casting weighted flies so they don't tangle with the line.

A narrow, or tight, loop has less surface area to cause wind resistance than a wide, or open, loop and results in longer casts. However, a more open loop is desirable when casting weighted nymphs, as the front part of the line with the weighted clutter is less liable to fall into the lower part of the loop and tangle.

For the beginning caster this isn't an immediate concern. You need to learn how to get the line out properly, and whether or not you have tight loops is not terribly important. It may be, in fact, that the issue of tight *versus* open loops is somewhat overrated in fly-angling schools of thought. I have a weak right forearm and wrist—even after all these years of fly casting—and tend to have a rather slow cast, resulting in much wider loops than many of my friends. Ask your casting instructor to explain this in more detail.

Getting the line out and false casting

When you feel confident in your ability to make a 30-foot cast, you will want to lengthen the distance. Several false casts—back and forward casts without letting the line come down—are used to get line out. At the end of each forward cast, a couple of feet or more of line are allowed to shoot through the rod line guides. This line has already been stripped from the reel, the bulk of it resting on the water at your feet. It is held and controlled in the line hand, and the line is released through the fingers at the end of the forward cast. When sufficient distance is achieved the cast is completed by allowing the line to settle to the surface.

A common mistake of novice fly casters is to false cast unnecessarily. Back and forth. Back and forth. Without actually doing anything constructive such as drying the fly, letting out more line or actively measuring the distance of the cast. Back and forth. Back and forth.

When you have enough line out and you are in control, complete the cast. Our kids' hockey coaches said, "You can't score goals in the penalty box or on your butt." And you can't catch fish with your line in the air.

At the end of the forward cast extra line that has been stripped from the reel is released to lengthen the cast.

The single haul

A useful technique for lengthening the distance of your overhead casts when casting large pike and bass flies is called the single haul. At the top of the back cast the line hand is moved up near the reel, and at the moment the casting arm is brought forward the line hand tugs sharply downward a few inches. This extra speed and power is usually enough to shoot flies a few more feet. Learn the basic cast properly before attempting this advanced technique. Ask your casting instructor about hauling line.

The single haul increases line speed and casting distance. It is useful for casting heavy pike flies. At the top of the back cast, the line hand is moved up near the reel to A. At the moment the casting arm is brought forward, the line hand tugs sharply downward several inches to B.

The roll cast

There are many times when the basic overhead cast will not work or when it cannot be used because of wind conditions or obstructions. Different casts or variations of the basic cast must be employed. One is the roll cast.

On small creeks or in tight spots on larger rivers, the roll cast can come in handy. It allows you to cast a fly when you are almost backed up to a high bank or streamside bushes.

The roll cast works well for casting small flies short to medium distances. But it is not a distance cast, and it isn't going to

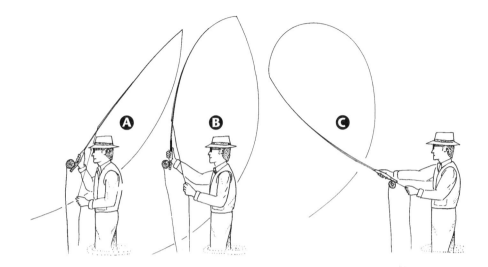

work too well for weighted streamers and nymphs—at least it doesn't for me.

To roll cast, lift the rod slowly so the line (which is stretched out in front or downstream) moves closer toward you. The rod is held upright or just past upright, and the near part of the line hangs slack down to the water while the rest is still out in front. The rod is cast forward with a quick forearm snap. If all goes according to plan, the line will roll ahead, lay out where you planned and not get hung up in the bushes behind you. Or not. Practice the roll cast if you're going to fish small creeks and streams with lots of bank clutter.

The roll cast is used when obstructions prevent a normal back cast.

The steeple cast

For one or two reasons the roll cast may not be an option. Perhaps you need more distance than a roll cast offers, or perhaps its splashy presentation will spook trout in a slow spring creek. (That wretched 7-foot reed grass along one of my favorite brown trout sections is a pain in August.) Try a steeple cast when shrubs or tall grass are behind you.

The steeple cast is used to shoot line high in the air to clear bushes behind. The line travels upward at about the same angle as the rod.

Instead of stopping the back cast at 1 o'clock, stop it much sooner and punch the line high up toward an imaginary church steeple high in the air behind you. The idea is to end the back cast with the line at a high angle instead of level to the ground as in the normal overhead cast. The steeple cast works well for light flies, but heavy nymphs and split shots are difficult to cast.

The reach cast

We often want to cast dry flies straight across a stream at a rising fish. This is fairly straightforward if the current is uniform. But often as not, the current between you and the fish is faster than where the fish is holding. This is not some fiendish plot but

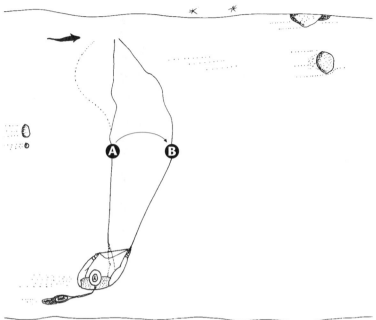

The reach cast. Instead of aiming the casting arm straight ahead to A it is arced upstream to B during the last stage of the forward cast. This places the line upstream ahead of the fly and lengthens the drag-free drift. If the stream flow is in the opposite direction the arm is moved the other way.

a fact of physics. Because of friction between water and the river-bed and bank, water flows slower along the bank than it does out in the middle. So fish often hold near the bank.

In this instance a modified overhead cast, the reach cast, is necessary. As the line extends during the forward cast, simply reach the casting arm and rod upstream. As your arm moves forward, arc it and the rod to the upstream side. This puts much of the line upstream of the fly instead of in a straight line between you and the fly. The center portion of the line then has some catching up to do before it starts to pull on the fly, causing it to drag.

Cross casting (wind cast)

If you are a right-hand caster, wind blowing from your left side is no problem because it carries the fly out of harm's way. But cast-ing with even a light crosswind coming from your casting-arm side

The wind cast. A strong wind from the left side would blow the line and fly into the caster. The wind cast is the same as a basic overhead cast except that the casting arm is brought high over the opposite shoulder.

is difficult and dangerous, especially if you are trying to throw out a heavy weighted nymph. (Weighted nymphing is often referred to as "chuck 'n' duck" for good reason.) On the back and forward casts the wind pushes the line toward you, and the fly can smack you in the back or head—possibly sticking in your ear. Even if it doesn't you will find this intimidating and your casts will be faulty.

The best way to overcome this problem is to bring the back cast over your left shoulder—assuming you are right-handed. In other words, make the back cast over your left shoulder instead of your right shoulder. Otherwise, the casting procedures used for the cross cast are the same as the basic cast.

A head wind can also interfere with fly presentation. Normally, the forward cast power is stopped at about 10 o'clock and the line is allowed to fall onto the water. Great in theory, but it doesn't work too well with a head wind. Delicate presentation may have to be sacrificed for accuracy by powering the forward cast down lower and punching the line toward the target site.

Powering the rod and line will also help you get under overhanging branches. Again, you may have to sacrifice delicacy just for the benefit of getting the fly near some slurping brown trout. Overcoming wind and branches by powering the line to the water may put some trout down, but what are your options?

The flip cast can often be used to cast nymphs upstream without a back cast.

The flip cast

When nymph fishing you don't always have to bother with back casting. Nymphs are sometimes fished until the line is more or less straight downstream. It depends on the type of water, type of nymph and what the fish are doing. Imagine you are standing in the water with the line straight downstream. You've got perhaps 30 feet of line out and feel the tension on the rod. If the line is raised slightly, so there is not too much drag, the line can be simply "flipped" straight ahead to make the forward cast. In other words, the current and drag on the line has loaded the rod already—there's no need for a back cast.

Controlling line after the cast

You need to maintain control of the fly line at all times. That way your flies will do what they are supposed to do, you'll scare fewer fish, your line will tangle less often, you will cast more effectively and you will hook more fish.

As with other fly-fishing procedures, you can't learn the details of controlling line by just reading about them. Of all the things we'll talk about, perhaps line management is the one that will come naturally with time on the water. Again, taking a class that gets you on the water will be a big help. However, some general principles deserve discussion to prepare you for classes and on-stream practice.

Line control is more complicated in flowing water than in stillwater because everything keeps moving. In flowing water there is a natural tendency for two things to happen. Slack develops and/or the line forms a U-shaped bow—things that are not desirable for many types of fly-fishing. In stillwater there is usually tight contact with the fly and there is rarely any slack line between the angler and the fly.

It will take some time on the water to become comfortable with handling and controlling line. After many years of catching more fish than I probably deserve, I still mess up once in a while. For whatever reason I occasionally drop the line from my rod-hand fingers when I hook a fish. Then I have to get the line back to the all-important rod hand while trying to keep the line tight and the fish on. Usually, the fish is lost.

Line control. Immediately after the cast the line is placed under the rod hand index or middle finger (or both). This gives the fly-angler better control of the line.

If the line is not held in the rod hand, line control is difficult. It is also hard to hook a fish and keep it on while the line is being brought under control.

To help us understand the key elements of line control let's review a basic dry-fly drift and describe the hand and line movements. To keep things simple we will consider a 30-foot quartering-upstream cast with a dry fly. From the point of the angler, the fly is placed on the water, say, about 25 feet upstream and a few feet out into the current—that's quartering upstream.

At the completion of the cast the fly line is held only in the left hand (with apologies to left-handed casters). Immediately, the line is handed over to the rod hand and hooked under the middle finger (or middle and index fingers) and grasped in the

After the upstream cast line is stripped toward the angler to prevent slack from developing in the line.

first joint of the middle finger. It is also still held with the left hand.

This sounds simple—and is—but its importance cannot be overemphasized. The middle finger (and/or the index finger) is now the master of the line. It is the brake and the clutch. You can now strip in line with the left hand, you can put a lock on the line if you get a hit and need to tighten up on a fish, and when a fish is on you can use the middle finger to control the tension on the line.

Back to the cast. Immediately after the fly lands on the water, it starts moving toward you. Let's see what happens if you fail to remove the slack between the fly and your rod-hand brake finger.

By the time the fly drifts down to within 20 feet, slack has developed in the line. Suddenly, a rainbow hits the fly. You have to tighten up to set the hook and keep the line taut so the hook doesn't come lose. You pull down on the line with your left hand and raise the rod in one motion. Nothing happens.

Well, nothing significant. A whole bunch of loose line flies up in the air, and still there's no feel of the fish. Even with the rod tip high in the air, there are 2 or 3 more feet of loose line between the rod tip and where the fish was—past tense. The verbal air pollution in the valley increases dramatically as you curse the scaly fiend that got away. You were unable to tighten up on the line because of all the slack, and the hook failed to set into the hard jaw of a 17-inch rainbow trout. Such experiences really encourage attention to line control.

Let's go through the same cast and keep the line under control this time. After the cast, you clasp the line with your rod-hand middle finger. Almost immediately, you pull down on the line

Proper line control with little or no slack line on the water between the rod tip and strike indicator or dry fly. The line is controlled with the rod hand fingers, and slack is removed by stripping in line with the other hand.

with your left hand and strip line through the middle finger of your rod hand. Being careful not to pull too fast, you carefully watch the fly and the line so the fly is not pulled along. You keep no more than 1 or 2 feet of loose line between the rod tip and the fly. The rod tip is near the water and pointed toward the fly, following it along. Suddenly, the same rainbow comes up again. You pause for a fraction of a second, and without thinking you simultaneously raise the rod tip and pull down with your left hand. (You remembered to keep the line under your rod-hand middle finger.) This time you've made firm contact, and the silvery rose-colored rainbow leaps 2 feet into the air, protesting wildly. Fish on!

Sometimes when you are short-line nymph fishing, you do not need to strip in line. A few feet of line is cast upstream and out into the run. As the indicator moves downstream, the tip of the rod is raised up to maintain minimal slack. As the indicator passes only a few feet away, the rod tip is then lowered again to feed line to prevent dragging the nymph. Remember:

1   Limit the amount of slack in the fly line when dry-fly and nymph fishing.
2   Use your rod-hand middle finger or index finger to help manage the line.
3   Strip the fly line with your left hand.
4   Use both hands to manage line when a fish hits.

Mending the line

As already mentioned, fly line tends to form a U-shaped bow between the fly (or strike indicator) on the water and the rod tip. Usually, this is not desirable because the line pulls the fly downstream in an unnatural manner. This is called drag. To remove the bend in the line, it is lightly tossed or flicked upstream. Usually upstream. Sometimes, when streamer fishing, line is mended downstream to add more speed or to direct it to a fish-holding spot. Controlling the line like this is called mending, or line mending.

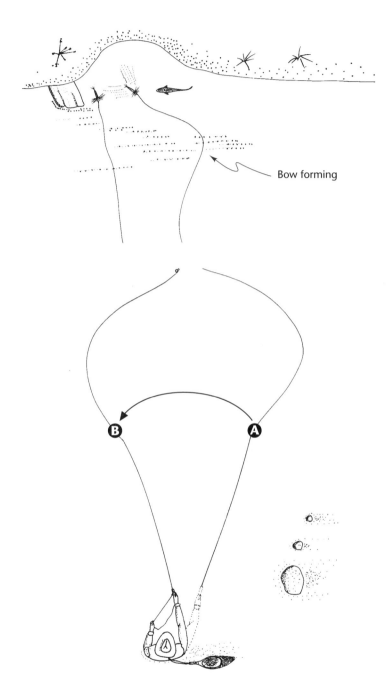

When the fly line moves faster in midstream than near the fly a bow forms and the fly is dragged unnaturally.

Bow forming

With a quick flick of the casting arm mend the line upstream from A to B to prevent or reduce drag.

The rod and line are flicked upstream (to the left) to remove a downstream bow in the line and reduce drag.

Left hand or right hand?

The line-management discussions in this book assume that you cast with your right hand and wind with your left—the way that's comfortable for a majority of fly-anglers. I don't switch the rod from my right hand to left hand when retrieving a fish or winding in the line, but a fair number of right-handers who cast with their right hand actually switch the rod to their left hand and wind with their right. It's a personal thing and you'll have to decide what's more comfortable for you. Switching hands makes no sense to me at all. But a lot of things don't make sense and this certainly is not critical to the continuation of civilization. If you want to switch hands, go ahead.

If you loaded the line on your new fly reel for right-hand winding and decide to try left-hand winding, you'll have to rewind the line. First, make the necessary changes in the reel mechanism to change from right- to left-hand winding. Then remove the line and backing from the reel—you don't have to untie it. Then rewind the line with the reel attached to the rod so it is wound on the "right" way. When taking the line off the reel be careful not to get it tangled or you'll have an awful job getting it sorted out. Walk around the house stripping the line as you go to keep it from piling up in one spot and tangling. In summer do it in the backyard as long as the grass is clean. Just make sure your dog is tied up or kept out of the way.

Playing fish

So you've managed and mended the line carefully and have a strike. You now have to control the line to keep your fish hooked.

Rule number one is always keep the rod tip up or at least to the side at an angle to the direction of the fish. The purpose of the rod is to act as a buffer so the line doesn't snap. Never point the rod at the fish because this prevents the rod from buffering the pulls of the trout.

The first thing you need to be concerned with is "getting the line to the reel" or "playing the fish from the reel." This means winding in the slack line around your knees, assuming you are wading. The fish is then played from the reel either by letting line out (and controlling drag with your palm on the reel rim or with fingers on the line or both) or by reeling in. Playing fish from the reel is recommended because it reduces the risk of getting piles of loose line caught around feet, legs or twigs, and thus causing problems when the fish wants to run. Quite often when fishing for small trout on a small stream, I'll simply strip the line in, release the fish and start casting again with all the line I need already out of the reel. But every effort should be made to play larger trout from the reel. You'll have better control and will be less prone to foul the line and break off the fish.

Unless you've hooked a real wall hanger most trout will start to come in right away, and you have to bring the line in to maintain tension so the fish doesn't shake loose. You'll have to hand

When a fish strikes, lift the rod tip and keep it up while playing the fish.

strip the line in because single-action fly reels do not wind in fast. Spinning reels retrieve line at high speed, something like 4 or 5 spool turns for each rotation of the handle, but single-action fly reels, which have no multiplier gearing, rotate one for one.

Normally, the fish is brought closer by stripping the line in with the left hand. After each strip you have to apply braking pressure to the line with your rod-hand middle finger (or with your thumb and index finger) to prevent the line from heading back out and to maintain some form of control over the line and fish.

If your hooked fish decides it has had enough of this and it's large, it will make a run and haul out some line. Since you haven't yet "got the fish to the reel" you have no drag system to help ease out the line. Here's where the middle finger, or thumb and index finger, come in handy. Now they're a clutch controlling the tension on the line as the fish runs out. Too much pressure and you'll perform the 40-foot release (or long distance release).

When winding line on the reel while playing a fish, the line can be placed under the rod-hand little finger. This removes line coils, and the line is wrapped on the reel spool tightly and neatly.

When you've stripped in a bunch of line and the fish is halfway in, the line is floating around your knees or drifting downstream. You should now wind in the slack line. You have to maintain tension on the line—again with the all important middle finger—while you reel in line like mad. If the fish swims toward you while you're doing this, you'll have to stop winding and start stripping again. When you reach a steady relationship with the trout, you can start winding in line.

While getting the line to the reel, it's a good idea to place the slack line—the line between the reel and the rod-hand middle finger—under your rod-hand little finger. If you hook the line under your pinkie finger you can apply pressure to the line that is being wound onto the reel so that it wraps on neatly without loose coils. Using your little finger also ensures that you will clear any kinks in the line before they are wound on the reel.

Once all the line is on the reel you now have pretty good control. You can directly hand crank the trout in closer for netting. If it's a fighter and wants to strip out line, control the speed of its run by gently applying pressure to the palming rim on your reel with your winding hand. This is very important if the drag on

*Palming a reel.
Drag can be
applied to the
rim of the spool
with the palm
or the fingers.*

your reel is less than ideal. Drags on cheaper reels tend to spin uncontrollably when a fish makes a sudden stop. You are then left with a rat's nest in the line and probably a lost fish if it runs again and your reel is fouled. Another long distance release. Land the trout and release it as soon as possible. Remember:

1. Immediately take up the slack by hand-stripping line.
2. When the fish is under control wind the slack to the reel.
3. Play the fish from the reel.
4. Allow the fish to run to prevent breaking it off.
5. Control the spool by palming the reel rim.

A net reduces time required to land larger trout.

Landing trout

Finally, your prize trout is within reach. Reel in enough line so you will be able to reach the fish with your net. Lock the line in place with your rod-hand middle finger and get your net ready. Landing trout is usually quite easy, but sometimes things go awry. If all goes according to plan you will lift up high with the rod and get the trout's nose out of the water. If it is tired, but not exhausted, it will skid across the surface, and you can gently slip the net underneath. If it's a smallish trout, hold the baggy bottom of the net in your net-holding hand so the trout is scooped out of the water and cradled in the shallow net.

Reach in the net and grasp the trout upside down to remove the hook. You can also grab the trout from the outside of the net and poke its head up through the net frame for hook removal.

Assuming you have debarbed your fly it should come out easily. A pair of forceps—hanging from your vest—makes for easy hook removal. The toughest hooks to remove are those imbedded in the bony maxilla. This is the hard "flap" that extends back from the upper lip. Just take it easy and gently work the hook out as soon as possible. Release the fish only after you are certain it is ready.

Polarized sunglasses reduce risk of eye injury and reduce glare from the water's surface. A hat shades the eyes and protects the head from wandering flies.

Eye and skin safety

Fly-fishing is hardly an extreme sport like hang gliding, yet has its share of safety concerns. Wear glasses and a hat when you are fly casting. Polarized glasses are excellent for screening water glare, and they also protect eyes from errant flies. A hat will protect you from sunburn, shade your eyes and protect your noggin from flies on the forward cast. Ball caps are popular with fly-anglers, especially where the wind blows, but they offer less protection from the sun than wide-brimmed hats. And, of course, sun screen is highly recommended these days.

Wading safety

Wading and casting. Wading and casting. That's how we fish in small streams and rivers. About the only things to say about wading are to wade safely and wade quietly. There are all sorts of things to throw you off balance when wading: slippery rocks, random boulders and loose pea gravel. You'll find them.

My brother (hope he doesn't mind) tells of the time he was walking along the banks of the Crowsnest River. He saw his campsite neighbors across the river, and instead of stopping to

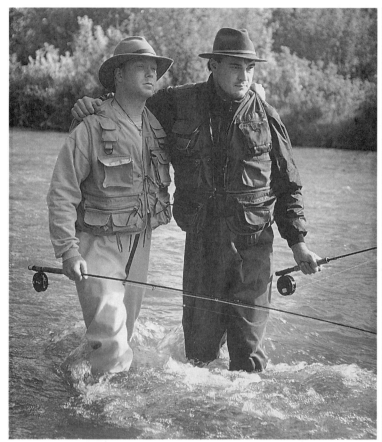

Cross fast water with a buddy to make walking steadier and safer.

wave he kept walking—right into the river. Not exactly a wading incident, but it shows that you have to pay attention. Most fly-anglers have taken a minor or major dunking.

Don't be in a rush when wading. Watch where your feet are going. If there are fish rising up ahead, chances are they will still be there when you arrive, whether you rush up or take it easy. And you are more likely to spook the fish if you rush toward them. Take it easy.

If you plan to wade in fast water quite often, consider buying a wading staff. I don't own one but often find a strong branch on the shore to help me across a piece of water I'm unsure of.

If you have to cross fast water and are fishing with a buddy, cross together. Stand close together with the less heavy angler on the downstream side. Put one arm around your buddy's shoulder and grab onto his jacket or shirt on the opposite side. He does the same to you. Hold on tight. Now wade across together. Barry Thornton from Vancouver Island showed me how to do this a few years ago when we were fishing for steelhead on the Oyster River. I couldn't believe how much more stable we were in the fast water. John and I now do this from time to time on the Bow River, and I'm always impressed with how much safer I feel. (I don't know how John feels about this, since I weigh 50 pounds more than he. If I go down and don't let go, well . . .)

And if you can't cross safely, don't try. You'll either get dunked or end up in serious trouble. The most that will happen is you'll lose a good opportunity to hook a fish. There will be another you can get farther upstream.

Safety belt

If you'll be wading in a fast river, secure a belt around your midsection. The belt will prevent your waders from filling with water and dragging you under should you take a fall. Neoprenes are usually quite snug and less likely to fill. Lightweight waders tend to be looser fitting and will quickly fill with water. Most models of lightweight and neoprene waders have belt loops to accommodate a safety belt. A fanny pack also can double as a safety belt.

In Craig, Montana, right on the bank of the Missouri River, there's small epitaph. It's on private property right across the fence bordering the public campground on the south side. A poem on the stone marker waxes about a departed angler who only fished with Wooly Worms on the Missouri. I talked to his surviving fishing partner a few years ago. Turns out the poor fellow, who refused to wear a wader belt, took a fall, was dragged under and drowned a few miles upstream. Don't let this be you.

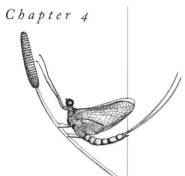

Chapter 4

Insects and Artificial Flies

All fish do three things in life: make more fish of their own species, keep from being eaten and eat. How much they eat is closely related to water temperature and, of course, their size. What they eat depends on what's available.

Trout and other gamefish eat an assortment of aquatic insects like mayflies, caddisflies, stoneflies and midges. Fish also eat terrestrial or land insects like ants, grasshoppers and beetles that blow or fall into the water. Many other aquatic animals like leaches, minnows, shrimp and crayfish, where available, round out the menu. Big trout, pike and bass are known to eat mice. All these creatures can be imitated with artificial flies. That's why we're on the water with our fly-fishing gear.

Many insect species are of special interest to fly-anglers because their immature stages live in water. Adult females of these aquatic insects lay eggs in the water that hatch into nymphs and larvae that spend a year or more in the water until they reach puberty —or until a trout or other fish eats them. Casual observers may be vaguely familiar with the air and land forms of these bugs they see flying around. But most don't realize that many insects spend the majority of their lives underwater as nymphs and larvae.

Insects like this mayfly are imitated with dry flies.

The classification of insects and other creatures eaten by trout and other gamefish is complicated. But the technical details really don't matter, for as Dave Hughes said in his excellent book *Handbook of Hatches*, "Trout don't speak Latin." However, a basic understanding of food insects and other animals and how to imitate them with flies helps fly-anglers catch fish.

Many fly-anglers feel that learning the basics of fish food is another special dimension of interest to the sport of fly-fishing. Others, however, consistently catch a lot of trout by blissfully ignoring the biology and using only a handful of generic patterns to attract and catch fish. They use flies like Adamses, Royal Wulffs, Hare's Ears and Wooly Buggers that often don't imitate anything in particular, but are buggy looking or simply look flashy enough to trout and other gamefish to eat. Whether you want to get technical or take it easy, the important thing is to do what makes you happy and gives you pleasure.

Selecting flies that imitate trout food

We imitate insects on the water's surface with dry flies, and we imitate insect stages below the surface with nymphs and other wet flies. Other aquatic animals like minnows and leeches are imitated with streamers or other appropriate patterns.

Some fly patterns, like Blue-winged Olive dry flies or stonefly nymphs, *imitate* one specific type of insect. They are tied to actually look like a specific insect. Other patterns, like the Adams or Hare's Ear, are tied to give a general *impression* of

Screening water is a good way of collecting and learning about aquatic insects.

insects without actually looking like anything in particular. They look buggy. They've got the shape, size and perhaps color of several species without looking a whole lot like anything specific. They may be tied with willowy fibers, like marabou feathers, that flutter invitingly and imitate the legs or gills of underwater insects. Still other flies are downright *attractors*, not really looking like anything at all, but flashy enough to induce a fish to strike. Many of the flies we fish with take on two of these three main characteristics. A Zug Bug, for example, is a flashy little item tied with peacock feather strands called herl. It is an attractor, yet it looks

This large stonefly nymph screened from a river bottom is imitated with a large wet fly called a nymph.

a bit like some mayfly nymphs. If you are trying to imitate or give the impression of a specific insect, select a fly pattern that closely resembles the size, shape and color of the natural.

Included with each group of insects and other animals discussed below are a few popular fly patterns that imitate them. There is no intention to suggest that these are the only patterns that will work. There are, after all, too many regional differences and too many species of insects to begin to list them all. The seven fly-pattern books on my shelves list between one and two thousand patterns, and I've heard there are over ten thousand published examples.

All species within an order (or group) of insects have the same general shape and really only vary in size and color. A ¼ inch blue-winged olive mayfly and a 1¼-inch *Hexagenia* mayfly look pretty much the same, except one is small and greenish and the other is big and yellowy tan. They both have the character-

istic mayfly shape of a tapered carrot. Accordingly, the dry-fly imitations look pretty much the same except for the size and color.

Underwater rocks are teeming with nymphs and larvae of aquatic insects.

Your best source of information about flies that work where you plan to fish is a local fly shop. And the closer the fly shop is to the waters you plan to fish, the better. The main sports store in my hometown has a great selection of flies, but since it's a three-hour drive to most trout streams, the owners can't be expected to know what flies are working on what streams.

A fly shop close to the water can recommend variations such as parachute styles, thorax ties or standard-hackled patterns. They can tell you if dry flies or nymphs are working better. And they can tell you about local patterns that work particularly well on local streams or lakes, but are not used anywhere else.

Mayflies

Mayflies, one of the most obvious groups of insects in trout streams, are of immense interest to fly-anglers because they can occur in large numbers and are a favored food of trout and other fish. The aquatic forms (nymphs) and adults (duns and spinners) lend themselves well to imitation with artificial flies. Fishing a good mayfly hatch can be pure delight.

Mayflies belong to the order Ephemeroptera: *ephemero*, meaning "short lived" and *ptera* meaning "wings." Adults are slender, winged insects with two or three long thin tails. They range in length from under ¼ inch to over 1 inch (4 mm to about 30 mm). Most species have four wings; however, only one pair is large and obvious. Wings of the first stage (the dun) tend to be dull or darkly mottled. After the adult mayflies have molted into the second land stage (the spinner), the wings are light and translucent. Spinner wings also may be mottled.

Mayfly adult.

Body colors range from pale to black with shades and mixtures of tan, gray, cream, green and brown predominating. Bodies are often banded with shades of colors because they are segmented. Mayfly bodies are often lighter on the bottom than top.

Life cycle of mayflies

Mayflies undergo incomplete metamorphosis, which means they miss one of the underwater stages common to some other insects. This cycle starts with an adult female laying eggs in water. The eggs fall to the stream or lake bottom and soon hatch into nymphs. Depending on the species, mayfly nymphs crawl around the bottom, cling to rocks, swim freely or burrow into silt. Most species spend one year in the water, and all but the burrowing types are eaten by trout regularly. The nymphs are imitated with wet flies we call nymphs.

Exactly one year (give or take) after the eggs are dropped into the water, the nymphs swim to the surface and emerge, or hatch, as we say. This is of great importance to trout and trout anglers. The nymphs that have spent the last year crawling around and under rocks now have to swim to the water's surface. During this brief trip they are vulnerable, and trout feed readily on them. At the surface, adults emerge from their skins, or shucks (more correctly known as exoskeletons), and pump fluid into their wings. They sit on the water's surface like little sail-boats for anything from a few seconds to a few minutes while their wings dry. They can emerge, or hatch, like this by the thousands and trout love them. We use dry flies to imitate them while they are floating down the river drying their wings.

The adults, called duns because they are usually dull colored, then fly to nearby bushes. After a few hours, or perhaps a day or so, the duns molt into a second land stage and are then called spinners. The spin-ners mate near or over water, and after a short incubation period, the females return to the water's surface and drop their eggs, thus completing the cycle. The females usually die on the surface with wings splayed apart. We call them spent spin-ners.

Mayfly nymph.

Most mayflies have one life cycle per year. However, some, like the many species of blue-winged olives, have two or more generations per year. Blue-winged olives hatch in the spring and again in the fall if conditions are right.

Mayfly patterns

An angler can get quite emotional about mayflies because their life cycle is all about living for a day or so, mating and dying, only to be regenerated in another season. And during this cycle, millions of mayflies become part of the food chain, thus perpet-

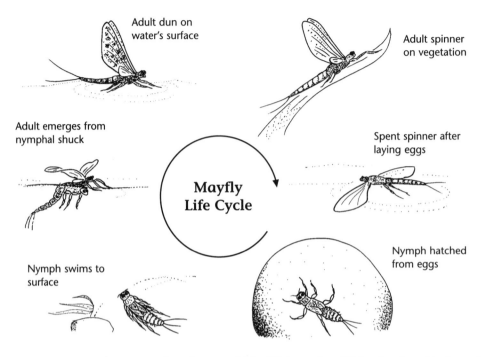

Adult dun on water's surface

Adult spinner on vegetation

Adult emerges from nymphal shuck

Spent spinner after laying eggs

Mayfly Life Cycle

Nymph swims to surface

Nymph hatched from eggs

uating other forms of life. This cycle of life, death, rebirth and sustenance is of such interest to fly-anglers because imitations of the various stages of mayflies are used to catch trout and other species of freshwater gamefish.

But before we get maudlin about this great natural event, let's remember that mayfly hatches are sometimes damnably tough to fish. Tough because it's hard to figure out what stage the fish are eating: nymphs near the surface, surface emergers, duns or spinners, all of which can be on the surface at once! All this confusion can be doubly tough because fish can be rising all around you, yet you can't catch them, and the last daylight is fading fast. It's happened to me many times. And although I've experienced this and know some textbook answers, it'll happen again. If fly-fishing were easy all the time I'd take up golf.

It is quite common to see trout rising to what appears to be a hatch of mayfly duns sitting on the water surface. You tie on the appropriate dry-fly pattern and congratulate yourself for being one smart person for not staying home and painting window trim. You cast away. Half an hour and ten patterns later, the trout continue to rise around you while ignoring your flies.

A couple of things could be happening. The most likely cause of the lack of hookups is that the trout are not eating adult duns drying their wings on the surface—the most obvious menu item on the water. Sometimes trout get locked on to nymphs as they approach the surface. Swirls near the surface may be mistaken for rises, when the trout may be eating emergers stuck in the film for a few seconds, or they may be eating crippled emergers. Occasionally, dying spinners, which have laid their eggs, may also be on the surface, and trout know they are not about to fly away.

If your mayfly dry flies are not working, look closely at what's happening. If the trout appear to be eating something else change to an emerger pattern, or float a nymph just under the surface. If you don't have emerger patterns, clip the hackles from the underside of the dry fly and try it. If it doesn't work, clip all the hackles and fish the fly wet just below the surface. Or tie on a nymph.

Something else may be going on. For reasons only the fish know for sure, they may not be eating the most obvious insect on the water—the one you've been trying to imitate for the past hour. Trout have a special fondness for small blue-winged olives and even smaller midges. A bigger insect might be on the water as well, but the trout may be quietly sipping away on the smaller bugs. Have a look.

Popular dry flies that imitate mayflies include the generic but widely effective Adams in standard and parachute styles; light-colored patterns, like Light Cahill, Light Hendrickson or Pale Morning Dun; Blue-winged Olive; and patterns like Dark Hendrickson, Quill Gordon or Rusty Spinner. Other mayfly dries of regional importance include forms of green and brown drakes. Typical hook sizes for many mayfly species range from #12 to #18; however, a few are much larger and some smaller. Popular mayfly patterns vary from east to west as the species change.

Popular nymphs that imitate the underwater stage of mayflies include the Hare's Ear, Pheasant Tail, Zug Bug, Prince Nymph and Blue-winged Olive Nymph. There are subtle differences in body thickness (or at least length-to-width ratios) between various types of mayfly nymphs. But the general shape and pattern of the popular Hare's Ear resembles most mayflies' distinctive carrot shape. Most mayfly nymphs can be successfully imitated with generic patterns (like Hare's Ears) tied in different body colors and a few sizes.

Emerger patterns imitate mayflies as they break through the surface film and out of their nymphal shuck. They are usually a hybrid of nymphs and dry flies. Typically, emerger patterns are a nymph with a ball of floating material like poly yarn or foam tied near the head. The idea is to simulate a nymph floating at the surface and starting to crawl out of the nymphal case.

Caddisflies

Caddisflies, like mayflies, are prevalent in many streams and lakes. There are few days from spring through autumn when there are not a few caddisflies flitting around the water's edge. Because of their frequent occurrence caddisfly imitations catch trout with reasonable consistency.

Caddisflies belong to the order Trichoptera: *tricho* meaning "hair" and *ptera* meaning "wings." They resemble moths in shape and tend to flutter around like moths when they are flying, but the caddisfly wingbeat tends to be much faster. Caddises have four wings, but unlike moths, the wings form a distinct "tent" when they are at rest. Caddisfly wings are large compared with the body and are typically half again as long as the body and usually hide it. Wing colors tend to be mottled brown, although there are many shades. The most common body colors are shades of brown and green. Some species have quite dark bodies, and this can be quite confusing because they have lighter brown wings. There's a message here. If you catch a brown-winged caddis and want to tie on a fly to imitate it, check the body color by turning the caddis upside down.

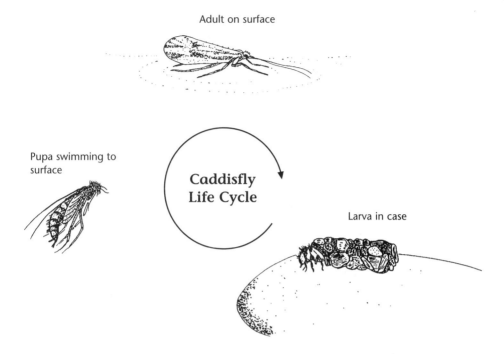

Adult on surface

Pupa swimming to surface

Caddisfly Life Cycle

Larva in case

Bodies of common caddisfly species range from about ¼ to ½ inch (6 mm to 12 mm) in length. The wings are longer than the bodies and range from about ½ to ¾ inch (12 mm to 18 mm). The biggest caddis I've seen is the October caddis, which has a beautiful salmon-colored body. Its wings measure up to 1 inch or more in length. This big caddis hatches late in the year—mid-September into October in Alberta.

Caddis pupae and adult caddisflies have two long antennae, but unlike mayflies the adults have no tails.

Life cycle of caddisflies

Caddisflies undergo complete metamorphosis, which means there are two stages, both underwater, between the egg and adult. The eggs hatch into larvae, which turn into pupae before they emerge as adults at the water's surface.

Caddisfly pupa in pebble-covered case.

There are three general types of larva. Species of case-building larvae build cases around their bodies with pieces of coarse material, like sand or small stones, if they live in fast water, and lighter material, like plant debris, if they live in slower water. They crawl around by sticking their thoraxes and legs out of the front of the case while their soft bodies remain inside. Larvae of the other two general types do not build cases. One is completely free roaming and forages for food on the stream bottom. Net-spinning caddisfly larvae build miniature nets to trap food. Some species are reported to live in the general area of their net, but the species of net-spinning caddisfly larvae I've found actually live inside the net.

All three types seal themselves inside the case, or cocoon, and remain there from a few days to a few weeks while they pupate. When they have matured they swim quickly to the surface and emerge as adults at the water's surface.

After emerging the adults live in and around stream-bank vegetation. Males and females mate, and the females return to the stream to lay eggs either directly on the surface or by swimming or crawling to the bottom.

Adult caddisflies gather along streamside vegetation by the tens of thousands. Some accidentally end up in the water, and, of course, there's a good chance many females will die there. Trout become quite familiar with caddisflies, and dry imitations can be very effective throughout the summer.

Caddisfly patterns

Larvae, pupae and adults are all eaten by trout, and all lend themselves to imitation with flies. This gets us into an interesting discussion about one of the primary differences between caddisflies and mayflies—or at least how anglers look at them. If you've fly-fished for a while and spoken to a few serious anglers, you might have noticed that some get quite technical when it comes to identifying mayflies, even using Latin names. The mayfly patterns often have specific names to identify specific mayflies. Flies called Pale Morning Dun are used during a pale morning dun hatch, and most anglers would never think of using a #16 pale mayfly.

But when it comes to caddisflies, well, they just "don't get no respect." The adults of the dozens of species of caddisflies are usually described by hook size and body color. For example, #14 tan or #16 green caddis. Not scientific, but practical and it works.

Select caddis dry-fly patterns to match the body color of the natural insects. The all-time favorite caddisfly dry-fly imitation is probably the Elk Hair Caddis. The hair type is not critical, and effective flies can be tied with deer hair in place of elk. Small hopper patterns, Stimulators and Adams-type dry flies tied in the color of the naturals work as well.

Trout love caddisfly larvae and pupae. Several patterns work well including soft-hackle wet flies in body colors to match the local naturals. Hare's Ear, tan or olive caddis pupa and sparkle caddis pupa patterns with and without bead heads will work. If trout are rising quite violently and slashing at the surface—and there are caddisflies around—try swinging a sparkle caddis pupa through the active area. It's probable that the trout are chasing caddisfly pupae as they swim to the surface.

Stoneflies

Stoneflies are not as abundant in numbers as either mayflies or caddisflies, but when they are active, fishing stonefly patterns can be productive. If stoneflies have recently emerged, trout will readily take a dry stonefly imitation. Or if nymphs are active on the bottom, stonefly nymph patterns work well.

Stoneflies belong to the order Plecoptera: *pleco* meaning "twisted"; *ptera* meaning "wings." There are many species that range widely in size from about ¼ inch to over 2 inches (6 mm to 60 mm).

Left: Stonefly nymph.

Right: Stonefly adult.

Species like golden stones and salmonflies are large, and you can't help but notice them if they are around. Smaller species include early brown stones, little black stones and yellow stones.

The wings of the adults are distinguished from caddisflies in that they lie flat on top, like a tabletop, when the adults are at rest. (The resting wings of caddisflies are always an inverted V-shape like a pup tent.) The dark nymphs of the larger species are very obvious when rocks are turned over on a stream bottom. Smaller stonefly nymphs look somewhat like mayfly nymphs, but stoneflies always have two tails (mayflies may have three), and stoneflies have two distinct wing pads as opposed to the single prominent pad on mayflies.

Stoneflies like highly oxygenated, rough-and-tumble water that you might think is too fast to hold trout.

Typical stonefly section of a western river.

Life cycle of stoneflies

Like mayflies, stoneflies undergo incomplete metamorphosis: adult, egg, nymph. After the females lay eggs in stony water (they are called stoneflies for good reason) the eggs hatch into nymphs. The nymphs remain in the water for two or more years. During this time they shed their exoskeletons many times as they grow, and there can be many sizes of nymphs of the same species. I know what a mature salmonfly nymph looks like, but I couldn't identify first-year or second-year specimens. Obviously, they are smaller, and I suspect many of the smaller nymphs some call black stones or brown stones are simply small salmonflies. It doesn't matter as long as you use a fly that's close to what the trout are eating.

Unlike mayfly nymphs, most stonefly nymphs don't swim to the water's surface to emerge. When ready to "hatch," they crawl along the streambed to the shore and climb on rocks or bushes to emerge. The hard nymphal shell splits along the back, and the adult emerges. Because they emerge on land there is no intense hatch on the water's surface and therefore no frenzied surface feeding at emergence. However, trout may gorge on active nymphs as they crawl to shore, no longer protected under rocks.

You'll know when you are in stonefly water when you see empty nymphal shucks on streamside rocks and vegetation.

Stoneflies and other aquatic insects that inhabit a long section of one river will not all hatch on the same day. Normally, the hatching of a particular stonefly species starts at the farthest downstream range of the insect. The hatch moves progressively upstream, peaking for a day or two at any given point. This has to do with degree-day accumulation—heat over time. The water at lower elevations—that is, farther downstream—will normally get warmer sooner, although the temperature downstream can be lowered by incoming streams.

Mature stonefly nymphs getting ready to hatch require a certain number of hours or days when the water temperature is above some critical minimum. This has to do with metabolic rates and the effect of heat on maturity. When the water has been warm enough for a certain length of time, the insects are ready to emerge. And they do. As water warms farther upstream, the insects start hatching there as well. It's all very fascinating when you think about it. It's just one big bug wave—teaming insect and fish activity surging upstream. And sports fans figured they invented the wave.

Stonefly patterns

Trout are routinely caught on both stonefly nymphs and dry patterns. Always carry some of each with you when you fish waters known to hold stoneflies. The nymphs are relatively large and there are many species, so trout see lots of them and eat them when they are active and not hidden under rocks. Although fishing stoneflies dries can be fast and furious, I'd guess more trout are taken on stonefly nymphs than dries because of the insect's prolonged underwater life. If stoneflies are hatching you can fish a dry imitation of the right size and general body color. Or, since the nymphs were recently active or are still active, you can fish a stonefly nymph imitation that, again, is about the right size and shade.

Empty nymphal shuck of giant stonefly or salmonfly. The mature adult crawls out of the opening on the back of the shell.

As with mayflies and caddisflies, there are many specific, named patterns to choose from. Stimulators, Sofa Pillows and Elk Hair caddises tied with the correct body color and size imitate natural stoneflies.

Stonefly nymphs are a fairly plain lot and, again, the Hare's Ear is a favorite stonefly nymph imitation. Stonefly nymphs tend to be quite dark, and all have about the same shape, which is well represented by the Hare's Ear or similar patterns tied fairly dark. Black stonefly nymphs like the Montana or Brook's Stone patterns are popular. Wooly Worm, Wooly Bugger and Bitch Creeks also imitate stoneflies—at least we presume they do. Who knows what the trout think?

Golden stoneflies are not well represented by generic stonefly nymph colors because they are lighter. Their bodies are a yellowy tan color (at least yellow is quite dominant in the body), and you'll need a few golden stone nymphs if you'll be fishing where golden stones are active. There are many named golden stone patterns using the words *golden stone.*

Standard dark nymph flies may be too small to represent the salmonfly found in many western rivers. The standard nymphs represent the early generations of this stonefly when they are still quite small, but by the time this beast is ready to emerge and is available to trout, it's much bigger than the average pattern. This is a huge stonefly—mature nymph bodies are up to 2½ inches (60 mm) long—and the body color is distinctly dark brown. If you will be fishing where the salmonflies could "be coming off any day now," make sure you stop at a local fly shop for a few large salmonfly imitations with long bodies on size #4 hooks or larger.

When stonefly nymphs are active in late spring and early summer, fishing nymphs in rough water can be very productive. When stoneflies are laying eggs or generally flitting around the water, dry-fly patterns like Stimulators cast to rough stonefly water will often promote a strike. Sometimes.

In June 1992 my brother, Gary, John Tunstall and I attended a full-blown salmonfly hatch on the Crowsnest River. First we saw these giant insects haphazardly fluttering over the water. As we got closer to the water's edge we could see hundreds of them clinging to the nearly blooming dogwoods along the banks. According to the gurus this is supposed to be *it.* The ultimate hatch. Fish abandon all caution and can be caught at will with any fly that closely resembles a salmonfly. But why weren't the trout slashing the water at drowning salmonflies? Why wouldn't they take our flies? When we shook the shore bushes these giant critters flopped to the surface by the dozens. Nothing. Not a rise in sight. Although I did land one trout on a salmonfly imitation that day, and other rainbows were caught on other flies, it was a disappointment. Sure, you can argue that we tie lousy flies. But why wouldn't they eat the real thing?

The only reason we could think of to explain our failure was that the trout were stuffed on the nymphs. Remembering the old standby logic we drove ahead of the hatch and fished salmonfly nymphs. Nothing. We went downstream to where the gluttony should have worn off and where they might remember what the flies looked like. Not much better. That's life.

In all fairness, I've talked to anglers who have hammered the trout as they attacked natural salmonflies.

Midges

Midges are the most abundant insect in numbers and perhaps even in biomass on many of our streams. Bigger insects like mayflies and caddisflies are usually more obvious because of their size, but midges make up a huge portion

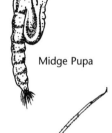

Midge Larva

Midge Pupa

Midge Adult

of the trout diet. Mayfly, caddisfly and stonefly activity comes and goes. But midges just seem to be around forever. In Alberta there aren't too many days during the fishing season that we don't see at least some midges. Their presence is often overridden by larger insects, but thankfully they are always around.

Midges belong to the order Diptera: *di* meaning "two" and *ptera* meaning "wings." These are flies. More precisely, they belong to the midge family, Chironomidae. The mosquitolike midges range in size from about ½ inch (12 mm) all the way down to no–see–um size—less than ⅛ inch (3 mm) in length. Larger midges are not uncommon on some waters. The most common body colors where I fish are black, dark charcoal gray and shades of brown. Green and red midges are found elsewhere.

Midges undergo complete metamorphosis. The larvae develop from eggs and turn into pupae before they emerge as adults. Midges hatch every month of the year (including in Alberta on streams where the water stays open). I've fly-fished every month of the year but have seen fishable surface hatches only in September, October and November. We've seen midges flying around in January and February; however, there weren't enough to interest cold trout. But small midge nymphs work well throughout the winter and spring and during cool summer weather when there's not much happening bug-wise on the surface.

A number of years ago my brother and I caught and kept a 16-inch Crowsnest rainbow trout because we wanted to see what these uncooperative trout were eating. The stomach was stuffed. There were partly decomposed bits of one or two stoneflies. But the majority of the contents were midge pupae. The conservative dimensions of the plug were ½ inch by over 2 inches (12 to 60 mm). The pupae measured about ¼ inch long (6 mm) and less than a pencil lead in diameter. Therefore, there were between 1,500 and 2,000 pupae in the stomach! These are important insects, and very small midge pupae imitations have caught many trout—sometimes quite large trout.

Midge patterns

Trout eat larvae, pupae, emerging adults and adults, and these are imitated with small "nymph" and dry-fly patterns. Midges are small, and hook sizes ranging from #16 to #22 will normally be required to match the natural size closely. Some keeners fish #26 and smaller imitations. There are a few larger species up to size #12 in some waters.

To imitate pupae use small Serendipity, Black Midge Pupa, TDC and chironomid or buzzer patterns. All of these can and should be tied or bought in colors similar to the natural midges you are trying to imitate. Black, charcoal, tan and olive are the common colors of midge flies, although some midge patterns are dark red and bright green.

Pupae imitations are usually fished near the bottom. Because they are so small I don't feel confident fishing them alone, so I always tie a pupa pattern with a larger fly. (This dropper method is discussed later in the nymph-fishing chapter.) Although I fish them along with a larger fly, these small flies catch the majority of fish. Over the past few years I have caught more trout on midge pupae patterns than any other single type of wet fly. Trout eat a lot of midges.

During midge hatches, when the little wigglers are approaching the top, pupae imitations can be fished just below or on the surface. This is done by applying fly floatant to the leader to within a few inches of the pupa pattern. Small tufts of white yarn or white foam also can be clove hitched to the tippet a few inches from the emerging pupa pattern to keep the fly from sinking too far.

Trout also eat midges in the surface film at the moment they are wriggling out of their shuck. Tom's Midge Emerger is a good imitation. As well, any of the pupae patterns listed above can be tied with a small tuft of poly yarn or foam at the head. This little life jacket allows the body to sink just below the surface while the fly still remains at the surface. Dry flies can also be used to imitate emergers. Clip the hackles flush with the body and fish it as a dry fly.

Adamses and Griffith's Gnats are common midge dry-fly patterns. Small dry flies the same color as natural midges can also be tied or purchased. They consist of a tail, tying thread or lightly dubbed body and sparse hackles.

Dragonflies and damselflies

There are hundreds of species of dragonflies and their smaller kin, damselflies, in North America. They are common to lakes and ponds although they are found in and around slower streams. These are the helicopter insects that hover around shoreline vegetation, eating midges and other small insects.

Fat dragonfly nymphs spend their underwater lives crawling on vegetation as they feed on larvae and pupae of small aquatic insects. Dragonfly nymphs live two or three years in the water after hatching from eggs. Depending upon species and where

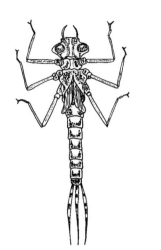

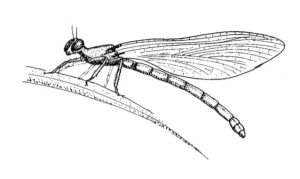

Left: Damselfly nymph.

Right: Damselfly adult.

they live, they can be intermittently available to trout and other fish. The most important time for fly-anglers is in spring and early summer, when the mature nymphs migrate over the pond bottom and vegetation to shore, where they emerge as adults. Dragonfly nymphs are short and thick, while damselfly nymphs are rather slender. Nymphs of both tend to be dark green and brown in color, and are imitated with appropriately sized and colored nymphs.

Popular dragonfly nymph imitations are Carey Specials, Wooly Buggers and Wooly Worms tied with olive, olive-brown or brown bodies. Dragonfly nymphs are quite stocky in build, and the nymph imitations should be tied to imitate this shape on hooks from size #6 through #10. There also is an assortment of named dragonfly patterns, usually sporting eyes to match the big eyes of the naturals.

Damselfly nymphs also hang out in pond or slow-water vegetation. They are vulnerable to predation by trout and other fish when they swim from weed beds to shore to emerge, usually in spring and summer. These slender, usually olive-colored nymphs swim by wiggling from side to side. Popular patterns are made with soft willowy olive marabou feathers that sway in the water, simulating the body and paddlelike gills at the tail end. Marabou damselfly patterns are recommended.

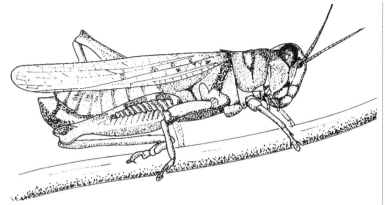

Terrestrial insects, like this grasshopper, and ants and beetles are eaten by trout and other fish.

Trout also eat damselfly adults that die or get blown onto the water. Specific damsel dry-fly patterns are available at fly shops. Several years ago I had been casting to two or three fussy Crowsnest rainbows in a slow back eddy and wasn't able to hook any. A few blue damselflies flitted around the water's surface, although none was taken by trout. None that I saw. But there were enough around that you had to figure the trout knew what they were. Earlier that year I had purchased two damsel dry flies in Missoula, Montana, because they looked cute. In frustration I tied one on and immediately hooked a good rainbow, only to break it of on the first jump a few seconds later.

If you'll be pond fishing in the late spring or early autumn, make sure you have some dragonfly and damselfly imitations.

Terrestrial insects

No fly-fisher should be astream without a few ants and hoppers. On a hot windy summer day grasshoppers are blown into the water and trout love to eat them. Always carry two or three sizes of patterns like Dave's Hopper and LeTort Hoppers for these days.

Until a few years ago I had never fished ant patterns—not until I watched my brother catch several rainbows in the rocks just upstream from a popular spot on one of our favorite rivers. He was fishing a #16 black ant both dry and wet—it didn't matter. Black ants worked well all that week, and I've since successfully used them on other streams. Carry a few black and red ants in sizes #14 or #16 at all times. Fish them near banks when more obvious patterns aren't working. Ants are around all summer long, and trout see a few every day, so they always know what they are.

Ants contain high amounts of formic acid, which must taste like candy to trout. Occasionally, a flotilla of flying ants will fall or be blown onto the water. I've seen it happen a few times on both lakes and rivers. The trout go nuts. The last time I saw it happen the ants were barely more than ⅛ inch long. The trout still went nuts. But they were fussy and locked solidly on to the small ants and wouldn't look at my smallest #18 ant fly because it was far too big. A #18 ant that's too big! I mean, have you ever seen ants that small?

Scuds and crayfish

Freshwater scuds, or freshwater shrimp, are permanent residents of water and never hatch into land forms. Their shrimplike bodies range in size from about ¼ inch to over 1 inch (6 mm to 25 mm) in length. Body colors tend toward light olives and gray-tans, and they often have a translucent appearance. When you pick up scuds, they always curl up, but when they are swimming, their bodies are held almost straight. Scuds live in and around vegetation and are a favorite underwater food of trout.

There are numerous freshwater shrimp patterns, most using *scud* in the name. Carry scud patterns that match the probable size and color of the naturals where you'll be fishing.

Crayfish are common to eastern North America and the West Coast. They look like small lobsters and range from about one to several inches. Different species are found in fast and slow streams, and ponds and lakes. Trout and bass eat crayfish. They are imitated by numerous patterns like Clouser and Whitlock Crayfish.

Small fish and leeches

An assortment of small fish species are eaten by trout, bass, pike and panfish. These include true minnows, dace, shiners, chubs and sculpins. As some gamefish get larger they even eat their own kin. Streamers are excellent imitations of these small fish. Popular examples include Wooly Buggers, Black-nose Daces, Muddler Minnows and sculpin patterns.

No doubt streamer fishing is seen as not being quite as virtuous as nymph and dry-fly fishing. Perhaps in some minds casting streamers comes close to chucking spinners, but you can't argue with their effectiveness. They are responsible for catching a lot of big bass and trout.

Streamer fishing is a great example of the versatility of fly-fishing. With the same outfit you can cast big streamers when nothing else is working, and when the trout start looking up, you can switch to dry flies. You can't do that very well on a lot of water with spinning gear.

Another big-food type popular with trout and other gamefish are leeches. These undulating segmented worms with the unsavory but realistic name of bloodsuckers inhabit most waters where trout are found. Their dark bodies are easily imitated with black marabou feathers that mimic the wavelike swimming motion of this fine fish snack.

I used leech patterns sparingly until a couple of years ago, but they are now one of my favorite fall searching patterns. If you're fishing a big river with slow sections where leeches could live, cast a big marabou leech across stream and allow it to swing around. Give it some life by twitching the rod tip. It's as good a method as I know for connecting to a large fall rainbow or brown. Carry weighted marabou leech patterns in hook sizes #2 to #6. Black Wooly Buggers with long marabou tails also probably imitate leeches. (Again, some fly fishers may fail to find the virtue in leeches, but don't let the name and associated "social disgrace" put you off them. Leeches are responsible for hooking their share of fish.)

Simplified fly selection for trout

All this detailed talk about fly selection can be very confusing. It's easy to tell you to match the color and size of dry flies or to match nymphs to the naturals. But what if you simply don't know what insects will be around where you're headed? What if you just bought a new rig, your brother-in-law showed you how to cast and you can get the line out pretty well. Now you want to head out for the weekend. Perhaps the staff down at the local sports store simply don't know much about fly-fishing. What's a new fly-angler to do?

When there are trout to be caught one or two sizes of a dozen or so flies will work fairly consistently because they represent a wide range of insects. But before getting into trouble with some who might not agree with the flies listed, I must restate that the best source information about flies that will work where you plan to fish is a specialty fly shop. The following flies, and variations of them, are popular in many places, but there are thousands of patterns and it is not possible to list all of them or list ones that may work better in a particular location at a particular time of the year.

Nevertheless, following are some popular flies used frequently by experienced anglers everywhere. Some are inevitably going to work where you're going. Use this as a starting point and refine your collection for the places you fish. Many of these popular trout flies also catch bass, panfish, grayling and mountain whitefish.

For dry flies have on hand two or three each of some or most of the following in one or two of the sizes listed:

1. Adams (#14 – #18)
2. Elk Hair Caddis with either green or tan body (#14)
3. Blue-winged Olive (#16 – #18)
4. Some sort of light-bodied mayfly such as Pale Morning Dun, Light Cahill or Light Hendrickson (#14 – #18)
5. Red Quill or Quill Gordon (#12 – #16)
6. One of the popular yellow-bodied grasshopper patterns like LeTort or Dave's (#8 – #10)

7   Humpy or Tom Thumb (#10 – #14)
8   A few attractor patterns like Royal Coachman, Royal
     Wulff or Royal Humpy (#12)
9   Black Ant (#16 – #18).

Popular nymphs include:

1   Hare's Ear (#10 – #14)
2   Pheasant Tail (#14 – #16)
3   Zug Bug (#12 – #14)
4   Prince Nymph (#14)
5   Black and Golden Stones (#8)
6   San Juan Worm (#10)
7   Marabou damselflies (#8 – #10).

Look for some of these nymph patterns and others tied with
bead heads. These small shiny metal beads are added to the head
of a hook to lend weight and sparkle. Bead heads seem to attract
fish. I know of one accomplished fly-angler who only uses Hare's
Ear and Pheasant Tail nymphs with and without bead heads.

Popular streamers include:

1   Muddler Minnow (#4 – #8)
2   Black-nose Dace (#4 – #8)
3   Olive and Black Wooly Buggers (#4 – #8)
4   Spruce Fly (#4 – #8)
5   Marabou leech pattern (#4 – #8).

Clearly, this is a generic listing, but it represents an excellent
arsenal to prepare you to catch fish. Refine it for your local
waters, and always ask around!

Chapter 5

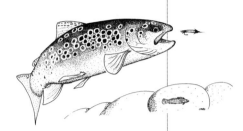

Trout, Trout Streams and Trout Senses

North American fly-fishing trout anglers spend the vast majority of their fishing time chasing rainbow, cutthroat, brown and brook trout. Several other trout species are locally or regionally important, but these are the big four. Other trout species sought by fly-anglers include golden trout, bull trout and Dolly Varden. Steelhead are a sea-running (anadromous) type of rainbow trout.

Trout are members of the Salmonidae family, the trout or salmon family, whichever you prefer. They are native to the Northern Hemisphere, although they have been successfully planted in the Southern Hemisphere where water temperatures are favorable. The trout family includes three subfamilies: one includes trout, char and salmon; one encompasses grayling only; and one includes whitefish, cisco and inconnu. All the true trout and char are native to North America except the brown trout which was first brought here from Europe in 1883. Trout are considered coldwater species as opposed to warmwater species like bass.

Brook trout, lake trout, bull trout and Dolly Varden are actually char by scientific definition and all are closely related. Two slight biological differences distinguish trout from char, but they are of little importance to anglers. First, there is a small

Trout are the preferred quarry of many fly-anglers, and the rivers they inhabit are as pretty as the fish.

difference in the configuration of the teeth on the roof of the mouth between the two groups. Secondly, chars lack black body spots common to true trout. These are not very scientific differences, but provide an easy way to distinguish between them.

The most easily recognizable feature of all sixty species in the trout family is the presence of an adipose fin. This is the spineless flexible fin on the back between the tail and the dorsal fins. If it has an adipose fin it's a salmonid, a member of the trout or salmon family.

Details of the classification and relationships among trout is somewhat clouded, and just a few years ago the genus name of rainbow, cutthroat and golden trout was changed from *Salmo* to *Oncorhynchus*. (There are a few *Salmo* fishing vehicle vanity license plates around. You'd need two rigs to fit *Oncorhynchus* on the license plates.)

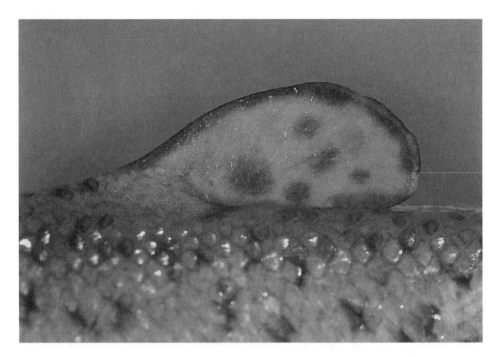

All members of the trout and salmon family, including grayling and whitefish, have an adipose fin.

The name change is of some interest, if not of any practical angling significance. *Oncorhynchus* is the genus name of the Pacific salmon like chinook and coho. *Salmo* is the genus name of Atlantic salmon and brown trout, both with roots in the Atlantic Ocean. The change recognizes that all the species of Pacific salmons and trouts are related and that Atlantic salmon and brown trout are related. Seems reasonable.

The subfamily of trout and salmon also includes char, lenok and taimen. The latter two are native to Asia and are found in Russia, Mongolia and other northern countries. The similarity of lenok and trout leaves no doubt about their relationship. In the summer of 1993, while working in northern Mongolia, I hired a driver and car to take me fishing and sight-seeing on a free Sunday afternoon. Just out of the capital city of Ulaanbaatar we crossed the river Tuul, where a family was fishing for lenok. We drove off the road and through the meadow to have a look. A young boy had caught a 14-inch lenok that I photographed. It

Popular Freshwater
Gamefish of North America

BROWN TROUT, *like this colorful specimen, are considered by some to be the wariest of trout. They are found across the continent where water temperatures support them. They originated in Europe and were brought to North America in 1883.*

ARCTIC GRAYLING, *which feature a spectacular dorsal fin, are a member of the trout and salmon family. They are found across the western half of northern Canada to Alaska and in a few western states.*

CUTTHROAT TROUT *have a distinguishing red or orange slash on the lower jaw. They are considered to be easier to catch than rainbows and offer excellent dry-fly fishing for novices in high western streams.*

EASTERN BROOK TROUT *are considered by some to be the easiest trout to catch and therefore ideal for the beginner. They originated in the eastern half of North America and have been transplanted throughout the continent where water quality supports them.*

RAINBOW TROUT *are respected for their fighting and aerial acrobatics when hooked. They were originally confined to the western part of the continent but have been transplanted to rivers and ponds over a wide part of North America.*

MOUNTAIN WHITEFISH, *also a member of the trout and salmon family, are common in many western trout streams. They take a wide range of trout flies and fight well even in winter months.*

NORTHERN PIKE, *like this mid-sized specimen caught in a small prairie lake, attack large streamers and are rugged fighters.*

LARGEMOUTH BASS, *like this small specimen caught on a streamer, along with their close kin, smallmouth bass, are North America's most popular gamefish, considering the time and money spent in pursuit of them. They belong to the sunfish family.*

PUMPKINSEED OR COMMON SUNFISH *are one of many gamefish in the sunfish family and closely related to crappies and bluegills. Collectively, they are called panfish. They are usually easy to catch and an ideal quarry for children.*

YELLOW PERCH, *a northern panfish, are ideal quarry for young fly-fishers because they readily take a wide range of small wet flies. Yellow Perch are related to walleye.*

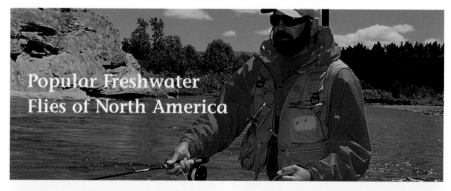

Popular Freshwater
Flies of North America

ADAMS: *a traditionally tied winged dry fly carried by most fly anglers.*

PALE MORNING DUN: *a wingless and clipped-hackle dry fly variation and one of several pale-bodied mayfly patterns.*

BLUE-WINGED OLIVE: *a wingless variation of the dry fly used during spring and autumn hatches of blue-winged olive mayflies.*

ELK HAIR CADDIS: *a palmer-hackled dry fly that is a standard caddisfly pattern and usually tied with a tan or green body.*

MAYFLY EMERGER: *a foam-ball pattern designed to imitate the unfolding wings of mayflies emerging at the water's surface.*

STIMULATOR: *a palmer-hackled dry fly tied in various sizes and colors and a standard stonefly imitation.*

ROYAL COACHMAN: *a popular attractor dry fly.*

HUMPY: *a popular high-floating deer-hair dry fly that is both an impressionistic dry fly and an attractor.*

SCUD: *an imitation of freshwater shrimp, or more correctly a scud, a common lake crustacean.*

MARABOU DAMSELFLY: *a popular lake fly that imitates damselfly nymphs.*

WOOLY BUGGER: *the color and size variations of this pattern collectively make it one of the most popular wet-fly patterns.*

PHEASANT TAIL: *a popular nymph tied in various sizes to imitate an assortment of mayfly and stonefly nymphs and midge pupae.*

STONEFLY: *a simple dark pattern that imitates stonefly nymphs.*

PRINCE NYMPH: *a pattern that is both dead-drifted to imitate nymphs and cast across and downstream to imitate emerging insects.*

BLACK MINK: *a new, effective impressionistic pattern that has caught several species of trout in rivers and lakes.*

HARE'S EAR: *an enduring favorite tied in various sizes (some with bead heads) to imitate a wide range of aquatic insects.*

MIDGE PUPA: *an effective and simple fly tied with a black thread body and gray thread rib.*

SOFT-HACKLE WET FLY: *imitates emerging caddisflies and usually fished across and downstream on a tight line.*

SPARKLE CADDIS PUPA: *a modern fly used to imitate emerging caddisflies.*

MUDDLER MINNOW: *one of the most popular streamers in North America used for many species of gamefish.*

BASS FLY: *a standard bass popper fly that is tied with several color combinations.*

PIKE FLY: *a large pike streamer with a dark top and light underside to imitate small baitfish.*

was quite similar in color to an immature rainbow trout. The snout was longer and more pointed—somewhere between a mountain whitefish and rainbow—but there was no doubt about the relationship. The boy's father showed me a handmade lure that he used for taimen, all of this information being passed with gestures and aided by my knowing the word *taimen*. The lure was a surface plug about 6 inches long with three or four treble hooks. When I repeated "taimen" and held my hands about 4 feet apart, the father nodded and smiled widely. There were two specimens of taimen in the museum of natural history in the capital, and one *was* about 4 feet long! These are big fish closely related to our lake trout.

I tried fly-fishing with a four-piece pack rod for about an hour, but never caught anything. It was worth the trip and had to be done. The driver made more money in 4 hours that afternoon than in a month—and it still only cost me $30.

Rainbow trout

Rainbow trout, *Oncorhynchus mykiss,* are prized for their fighting ability and aerial acrobatics, and are the primary target of anglers throughout the world. Lots of fish fight well, but a spunky rainbow is tops. I've caught rainbows, browns, cutthroats, brookies, lake and bull trout, chinook, coho and Atlantic salmon, but pound for pound, a late-summer Bow River rainbow is without doubt the hardest fighting trout anywhere. A fat feisty 4- or 5-pound 22-inch rainbow will haul out more backing than you've seen all year and take many minutes to land.

Like other trout, rainbows were made for fly-fishing because they eat insects that are easy to imitate with flies. So here we have a hard-fighting, acrobatic, fly-eating trout. Ideal.

Rainbows are native to the western part of the North America and the Pacific coastal regions of Asia. On this continent they range from northern Mexico all the way up to the Aleutian Islands in Alaska. Some strains run to the ocean and are called

Rainbow trout from a small pond.

steelhead, but the majority of strains live in freshwater their entire lives.

There is a wide variation in the coloring of rainbow trout that is the result of their environment, including food types, water and season. Genetic variation and sex also play a role in coloration. Generally, their bodies are silvery with a rose-colored band along the side. Their backs range from dark olive-green to olive steel-blue. Sometimes there is pronounced red coloring on the gills, although the gill blushing may be faint or nonexistent. They are covered with many black spots from head to tail with the spots concentrated on the upper half or upper two-thirds of their bodies. Rainbows in some waters are almost completely silver with black spots, have virtually no red or rose coloring and do not have the characteristic silvery bluish background hue. Rainbows lack the cutthroat trout's crimson slash on the lower jaw, although rainbow–cutt hybrids have a faint red slash.

Cutthroat trout

Cutthroat trout, *Oncorhynchus clarki*, were formerly *Salmo clarki* and are native to western North America. Two forms are recognized. The Pacific, or coastal, form ranges from Alaska to northern California. The coastal form can be either sea-running (anadromous) or live only in freshwater near the coast. The interior form, called the westslope cutthroat, originally ranged throughout the western states, British Columbia and southwestern Alberta. Despite its name it occurs on both the east and west sides of the Rockies.

Cutthroats look somewhat like rainbow trout, but their bodies tend to be shaded with light olive compared to the usually silvery rainbows. There is a wide variation in body colors and spot distribution, presumably depending on strain, water conditions and age. Because of variations, specimens of both cutthroats and rainbows can look similar. However, all pure cutthroats have a distinctive crimson slash along the lower jaw that is missing from pure-strain rainbows. The two species interbreed and produce hybrids called cuttbows or cuttbow hybrids. The intensity of the throat slash on the hybrids varies depending on the ratio of species mixture.

Cutthroat trout don't jump like rainbows, but they still are great gamefish. They are made for kids or anyone learning to fly-fish because they are opportunistic feeders, meaning they tend to feed with less discrimination than rainbows and tend to live in less spooky water than browns. They typically live in cold rough-and-tumble mountain streams. Sure, they'll inhabit slow deep pools, but you won't find them in lazy meandering farmland streams.

Usually, cutthroats will eat a wide range of flies, and casts don't always have to be precise and delicate. When they are on the feed they'll often come up to dry flies, even when there are no natural bugs on the water. If you want to catch trout on your new fly outfit, buy some Royal Humpies, rig up and head to a cutthroat stream in August.

Cutthroat trout about to eat a stonefly nymph.

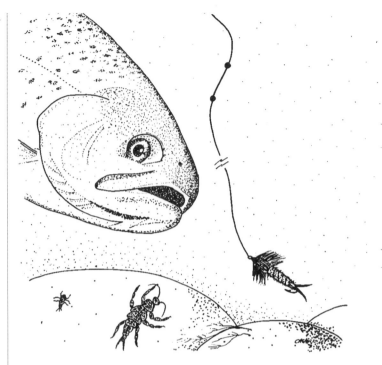

I took a 13-inch cutthroat late one evening on Mill Creek in southwestern Alberta, back when I could still eat fish. (That's another story.) Its gut was filled with body parts of a mishmash of insects: two or three undigested grasshopper drumsticks, some black ant or beetle parts, what appeared to be stonefly thoraxes and some partially digested mayfly nymphs. This was certainly an opportunistic trout feeding on whatever looked like food—including my caddisfly dry—that drifted on the surface or tumbled through the water. Although I caught it on a caddisfly it would have presumably eaten just about any reasonable fly. Some days it's nice to catch trout like cutthroats that perhaps couldn't catch if they were any smarter or more spooky.

Another feature of fly-fishing for cutthroats that attracts many people is their habitat. At least in my home province of Alberta, they are found in some of the prettiest mountain and foothill country you'll ever have pleasure to visit.

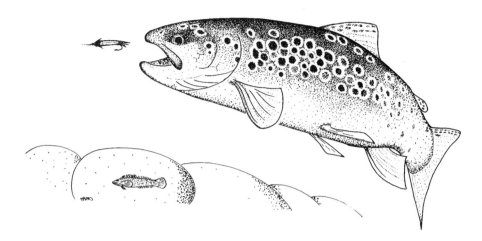

Brown trout

Brown trout chasing a streamer.

Brown trout escaped a scientific name change and are still called *Salmo trutta*. A close kin to Atlantic salmon they are native to western European coastal rivers and various parts of inland Europe. First introduced into Michigan in 1883 and into Canada in 1884, they have become established in major trout systems throughout North America. Plantings originated from different sources, and it's not uncommon to hear about Loch Leven browns (which originated in Scotland) and German browns. Brown trout also have been introduced to the Asian and African continents, and New Zealand has become a popular destination for well-healed brown trout anglers.

Like rainbows, brown trout vary widely in overall body and spot coloring, and in spot distribution. Body colors vary with the type of water and perhaps their ancestry, whether Scottish or German. Colors range from golden yellow to silvery tan. A distinguishing feature of many brown specimens are halos surrounding large black spots along the sides and back. These halos are lighter in color than the overall body color. Some browns have pronounced red spots and other specimens have none. The result of all this variation is that a novice could look at two specimens of brown trout and not believe they are the same species. There may even be difficulty identifying a specimen as a brown trout. I recall the first brown trout I caught on the lower-lower Bow River, well below the popular and crowded stretch. Its overall body color was silvery tan, and it had no red spots at all. I identified it by elimination. It *was* a trout. It was *not* a rainbow or cutthroat, well . . . just because. So it *had* to be a brown. Honestly, it sort of went like that. I have a picture of that specimen and it looks remarkably like an Atlantic salmon I caught and photographed.

Brown trout have the reputation of being extremely wary and hard to catch. Again, at the risk of going against the grain of accepted notions, I disagree. Sure, in hard-fished popular streams they may be "educated" and fussy about fly patterns—just like other trout wherever they are fished hard. But I believe that brown trout, if not heavily fished, are opportunistic feeders and will take a wide range of patterns presented well. I suspect they get the reputation of being difficult and wary, in part, because of where they live. They often inhabit slow smooth water. Quiet water. Spooky water. Water so quiet that a hard step or stumble along the creek bank may put feeding browns down for several casting lengths in both directions.

Slow brown-trout water also means that casts have to be well presented—quiet and not splashy. The fly has to be on target. Not so close that the landing rings spook a fish, but not so far that the fly line lands over a riser. In smooth brown trout water one sloppy cast will send an active feeder scurrying for cover.

A few years ago Bob Scammell, who is something of a legend in Alberta's west country, guided me to a secluded section of a certain brown trout creek and presented me with a large feeding brown. It was well past sunset and a few brown drakes were emerging, but not so many as to really call it a hatch. I had a Brown Drake fly on that Bob had kindly donated as my smaller dry patterns weren't nearly big enough. After a couple of casts that were too far out in the stream for this bank feeder, I finally made a cast just a few inches to the side of where it was coming up. The fly landed a few feet beyond the riser, but not so far that the fly line spooked it. In the seconds before he took my fly, the big brown came up twice and ate two other bugs as they floated a foot or two ahead of my imitation. My memory recalls the insects as a small caddisfly and a midge. I could be wrong, but they certainly were not brown drakes. The point is, this brown fed on three different species—including the fake—and was not fussy about what he ate. It was a hard-fighting 22-inch male. Nice fish.

All trout—indeed all gamefish—are great and each has special characteristics that heighten the chase. But I have to fess up and say browns are my favorite. I have no rational explanation for this affection. I fish for them far less than for rainbows and pike, but they hold a special spot in my angling-addled brain and heart.

Brook trout

Brook trout, *Salvelinus fontinalis,* are chars native to northeastern North America from Georgia to the Arctic Circle. They have been successfully introduced into creeks and rivers throughout western North America. In some waters they have a tendency to overpopulate and remain small. Most large specimens are caught today in parts of Canada from northern Manitoba to Quebec and Labrador. Brookies require clean, clear water and have suffered from man's invasion of their original habitat in many parts of eastern North America.

This most colorful of trout has red spots with blue halos along the sides and darker worm-shaped markings (vermiculations) along the upper part of the body and on the fins. All trout are pretty, but brookies win the prize for the most bizarre array of colors. Their fall breeding colors are positively dazzling: bright orange bellies, white and bright red fins, red body spots with neon blue halos and mottled olive upper body.

Like cutthroat trout, when brookies are on the feed they readily take dry flies and nymphs and are a fish for kids or beginners looking for success.

Small beaver pond brook trout about to eat an Adams dry fly.

Nothing transports my memory back to childhood fishing more than seeing a brookie. My first big trout was a monster 13- or 14-inch brook trout caught in Jasper Park, Alberta, when I was about twelve. At the time I couldn't get over the size. The memory has sinister undertones. The brookie was caught in the twilight, well after sunset, on a small brass lure I had hand painted with glow-in-the-dark paint—a substance then banned. I think it was past the legal angling time as well. Of course, I kept the trout and my dad took a picture in the morning of me holding it in front of our tent. Attitudes toward taking fish were different then.

I also recall walking to some beaver ponds with my brother—always on the lookout for black bears—in Banff National Park. These eerie ponds were filled with dead spruce trees, crystal-clear water and mounds of mossy emerald green aquatic weeds. Brook trout were easily seen swimming lazily through the ponds. Wayward red-and-white bobbers hung like Christmas ornaments from broken fishing lines snagged on sun-bleached spruce limbs.

A surreal angling scene to match the flamboyant colors of the small brookies we caught.

It was unnerving to watch little brookies swim lazily toward my salmon eggs and worms suspended a couple of feet below the two-toned plastic bobber Dad would have bought at the Army and Navy for a dime. More than one of my bobbers was added to the dangling collection high in the dead spruce trees.

I've only fished for brookies twice in the past few years. Once was in a small beaver pond not unlike the one described. Although they were small they were typically colored and readily came up for small Adams dry flies. This spring I fished for brook trout in a high lake where they readily took a Black Mink nymph.

Golden trout

Golden trout, *Oncorhynchus aguabonita,* were formerly called *Salmo aguabonita.* They are native to high lakes in the Sierra Nevada Mountains in California, but have been introduced to mountain lakes in several states and in my home province of Alberta. They are similar to rainbows, but have fine scales, fewer spots and are usually more brightly colored. I have never fished for golden trout, using the old afraid-of-bears excuse. But really I haven't worked up the ambition to hike several hours up to one of the beautiful lakes where they have been stocked. From all reports it's a worthwhile venture, and if you live out west and are getting into fly-fishing for the exercise and scenery, this a fish is for you.

The other chars: bull trout, Dolly Varden, lake trout

For decades bull trout and Dolly Varden—actually chars, like brookies—were considered the same species. However, in 1978 they were shown to be two distinct species. It's all very confusing and I'll make no attempt to sort it out. To quote one fish taxonomy reference, "The state of char taxonomy is unsettled. . . ."

Bull trout.

Dolly Varden were originally confined to the very western part of the continent from northern California to Alaska. The bull trout originally ranged further inland on both sides of the continental divide. Like their lake trout cousin these are aggressive fish-eating chars. It's this aggressive nature that has caused problems for them, and most jurisdictions are trying to reestablish populations or prevent further decline.

Bull trout populations have declined dramatically in the past few decades throughout their original range, and many jurisdictions have reduced limits to zero. The decline was caused by at least three factors. Bull trout grow to many pounds, and large breeding fish spawn in the fall in small feeder creeks, where they are easy to catch. Apparently, some folks couldn't pass up killing a 6- or 8-pound bull trout if they saw it swimming in a small creek. Bull trout were considered by some to be inferior to other trout like rainbows. There are stories of trout anglers catching bull trout and tossing them in the bush because they competed with the "better" species of gamefish. It also didn't help that bull trout are quite aggressive and will attack spinner lures and bait.

Bull trout surface feed and take a dry fly as pretty as any rainbow or brown, but they don't jump. A couple of years ago I fished a small creek west of Rocky Mountain House, Alberta, where both brown trout and bull trout live. I found a riser—what seemed like a good fish for such a small creek—feeding a couple of inches from a grass bank. It was feeding every few seconds and just coming up to the surface and poking its nose out. There was an assortment of bugs on the water including grayish mayflies. (There really is an Adams mayfly—at least I think so.) I figured the trout must be a brown because of the way it was rising. I made a couple of casts that carried the fly about 6 inches from the bank, but it wouldn't take. A fussy brown for sure. After a couple more casts I finally landed the Adams in the grass just a few inches upstream. I gave it a tug and it dropped onto the surface and was eaten by what turned out to be a 15-inch bull trout. The lowly bull trout—no way!

If you are fishing in a stream with zero limits on bull trout or Dolly Varden please release them unharmed. Bull trout are the only trout with no black marks on the body or dorsal fin. In the fall, during spawning, they could be confused with brook trout, but brookies have black vermiculations (wiggly marks) on the dorsal fin. *No black, put it back!*

Lake trout are a northern char species confined to the northern parts of Canada and some northern states where water depths and other conditions are suited to its needs. They live primarily in stillwater, but can be found in flowing water where a river enters a lake. They also travel flowing waters between lakes. These large chars are aggressive feeders and will take flashy streamers that imitate whitefish, grayling and small food fish.

They will even attempt to eat a hooked trout. If you are fishing for grayling or cutthroat trout and lake or bull trout are in the same water, be prepared for an aggressive laker or bull to chase and catch a small fish you have hooked. An unintentional reversion to baitfishing. My brother and I were fishing a grayling rapid in the

Northwest Territories a few years ago, when a large laker grabbed a hooked grayling and immediately stripped out line to almost the end of the backing. Gary checked the run by braking the reel and forced the tippet to break before he lost the entire line. Another hundred yards of backing might have helped, but I doubt it. In a similar fashion, I hooked a 10-inch brown trout this summer in a beaver pond. A large bull trout immediately latched on and held on for several minutes before letting go.

Trout streams

Rivers, streams and creeks are as fascinating as the trout they harbor and nourish. There's a whole lot of chemistry, pH factors and nutrient loading that come into play in the creation of a trout stream. And, of course, there are the insects that we've already discussed. In imagining an ideal trout stream with all the right types of water, we'll assume everything in the chemistry department is satisfactory and there are enough insects to feed our trout. To fly-fish our stream successfully we'll have to understand its physical shape and form.

Streams vary widely. Slow-flowing spring creeks meander through pastureland and change little with time. Rivers and streams fed with melting snow and rainwater babble peacefully through mountain gorges and get larger as they head downstream. But these sometimes peaceful waters have another face. Spring rains coupled with high temperatures that melt upland snow can turn them into raging torrents of silt-laden fluid inflicting destruction to stream banks and folks living in the flood plain. Rivers can be brutal to the fish, too, and it's a wonder they survive at all. But all this mayhem has been happening for millennia and will continue for a while longer if we have the wisdom to protect our watersheds.

The flowing, scouring, wearing and grinding of rivers carve a path through the geography. From this action the streambed develops a many-sided character that provides hiding, feeding and

breeding places for trout. Four general types of water have been etched into our ideal trout stream by the flow of water: riffles, runs, glides and pools. They are enhanced by the lay of the land and building materials—rocks, soil and vegetation. There are all sorts of less-distinct hybrid water bearing characteristics of two or three of these types. Within these four general types of water are places where fish tend to congregate.

Trout often hold at the bottom of a deep run like the one running from the upper right to the lower left.

A riffle is a fast choppy section of shallow water. The speed is determined by the slope, and the roughness is caused by stream-bed rocks. This water is highly oxygenated and can hold incredible numbers of insects. During significant insect activity trout will often move into riffles to feed on nymphs that are about to emerge.

A run is a section of fairly fast and deep water. Depending on depth and stream-bed rocks, the surface can be choppy or smooth. Runs are often faster portions of wider sections of rivers bordered on one or both sides by a wider shallow shelf. Trout often hold at the bottom of runs or in seams between the actual

Top View　　　　　　　**Cross Section**

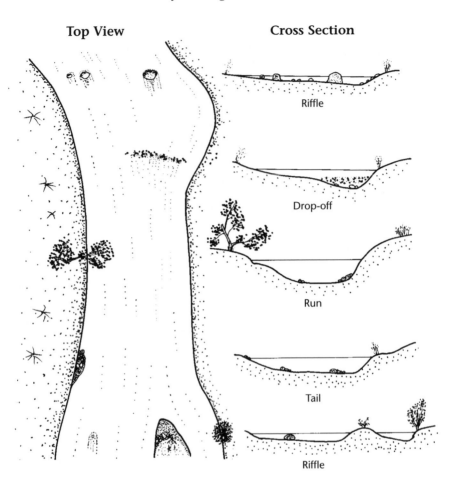

Riffle

Drop-off

Run

Tail

Riffle

Anatomy of a trout stream. The cross sections at the right correspond to the adjacent overhead sections on the left.

run and slower adjacent water. The head, or upstream end of the run, is usually a drop-off just below a riffle. Fish will hold at the head of a run, waiting for dislodged nymphs to float along or for insects that emerged in the riffle. The end of a run is called the tail. (The word *run* is sometimes used by fly-anglers to identify sections of streams and rivers—such as the Dog Run or Deer Run. These locations include several types of water.)

A glide, or flat, is a section of slow smooth water. Most are a few feet deep, but some are quite shallow and smooth because of slow water speed and a smooth streambed. Glides can be very

difficult to dry-fly fish and often require very long and light leaders. The smooth slow water allows the fish to get a clear and close look at a dry fly. Wading quietly is critical because of the surface smoothness and lack of natural water noise.

Pools are relatively slow deep sections of a stream or river. They often occur where a severe drop-off has carved a deep pocket. Trout tend to hold in pools during hot weather and in winter. Pools are considered to be favorite haunts of large trout. Because of their depth they can be difficult to fish.

A section of prime trout water.

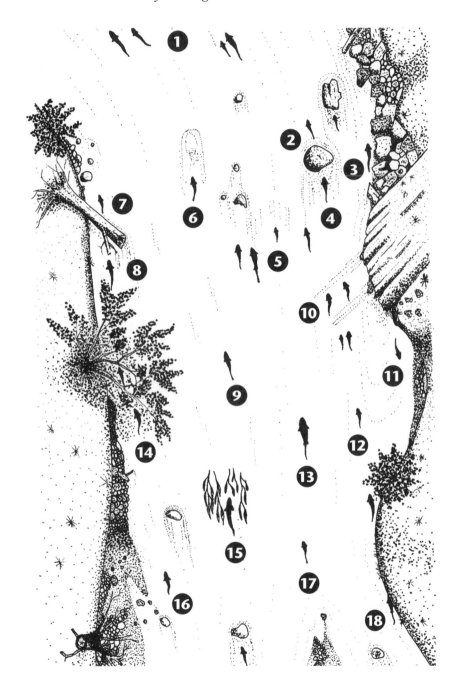

Favored holding spots of trout
in a typical section of river

Trout often hold and feed in identifiable parts of a stream:

1 In riffles and shallows, especially during insect hatches.
2 In front of boulders, where the water speed in front is slowed by the rock behind. This is a popular spot during heavy hatches.
3 Along banks where the current is slower and terrestrial insects fall in.
4 Behind boulders that offer protection from the current.
5 In drop-offs between riffles and the heads of runs that offer protection from the current and a steady supply of food.
6 Behind submerged boulders or other protective pockets.
7 In front of surface obstructions that can trap food insects.
8 Behind logs that offer protection and possibly ants.
9 At the floor of runs where the water is slower and food is plentiful.
10 In quiet holding pockets between subsurface rock ledges.
11 In back eddies where the current is slower and where insects tend to collect.
12 In seams between slow and faster water where the current isn't too strong and food passes nearby.
13 At the bottom of a deep pool.
14 In the shade of overhanging streamside trees protected from view.
15 In and around weed beds that offer food and protection from the current.
16 In gravel bar shallows in late evening.
17 In the tail of a run where the current is slower.
18 Under or inside undercut banks.

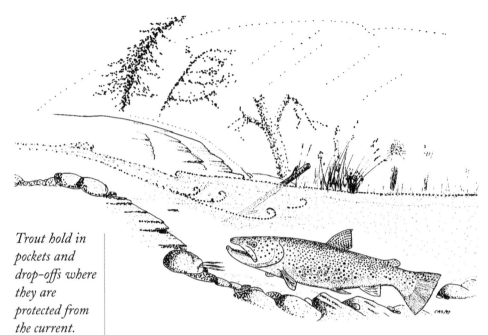

Trout hold in pockets and drop-offs where they are protected from the current.

These water types are often connected in some predictable way, yet the combinations are infinite. Water in a typical section of a river might run through a riffle that drops off into a deeper run. The deeper run may have shallower side sections. The run may become shallower and evolve into a glide or flat. And as the gradient changes it may narrow again, forming the tail that speeds up and transforms into yet another riffle that becomes the head of the next run. And on and on . . .

Our stream will have all of these features because they create environments for a wide range of insects and add dimension to our fishing opportunities.

Reading trout water

Figuring out the fishy parts of a stream is called "reading the water." You can learn a lot about reading water by taking a class on fly-fishing. And you will learn from experience. When trout are rising you know where they are. It becomes a bit trickier if they are feeding down below and you can't see them. When you are on the water, pay attention. Ask yourself: If I were a trout, where would I hold? Where would I be protected from the current and predators, and have access to a steady supply of food?

Polarized sunglasses are useful for reading trout streams and helping you see fish in the water. They eliminate most of the surface glare and often allow you to see structural variations that create the different types of water that hide fish.

Within the four general types of water, trout tend to hold where they are safe from predators, where the current isn't too strong and where there is a ready supply of food. Any place in a river that can provide all three at the same time is a prime holding spot, or prime lie. When there is intensive insect activity, either on the surface or below, trout will let their guard down and move into shallow water or to the surface. They also often move out of the runs into shallow water as night falls.

Trout *tend* to hold at the bottom of deeper runs, just below drop-offs, and behind rocks or other obstructions in the stream. They also hold under streamside vegetation or in undercut banks.

Large boulders within a riffle or run form what we call pocket water. Trout hold in front and behind rocks where the water speed is buffered. Conflicting currents make dry-fly and nymph fishing difficult in pocket water.

Seams are transition layers between two sections of water flowing at different speeds. There is often a noticeable seam between shallow slower water and a fast run. Trout often hold in the slower water and have the added benefit of a nearby steady flow of food passing by.

Back eddies are also favorite holding spots. Again, the water current is usually slow, and there is a nearby food supply in the faster water on the outside of the eddy. During a hatch insects often get caught up in the slow swirling currents in a back eddy. It is not uncommon to see trout noses sipping bugs in the back eddy foam. Because of the conflicting currents, back eddies are usually difficult to fish.

Water temperature and trout feeding habits

Trout feed when there is food to be eaten. The amount they eat depends, of course, on their size, on water temperature and therefore on their metabolic rate. And presumably their eating habits depend on things we don't understand. According to many sources each species of trout has an ideal temperature range in which it feeds the heaviest. But this is invariably of more academic interest than practical use to most of us out for the day or away on vacation. If you've just driven across three states or two provinces to fish a famous river and the water temperature is outside of the reported ideal range, what are you going to do? Drive home? No. You fish and make the best of it. Perhaps the temperature may explain why we are not hammering them, but what's the sense in complaining about it, right?

A few years ago I met a man from Rhode Island sitting on a bridge crossing the North Raven River in central Alberta. He was enjoying a cigar and generally taking it easy. I had stopped by the stream to kill a few hours in the afternoon while waiting for the main event later that evening on nearby river. Neither of us caught fish in the couple of hours we were on the water.

Out of the willow-tangled meadows emerged a local angler all bedecked in the latest gear. He inquired how we had fared and then told us he had caught *only* seven browns and the fish were decidedly off compared to a few days before when he had caught many more. He told us the water temperature was way down and well below the ideal brown trout range. He might as well go home, he said. Clearly not an option for us. We fished on, content to know that being skunked on a beautiful stream beat the hell out of a lot things in life.

For the record here are the survival and feeding-activity temperature ranges for trout published in a popular fishing text. The survival range for trout is published at $35°$F to $75°$F ($2°$C to $23°$C). And the optimum feeding range for most trout species is between about $50°$F and $68°$F ($10°$ to $20°$C). Cutthroats and brook trout feed optimally at slightly cooler temperatures.

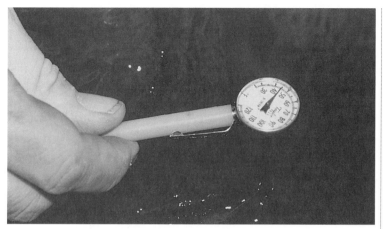

Trout are most active between about 50°F and 68°F (10°C and 18°C). They feed at lower temperatures but not as actively.

I am doubtful about the reported optimum feeding temperature ranges for trout. My brother, Gary, has a theory that, within reason, the trend in temperature direction is more important than the actual temperature. He believes that at the lower range the absolute water temperature is not as important as whether it's getting warmer or colder. If the stream temperature rises from 45°F to 50°F (7° to 10°C) the trout will get jazzed and increase feeding—perhaps not as aggressively as they might at, say, 60°F. But if the temperature drops from 55°F *down* to 50°F (13 to 10°C) they will go off their feed. Trout feed better on the upswing than on the downswing. So you could have two identical water temperatures in the same creek, perhaps two or three days apart, and the feeding habits could be totally different. (Of course, this may be complicated by the relative insect activity as well. The bugs also may be turned off by falling water temperatures.) This theory may or may not be so, but on-stream experience seems to bear it out often enough to make it intriguing.

Gary's theory may be written up in the scientific literature somewhere. If not it would make an interesting research study for a young graduate student: "The effects of absolute water temperature and the direction of temperature change on the metabolism and feeding rates of *Oncorhynchus mykiss* (Rainbow trout)." Great topic.

Higher temperatures definitely cause feeding activity to drop off. Trout fishing at lower elevations can be quite poor when we have a long hot spell. If the water temperature gets too high the dissolved oxygen content can fall to fatal levels.

A final issue about the published temperature ranges is that they just don't seem to hold true at the lower end. They imply that trout simply will not eat when the water temperature hovers just above freezing. So why then are we able to catch trout in western streams from November through March when there are often ice flows in the water—a strong indication that the water is barely above freezing? Sure, the fish are sluggish, but they do eat our flies, and I have seen rainbows actually chase nymphs in ice-cold water.

Trout and their senses

You've heard of horse sense. We'll, trout seem to have a lot of it. Their brains may be small, but they are acutely in tune with their environment and evolved that way by selection. Any critter that can't sense food and predators is not long for this world.

Fish, like all other animals, basically live to do three things: make babies, eat and keep from being eaten. So they are always alert to threats to their safety. Clearly, they figure some stumbling rock-bashing neoprene-covered monster is more likely a predator than a sex counselor or food bearer.

Gamefish see and hear very well. They can hear you coming. They can see you coming. Fish "hear" with sensors along their lateral line and with earlike organs in the skull. The ear structure in the head obviously has no external opening, but it nonetheless picks up sound vibrations in the water. Fish can apparently hear aquatic insects and other foods in the water. (Sort of makes you wonder how grad students figured that out, right?)

Of most significance to anglers is their ability to hear sounds made by clumsy wading and stomping along the banks of quiet streams. Years ago my brother and our youngest son, Mike, fly-

Splashy wading will scare trout.

fished a small sluggish brown trout stream. (It was Mike's first fly-fishing trip and he did well, landing three or four small browns that afternoon.) The banks were made of spongy peat, and you could feel the earth vibrate slightly under foot. The slow meandering water made no sound to mask bank noises. Brown trout rose every now and then up and down the creek. What became obvious in a hurry was that you had to walk gingerly along the banks. One slight stomp on the ground put feeding fish down for 50 feet in either direction. It took several minutes before they started feeding again.

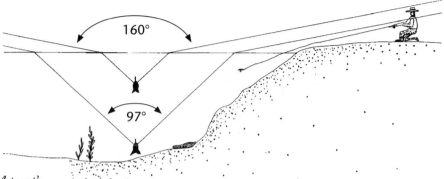

A trout's field of view to the water's surface is 97°. The field of view widens at the surface because of light refraction. The deeper a trout is in the water, the lower on the horizon it can see. Surface riffles interfere with vision.

In addition to bank vibrations you'll create two other types of noise when wading: splashy water noise and grinding, kicking, stumbling rock and gravel noise. Obviously, you will be aware of the surface water noise—or should be. However, pay attention to the noise as your feet grind along the bottom because sound travels well through water. If you can feel your feet grinding the stones you can bet trout for some distance around can hear it, too. Take it easy. Go slowly. Be quiet.

Take the time to watch someone else wade and imagine you are a fish near the wading angler. Would you put up with the noise created by the person you are watching? If the wader is quiet be quiet like him. If the angler is noisy—and you wouldn't tolerate the noise if you were a fish—then learn from what you see.

Trout can see to the side and ahead but not behind.

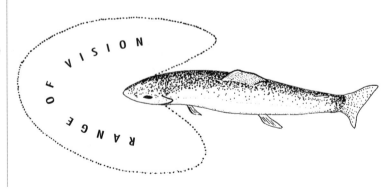

The physics of fish sight are complicated by the placement of the eyes, their natural field of view and light refraction at the surface. Suffice it to say that fish can see almost all the way around them and they have a wide angle of view above.

Since fish can see outside of smooth water, stay as low as possible when approaching, especially from the side. Provided the water is clear enough, the deeper a trout is in the water, the farther afield it can see. The only reason we can approach fish at all is by the saving grace of surface imperfections that are present on all but the glassiest of water. About the only time they potentially can't see you at all is when you are directly behind. Stay low and behind the fish if possible. You may have to stay well back of the water's edge. Wade quietly and keep low.

Fly-anglers may have to keep low and well back from the edge of a stream to avoid being seen by trout.

Chasing rainbows

Chasing rainbows is the pursuit of dreams that are not possible to catch. Reminds me a lot of fly-fishing for trout. Unlike the mythical pot of gold at the end of rainbows, we find and catch our share of fish, and we are content in our sport because of that. Or at least content in a strange sort of way, for it seems we are never totally satisfied. There's always a trickier trout to catch, a different fly to tie and try, a new rod to build and always another stream to explore. Chasing rainbows.

One of the true joys of fly-fishing is finding your own places to fish—the ones that aren't in the fishing guides or posted on the Internet. The pleasure in seeking out these places is rooted in the old work ethic that we appreciate things better when we have to work for them. I don't mean to imply that there are a whole lot of never-fished-before places left. But there are places that perhaps aren't quite as publicized, and a little effort will help you find them.

My neighbor and fishing partner, John Tunstall, and I have found our share of "exclusive" waters, and finding them is every bit as good as catching fish. Not better, but the fish we catch in the places we've found are always sweeter for it.

I have fished one well-known Alberta river for many years, but for the past six years I've fished where others don't fish—other than the few friends who come along from time to time. To find these places I bought some high-scale maps and scouted around. Burned some gas and hiked a lot. Found plenty of places where not to fish and a few superb spots that are perhaps among the best dry-fly stretches in Alberta. In that finding there was as much satisfaction as catching the fish that reside there.

John and I fished one of these stretches together for a year, and we were delighted with the results. Not a lot of fish, but they were big hard-running rainbows. There were a few browns. There were no other fishers. And I mean no other fishers. For a while we were content and sought no other places. Why should we?

Finally, it occurred to us to search farther afield. I don't recall any specific discussion, but I am certain of our reasoning. If this particular stretch was good, there have to be more runs just as good or better than the ones we'd been fishing. Right? And if we couldn't chase down some hot new places we could always return to the old ones—everything to gain and nothing to lose.

Maps were located, and we looked for river and land patterns similar to those that had already produced well for us in that river system. We were rewarded when we ground-proofed a new stretch of river on a warm September weekend. As John is my witness—and I his—the first rainbow to come out of the new place was a whopping 22 inches. It was taken on an Antron Adams on the third cast. From about 25 feet away. Went to the backing. And nowhere along this stretch was there a hint that other anglers had ever been there. (You've got to trust me on this point. There are still a few relatively unfished places like this in Alberta.)

Let me start at the beginning. Our map showed some trails that took us near where we thought we wanted to be. From time to time we caught glimpses of the water from the trail. It looked promising. We meandered down in the direction of the water and parked the 4x4 as close as we could get to a likely spot. After a short walk we came upon what looked like promising trout water.

We halfheartedly tried a couple of likely runs without success and slowly made our way upstream. Our primary objective was fish, but we were also in a mood for exploration.

"There have to be trout somewhere along here," we both chanted, perhaps refusing to believe anything different. We walked the gravel shore of a fair-looking 100-yard run and riffle, but passed it by in favor of the jackpot we were certain was some-where nearby. If you had seen this section of stream, you'd have felt no less certain that fish were about to be caught.

At the head of the run we reached a glide that had to be crossed if we were to continue exploring upstream. We slipped into the hip-deep water and waded across. We managed all of this without making lots of waves and noise. Sometimes you've just got to wonder what makes you do things right. I guess we were wired for fish and subconsciously slid in quietly. When stream fishing it always pays to assume there are fish in the neighborhood.

After wading about 20 feet I looked back over my left shoulder and saw the smallest of rises. Had I looked a second later it would have been gone. This was not one of those "car-hood-sized" rises we've all read about that ripple on the surface for seconds. These were the smallest rings. Almost not discernible as a fish rise.

"Hey, John, there's a rise near the bank, upstream. I think it's just a small fish. It may not have been a fish at all. The rings were awfully small." The fish rose again . . . and again.

The rings had none of the characteristics of a big fish sipping flies. Large fish usually make an audible slurping sound. On a quiet day like that one you can usually hear and see an air bubble as it's burped from the mouth or gills. There were no signs of big trout. And even at this close distance we were unable to see the fish because of the low angle and sun glare.

We later compared the rise rings to those formed if you dropped a pea into the water from a height of few inches. *Plip.* These were small rings. Plips. Nothing at all. But as we had yet to catch a fish in the soon-to-be classic (and soon-to-be-named) Duckfeather Run, anything was worth a try. I mean, wouldn't you give the first riser of the day a shot even if it were small and you were in mood to explore?

We couldn't see for sure what the trout was sipping on. There were a few very tiny surface insects.

"You give him a try. I've got a hopper on, and he's taking something smaller. Midges or blue-winged olives or something in the film," I said.

John must consider it his obligation to let me have first crack at a fish or run.

"No. No. You're closer than me, and I haven't got a fly tied on," he replied, even though he was only four feet farther in stream, and as it turned out I had to tie another fly on anyway.

The cast was simple: quartering-upstream, 25-foot, no wind. A classic dry-fly setup that would meet with the approval of the purest of dry-fly purists. They are rarely this perfect.

After two casts it was clear this fish was not eating hoppers today—at least not mine. But had I put it down? Unlike educated rainbows in the more heavily fished parts of this river system, it hadn't gone off its feed and continued to rise every few seconds to invisible critters on or near the surface. This is an advantage of fishing streams largely untainted by anglers. The trout aren't as quirky.

John insisted that I continue to try for this small trout. What could I say? So I tied on a small Antron Adams, a good just-emerged midge and mayfly imitation that floats well with its Wulff-like tail.

You know the rest already. First cast with the new fly and— *plip.* Just a sip and the fly was gone. I'll spare you all of the line-to-the-backing details, but the female rainbow measured an honest 22 inches and would have weighed well over 3 pounds. I should have talked to John about being so obliging.

A chunkier 22-inch rainbow caught the next day less than 100 yards away would have tipped the scales at well over 4 pounds. We caught and released over two dozen big silvery rainbows that weekend. We felt downright saintly because we had hunted out the place with no directions or hints from anyone. This was our stretch of river.

We can't forget that actually catching fish is the reason we fly-fish in the first place. Walking and looking without catching fish is called hiking or golf. So I still spend most of my fishing time at the popular places because of time and accessibility. But tracking down new fishing spots adds another dimension to fishing.

Finding new places. Naming your stretch. Catching trout. Once in a while catching a really big rainbow, brown or cutt. Tying and trying a new fly that works. These fishing experiences are the stuff of dreams, but unlike chasing rainbows in the sky, sometimes they come true down below on the water. Chasing rainbows—and catching them.

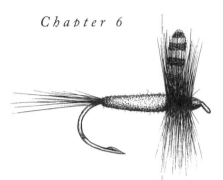

Chapter 6

Dry-Fly
Fishing

Dry-fly fishing. The main event. What we waited for all winter and much of the spring.

When the trout are looking up it just doesn't get any better. I love to nymph and streamer fish, but there is something about catching trout on dry flies, especially when casting to specific fish and watching it all happen.

We'd all likely catch more trout if we never tied on a dry fly, but instead pounded nymphs persistently hour in and hour out, week in week out—at least in many high-plains, foothills and mountain streams. You'll read articles by some anglers who ignore hatches and rising fish and cast nymphs of the hatching insect instead of dry flies. They claim to catch more fish that way even during hatches.

That's fine if numbers are important to you. But do we always fly-fish to catch the maximum number of fish? Don't get me wrong, I like to catch trout. But dry-fly fishing is a blast and a rise or two is often enough to make me break down the nymph gear and try a dry fly. If the nymph action has been slow I have nothing to lose anyway. I also may try it just for something different even if the nymph fishing has been good. But mostly I do it because it is just so neat to cast to rising a trout and watch it take the fly.

If the occasional trout is caught on a dry fly during sporadic feeding periods—perhaps only one or two trout instead of the five you might have caught during the same period on nymphs—that's okay. In fact, it's pretty satisfying. It could be easy to become smug and think of yourself as a very cool and selfless angler for catching a few trout on dries when you "could've slayed 'em" on nymphs. But there's no need be become boastful about it. You caught several fish on nymphs yesterday and fewer today on dries. It was different. You had fun as you always do—and that's what counts.

Mayflies are favored by trout and worshiped by dry-fly anglers.

Once in a while hatches and feeding fish can be difficult to figure out because, as I mentioned, it may not be apparent what the trout are eating. You can see adult mayflies or whatever on the surface, and you see trout eating something, but no matter what imitation you try, they ignore it. The #16 yellow mayfly dry was the first you tried, but that was six or eight patterns ago. Damn, what are they eating? Reminds me of when Butch Cassidy turned to the Sundance Kid and asked, "Who are those guys?"

Rainbow trout caught on a foam-winged caddis dry fly.

It could be one of those masked hatches, where there's a less obvious insect on the surface that the trout are feeding on and you don't notice it. Or the trout could be locked on emergers, and you think they're eating adults. Or they're eating spinners that hatched yesterday and are dying today in the midst of today's new crop of adults. It's doubly satisfying to get one of these tough hatches figured out. But it's frustrating if the hatch comes and goes before you find the solution. It's happened to me before and will happen again.

The best hatches of all are the "no-brainers." You see the insects hatching on the water and you know what they are: say, #16 pale mayflies. The guy at the fly shop said something about Pale Morning Duns, but to you they are smallish pale-colored mayflies. You catch one of the natural insects in your hat and they're quite pretty. There is no mistake with this hatch because you watched a few duns floating along and they all disappeared in quiet rises. You tie on the appropriate imitation dry fly and bingo. Trout are caught. The trout are on and you've got them figured out.

During a hot hatch, after you've landed a few fish—was it five or seven?—you momentarily think about wading to shore and relaxing while you watch fish rise. Maybe have a cigar. It's permitted; after all, you're in the smoking section. But you regain your senses, remembering all the times when the trout weren't rising, and you contentedly fish the hatch to the end, catching three or four more before the bugs and the rising dwindles. You feel cheery and content. Lord knows you've paid your dues in the past few weeks. This will make some good storytelling with the gang when you get back.

Hatches never last forever. Perhaps a couple of hours if you live a charmed life. Only a few minutes sometimes. A full-blown hatch should never be ignored because you just never know when the bugs, the trout and you will be at the same coordinates again. You can show up tomorrow at the same time and same place and under the same sky. The wind could stay down again for the second day in a row, and according to the nice man at the local fly shop, this is a solid hatch that will go on for at least one more week. And . . . nothing.

When you see insects emerging and trout eating them at the surface, take advantage of your fortune because you just never know how long it could last. Late last summer John and I hit three or four of what we came to call six-minute hatches. Twice we were having coffee on a high bank, waiting for something to happen and it did. Suddenly, trout were rising everywhere, not more than 50 yards away. But by the time we put stuff away, grabbed rods, locked the truck, clambered down and waded in, there were only a few straggler blue-winged olive mayflies drifting down. The trout had quit for lack of numbers. It wasn't that we couldn't figure it out. By the time we got in the water it was over, and we knew exactly what we had missed. A six-minute blue-winged olive hatch. Hell, we would've slayed 'em, eh John?

Fly selection

What fly to use? You'll have to make that decision. Usually, you should select a dry fly that is the same size and color as the naturals you are trying to imitate. It's called matching the hatch. If that doesn't work, and you are certain what the rising trout are eating, try a smaller fly or one that's lighter in color. You might clip the hackles from the underside so it floats lower in the water. If that doesn't work perhaps use a thinner tippet. Check for drag. Tie on a Royal Coachman.

A couple of Octobers ago Art Kruger and I were fishing a run together on the Crowsnest River. A few fish were rising to what seemed to be small gray or tan midges. It was never clear. I tried fishing small midge dries in an effort to match the hatch, and, well . . . I caught squat along that run. I had failed to match exactly what they were eating. Art used his favorite #14 tan caddis dry fly and caught three or four nice rainbows. The trout were not rising to natural caddisflies, but they knew what they were and came up for a good caddisfly imitation presented well. On the other hand, my attempts to fool them with what they were supposed to be eating failed.

There's an ongoing debate in fly-fishing literature about what's more important: fly selection or fly presentation. There are presentationists and there are selectionists. And then there are experts who righteously claim both are important. You can only do the best you can. Select your closest fly and cast as well as you can. Try to learn something that will help prepare you for your

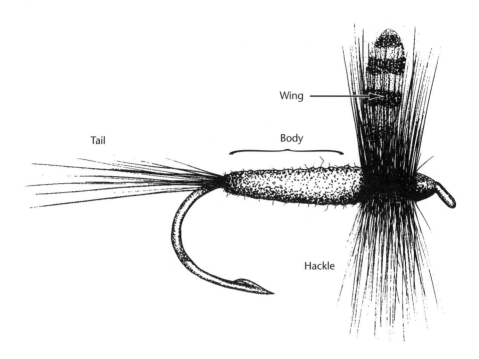

Tail

Body

Wing

Hackle

next outing. Perhaps you need a few more flies. Perhaps you need to work on your casting or practice another type of cast.

A standard dry fly.

Rigging for dry flies

Rigging for basic dry-fly fishing is simple. Normally, you will be using one fly only, and there are no split shots or strike indicators to worry about. Normally.

A typical setup is comprised of the leader, one or two tippet sections and the fly. Say you have a 9-foot, tapered, 2x leader attached with a nail knot to your fly line. Tie about 2 feet of 3x tippet to the end of the leader with a surgeon's knot. You can tie #8 or #10 grasshopper or stonefly imitations directly to the 3x tippet with a clinch knot. Treat the fly with floatant and start fishing.

If later on you decide to try a #14 Adams, first remove the

Mayflies of different sizes tied with hackles but no wings.

larger fly and tie on another 18 inches or so of 4x tippet to the 3x tippet, again with a surgeon's knot. Now tie on the Adams and you're away. If you have to use smaller flies yet, you have two choices. You can add a thinner, third section of 5x tippet to the 4x, but if you add up the total length of the leader it's pretty long already. You've got about 9 feet of tapered leader, 2 feet of 3x, 1½ feet of 4x for a total so far of over 12 feet. It may be a bit shorter now if you've changed flies a few times, but it's still plenty long, and adding another tippet section is too much. The second option is to cut off the 4x tippet and replace it with a 1½-foot section of 5x for the smaller flies. So what you have is a tapered 2x leader followed by a section of 3x tippet and now a short section of 5x tippet.

This little bit of confusion emphasizes the need to buy three

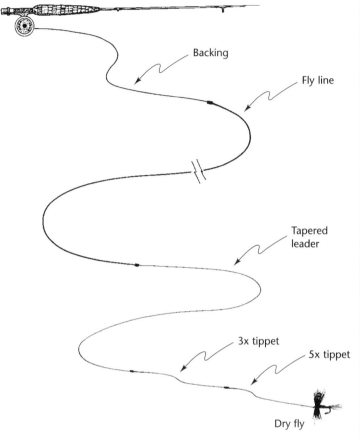

or four spools of different sized tippets. They can save you a lot of time and money. You could buy a number of leaders in different end thicknesses and change the leaders each time you move from one fly size to another. This is both a waste of time and leaders. Every time you change flies you lose a couple of inches of leader, and soon they are too short. Leaders cost about $1 a yard and tippet line costs about 10 cents a yard. So the thing to do is to tie on a section of, say, 3x tippet to the thin end of a 2x leader and you never have to change the leader. (Well, not exactly never, but it will last a few trips.) Just use different tippets when you change fly sizes. When the tippets get too short you replace them.

Reading rise forms

Rise forms are the water patterns—ripples, rings, bubbles and swirls—made by trout feeding at or near the surface. Individual forms are of interest, but there are two important things to learn and accept first. A rise only tells you there is a fish in the water. To figure out what the fish is eating and how to catch it, you may have to pay close attention. As Yogi Berra said, "You can see a lot by looking." If he wasn't a dry-fly fisherman he should have been. If you take the time to watch and try to understand what it is you are seeing, then half the battle of dry-fly fishing is won.

"This is starting to sound like bull, to me," you say, "The fish are rising, so all we do is tie on a brown fly because there are brown mayflies on the water."

Hopefully, that's true. You see fish rising; you take a quick look at the water and see some bugs floating by; so you tie something on that's close. Hopefully, that's all you have to do. But as often as not, what you think you see is not really what's happening. You might flog your brown fly all afternoon while trout merrily rise around it and ignore it.

When you see bugs in the water and trout rising, you first have to determine if they actually eating the floating bugs. Often they are, but, as mentioned earlier, trout love to eat some insects, like mayflies, just at the moment they are emerging. So there may be all sorts of adults drying their wings on the surface, but, in fact, the trout are not eating them. They are eating emergers stuck momentarily in the surface film, and you can't see them.

Watch the precise area where a fish is rising. If there are obvious insects floating down, you should be able to see the fish take the surface critters. If the trout continues to rise, yet all of the obvious insects go unnoticed, then it is likely taking emergers at the surface or nymphs a few inches below. There's another way to tell. A trout that takes a bug off the surface almost always leaves a bubble behind. When they suck in the bug they "burp" air out their gills, leaving surface bubbles. If the trout is eating insects

Because there is no surface air bubble, this rise indicates that a trout has taken a food item just below the surface.

just below the surface, and therefore it's mouth does not break the surface, there are no bubbles. If so, try tying on an emerger fly.

Trout can flip their tails at least a foot under the surface and still create a visible rise form. If trout are "rising" like this and you're having no luck with dry flies and emergers, try switching to a nymph and fishing it just below the surface. This may imitate the nymphs as they swim near the surface. Say there are medium-sized tan mayflies (#14s) on the water, but you've determined that the trout may be eating emergers, since you tried a tan-colored dry fly pattern and it didn't work. You also probably have tried a #16 tan mayfly, a #14 Adams, a small tan caddis and perhaps one or two emerger patterns. (There's nothing like trout eating bugs near the top to get you to try so many different flies. You just don't want to accept that they are not eating what seems so obvious.) Tie on a #14 Hare's Ear nymph. Apply fly floatant to the leader to within a few inches of the fly. Try casting this to the "rising" trout. If the imitation is close and the fish are eating nymphs near the surface, they may take your subsurface nymph.

It will be hard to tell where your fly is because you can't see it. This isn't a major problem if you're casting to a single fish. If

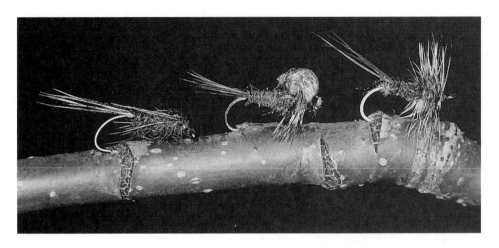

Left to right: Mayfly nymph, emerger and dry fly.

you see a swirl in the general area, you raise the rod. But if fish are rising all around, you've got a problem. Is one of those many rises your fly being eaten? Here's what to do. First tie on a buoyant Elk Hair Caddis dry fly. Then tie a few inches of 4x or 5x tippet to the bend of the dry-fly hook so the new tippet section hangs down below. Then tie on your emerger nymph. The dry fly is now a strike indicator, and because it looks something like a bug it won't scare the trout like a brightly colored strike indicator might. And you never know, you might catch a trout on it, even though you've already tried umpteen dry flies.

After casting the two-fly rig (the nymph is now called a dropper fly) manage the line to keep the flies from dragging and keep a close eye on the dry-fly indicator. If it goes under, raise the rod.

Rising trout may be taking the same species of mayfly you see floating down the stream, but they may not be eating the obvious newly emerged adults or even the less-obvious emergers. Most species of mayflies hatch over a few days. Some yesterday, some today and some tomorrow until it's over. The bugs that hatched a day or two ago have already mated, and the females, the so-called spent spinners, may be laying eggs today and then dying on the surface amidst the new adults. Usually, the spinner adults lay eggs and die at a different time of day than when they emerged, so there is usually not this much confusion—but I have seen it.

The difficulty with spinners is that they lie flat on the water and are difficult to see unless you pay close attention. In the past decade of fly-fishing I have only once seen trout eat spinners exclusively and not look at another thing. The strange thing was these were cutthroats, which are usually opportunistic and will eat pretty much anything when they're feeding. These cutts were eating dying drake mayflies of some unknown species—at least unknown to me. That's what they were eating and nothing else. After catching nothing for twenty minutes while cutts rose frantically, I finally used a #12 or #14 Adams (I forget which) and clipped all of the hackles from the bottom so it would lie flat on the water. Caught a nice cutt immediately and then they quit feeding.

There will be lots of time for you to study how fish feed and to make your conclusions about what they are actually doing. But do take the time to watch trout feeding. It's both fun and enlightening.

Approaching fish

Whether you're casting upstream or down, it's important to know that trout always face upstream in flowing water. This is quite significant. The most obvious reason is that it directs your approach to a fish-holding pool. Because trout are facing into the flow, you can approach them from behind without spooking them and, assuming you wade carefully, sometimes get amazingly close.

Approaching a stretch of water from downstream gets a bit tricky if you come upon a back eddy. Back eddies are favorite holding spots for trout because the water tends to be slower and they have close access to food drifting by in the main stream. Emerged insects often get caught up in back eddies, and it is common to see trout sipping bugs through the collected foam. But as you approach a back eddy you might come into view of fish facing toward you, downstream to the main flow. Be careful.

Marking a fish

When you walk stretches of rivers specifically looking for risers, you'll soon learn about the importance of marking a trout's position. Let's say you come around a bend and see a rise in the evening light. The silvery pink light on the smooth water is perfect for seeing a rise ring from quite a distance. Hurriedly, you advance along the bank. You might see the fish rise once more. You get closer and if you're lucky you realize just soon enough that you don't know exactly where it's holding, so you stop. Again, it rises two casts away.

This time the gods were with you. At first you didn't mark the exact spot where the trout was rising but were lucky to stop in time. Other times you'll get to where you think you should be and never see the trout rise again because you got too close. I've approached risers I thought I had marked well only to see a bow wave shoot away from the bank, indicating I'd walked too close.

When a trout rises, mark the exact spot against some landmark along the shore or bank: a clump of tall grass, an extra large rock along the shore, a willow clump, whatever. From a distance you'll never get the spot right on, but at least you'll know the general stretch. As you approach, stop and wait for another rise. This time you'll be close enough and can locate the trout next to a more precise landmark. You might think to yourself, "It's a rod length past the root sprig beyond the big rock." You walk quietly up within casting distance. If it's an infrequent riser you might take a break before stripping out line and measuring the cast, readying for the final rise before you give it a go.

Casting dry flies

Learning to cast is one thing. Learning to present flies is another. Casting—discussed in the second chapter—involves getting the fly somewhere with accuracy. Presentation is how you get the fly to a fish or fishy part of a river in a way that will

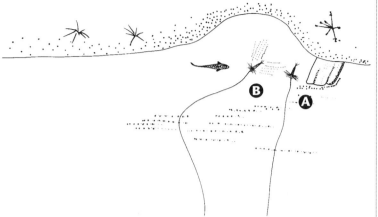

The fly and line should land at position A, but faster water in midstream quickly pulls on the line and causes the fly to drag as it drifts to B. The drag-free time can be extended by mending the line, in this case to the right.

impress the trout. Presentation depends on the position of fish, what they are eating, how fussy they are, the currents in the water, the obstructions and your ability to position yourself.

Usually, dry flies and nymphs are cast in an upstream direction—usually up and away and not directly upstream. As the dry fly or strike indicator travels downstream, the slack line is normally stripped in. If there are a bunch of loose loops floating on the water and you get a hit, you will not be able to tighten the line on the fish. When stripping in line, however, don't pull on it to the extent that the dry fly or nymph is dragged downstream.

As the dry fly or indicator drifts along, the drag-free drift is extended by mending the line. When the drift is complete the line is quietly lifted from the water, the back cast is made (possibly one false cast is required to change the direction of the line) and the line is cast upstream again.

There are times when you can't cast a dry fly upstream the traditional way. For example, it's not uncommon to find a trout rising in front of a streamside branch lying in or on the water. Casting from an upstream position down to the riser may be the only way to drift a fly over the trout. Other times you'll find that you simply cannot get a drag-free drift if you cast upstream to a rising trout. Conflicting and variable currents immediately tug and pull on the fly line and leader, and the fly acts unnaturally.

Fish in heavily fished rivers may be extremely leader shy, and the only way to present a fly that they'll hit is from upstream.

Normally, when casting upstream the line is extended fully on the forward cast as it falls to the water. You aim the cast perhaps 3 or 4 feet ahead of the rising fish. (Immediately, the current draws the fly closer and you have to strip line in.) When casting downstream you can't cast out the full section of line. If you do, the current instantly carries the line and fly away from you, and the fly will drag in the current, likely spooking the fish. You have to put slack into the line so the fly can drift along without dragging in front of the rising trout.

There are a couple of ways to put slack into the line. The first is to false cast a couple of times to measure the cast so the fly is a few feet past the fish. On the final forward cast, as the line is heading forward and more or less fully extended, the rod is pulled back so the fly falls short of the target. Now you have a few feet of extra slack line on the water. There's a bit of a dilemma here. You need the slack to prevent drag, but because you have slack you are not in immediate control of the fly should the trout come up for it. You'll have to figure out just how much slack you can get away with and still be able to tighten the line when the trout comes up.

The second way to add slack line for a drag-free downstream drift is to make a standard cast, and as the fly is drifting down, the rod tip is wiggled back and forth. This is commonly called the wiggle cast. Free line that you have stripped from the reel also can be fed through the line guides and onto the water.

When developing your presentation skills you will make your own discoveries—like the wiggle cast. "Wow," you'll say, "and I never even read about this." And you'll feel happy as a clam because it helped you catch a dandy brown trout. Then two weeks later you'll pick up a magazine or fly-fishing book and find that experts have been writing about your method for years.

Slack-line casting is very useful on streams and rivers. Once you start paying attention to where fish are and how they're feeding, you'll find many occasions when it will help you out.

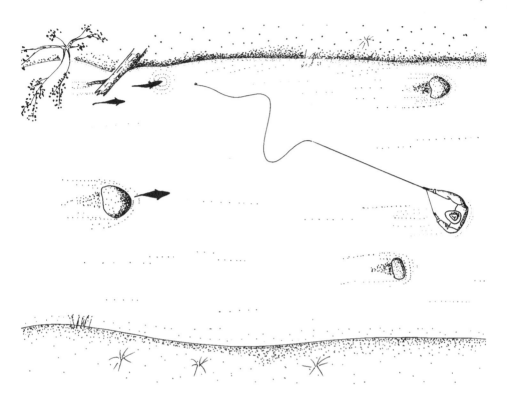

I was fishing at a favorite spot one September evening on the Crowsnest River, where normally I wade up the south bank and cast inward to midstream channels and to the north bank. This very short 75-yard section is usually good for a fish, and occasionally several can be caught there.

Once in a while there is a bank feeder along the south bank, so I've learned to have a close look before wallowing over. On this night there turned out to be a total of five bank feeders, all gulpers feeding every few seconds along the south bank. One was immediately in front of a bush that had trapped a small log. The trout was only a few inches from the bank and was literally holding in an upstream corner. The other four were all hugging the bank, again only a few inches out. There were bank bushes interfering with an upstream cast to a couple of these. But the kicker was the current.

The down-stream slack-line cast is used to present a dry fly to a rising fish when it is not possible to cast upstream because of obstructions.

After successfully casting downstream and catching the one holding in the bush and log corner, I tried casting upstream to the next trout feeding near the bank. The current allowed me little control over the fly, and I just couldn't get it over close enough and not get drag. Carefully, I waded as far out into the stream as possible and then slowly and quietly up past the feeder. This is the sort of thing you can't get away with in the daytime. Thankfully, trout are less aware of movement in fading light. I was able to cast toward the bank from my new position several feet out in the current and upstream from the trout. When the fly landed too close to the edge, I could carefully pull back and get it in the feeding lane. Line was fed out to keep the fly from dragging.

After I had spent 20 minutes or so in one place, rainbows twice moved over to the downstream bank where I had already waded. And so it went for nearly two hours until it was too dark. It's rare that I cast to five rising rainbows and catch them all, but on this great evening I managed to do just that—all with the downstream cast.

I have to confess that part of the reason for the success that evening was actually tying on a fly they would eat: a Griffith's Gnat. Some careful observation, but some luck, too. I think they were eating midges, but when I screened the surface all I came up with was a few empty shucks. Seeing feeders in the Crowsnest doesn't mean you're going to catch them. When there is no major hatch I swear that Crowsnest rainbows are the fussiest feeders on Earth and that other times they rise to dust particles. The next night in the same spot the rainbows wouldn't look at a Griffith's Gnat.

Leading a fish

The fly should land several feet ahead of a trout rising in smooth water so the landing doesn't spook it. In rough water this isn't too important because the surface ripples mask the landing rings and microsplash of the leader. Your ability to lead the fish varies with the type of water and whether you can get a fairly long drag-free drift. When all sorts of conflicting currents are between you and the fish, and the drag-free drift is short, you'll have to gently land the fly close to the riser. If you have the choice between a fly that is dragging by the time it gets to the fish and one that might land a bit too close, go with the latter. Or try the downstream cast.

Pay close attention to where a rising fish is actually holding between rises. The holding position in fast water can be a bit deceiving. Unless you're watching closely, the current may have moved the rise rings a foot or two by the time you see them. Trout will sometimes follow insects for a foot or two before eating, so the actual holding spot of your trout may be even farther yet—perhaps 3 or 4 feet ahead of where you originally thought. It all depends. The point is pay attention and aim ahead when possible.

Casting to the single riser

If you're like me you'll get the most enjoyment out of casting to solitary rising trout. You see a fish holding alone in a confined spot. The fish noses up every few seconds or sometimes only every minute or two. But it's there. Sometimes like clockwork, sometimes coming up at random intervals. Sometimes quitting for, say, 5 minutes or more and making you nervous. It might be in spooky water. It may be near a bank, perhaps with a willow branch right above it. You may not be able to get to it from the traditional downstream position. You may have to approach from upstream and cast down. However you do it, this fish is yours.

The thrill is enhanced when you can actually see insects drifting down toward the feeder. Gulp. (That may be the fish or you.) Sometimes trout rise nonstop and eat every mayfly or caddisfly that comes near. Catching these trout can be a breeze.

From position A the trout can see the leader, and if the line is cast too far upstream it will land over the trout, and it will be "lined." From position B the fish will not see the leader until the last moment, if at all. The cast from this position is made a few feet ahead of the rising fish.

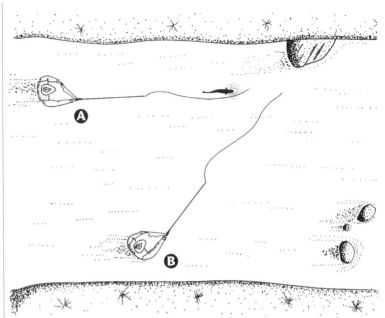

Sometimes you watch a fish consistently feeding on every bug, and then abruptly it ignores a few even though they pass right overhead. You take a close look at the ignored bugs. Are they the same? You check your fly. Do you change it? No, just wait. Then the riser starts feeding regularly again. No mistake this time. It's feeding and eating what your fly is supposed to imitate. Carefully, you strip out line and make a few false casts, lengthening the line each time. If there are no casting obstructions you might lay a practice cast on the water several feet to the side of your target to check the length. The distance needs to be just so. The false casts and perhaps a practice cast to the side are called measuring the cast. The fly has to be above the feeder, but not so far ahead that the fly line lands over it. This is called lining a fish.

The key now is to time your false cast with the feeding rhythm. Wait to drop the fly until what you think is, say, halfway between the timing of the rises. Don't land the fly above the trout a second after it just fed. Wait. False cast twice more. Now.

A word of caution. When a dry fly has sunk—perhaps as you strip in a few feet of line for the next cast—it may become water-logged. When you make the next forward cast, perhaps a measuring false cast, the water in the fly will come spraying out of the fly. This is not an issue on rough water, but in slow smooth water these fine water droplets can spook some finicky fish. Direct the first one or two forward casts away from your prized riser so the fine droplets settle away from it.

Casting to several fast-rising fish

Sometimes there will be so much rise action that you can't really pick out one fish. There may be as many as a dozen or twenty trout in an area no bigger than your living room. Each fish is perhaps holding in an area no bigger than a couple of square feet. But they are overlapping each other's turf since you've seen two rise in a small area at one time. It's happened to me a few times. And I'll tell you it can be fairly intimidating. I've become so excited that I've had trouble tying a fly on.

Or there may be fewer trout frequently rising, but after you've watched for a while it's apparent that each is casually meandering about. No single fish is holding in a small area, and perhaps each is covering an area as big as your truck box. Back and forth and from side to side. Cruise and pick. Cruise and pick. In both cases you can't pick out one fish, and at first you may be so rattled you don't know where to cast.

Assuming, of course, that you know what they are eating and have a fly that'll fool them, all you have to do is cast into the fray—like flock shooting. You watch your fly like a hawk and gently lift the rod when a trout takes the fly. Sounds simple all right and it can be. But it is not without problems, especially if you are having difficulty keeping an eye on your fly. If you can't see the fly, how do you know when to raise the rod in the midst of rises all around you? Was that rise at your fly or just close? Again, there are worse problems to have. One solution is to use special strike indicators to help you keep track of your small dry flies, something we'll turn to later in this chapter.

Working a pool or run

When you come across a section of water and many fish are rising, you have a problem. You want to catch a whole bunch of them, but how do you do that and not spook the whole pool? Many books talk about starting at the tail end and working your way up through the group—taking a fish here and there and hopefully not spooking too many. Nice in theory and it can work. I've had some success with this technique.

Of course, this requires that each fish at the lower end is played downstream away from the feeding masses. Trout can be a bit unpredictable when a hooked brethren thrashes through the cafeteria. They are prone to quit feeding at the surface for a while. A couple of times I have seen trout come over and check out the hooked specimen, apparently oblivious to its plight. You may have some success by starting at the lower end and working up through the horde. With some luck you'll catch a few trout before they've all been spooked or the hatch is finished.

There is, however, a downside to starting at the lower end of a group of fish and working up through them. Quite often the larger fish will be at the top end of the glide, run or riffle. Fish are territorial, with the bigger fish getting the best spots, and the best spots are frequently at the head of the pool. Some mayflies emerge in riffles. The trout, for reasons we'll never know, may not move into the riffles where there is good nymph and emerger activity. They may be content to hold in the downstream pool and pick off mayfly duns as they float down, drying their wings. As often as not, the head of the pool, just below the bug-producing riffle, will have a comfortable little drop-off where the big guys like to hold, waiting for food.

I've been known to pass over smaller fish in a group at the lower end of a pool and pick out a larger trout. There are a cou-

ple of pretty good reasons for doing this, both based on my preference for catching larger fish. First, a small trout hooked downstream may splash around and spook the bigger trout upstream.
Could happen. And second, you never know for sure how long
the hatch and rise will last. You could spend an hour or so fool-
ing around—albeit having serious fun—with a few small fish,
perhaps landing three or four and feeling pretty good. But as
quickly as the rising started, the surface bug numbers could fall
off, and the big trout could move to underwater feeding.

Whether or not I'll go straight for the larger fish depends on
a whole bunch of things. Am I on a four-day vacation and coming back tomorrow? Are the smaller fish at the tail easier to cast
to? Do I have to be back at camp for something more important?
(Can't imagine what.) Do I think the rise will last awhile longer?
Is there another good spot around the corner? It all depends. And
there are no textbook answers.

Pounding 'em up

Caddisflies and particularly stoneflies don't hatch in huge
numbers like mayflies and midges. But they live for longer periods in streamside vegetation, and over time their numbers build
up. Even if females are not laying eggs a few inadvertently fall on
the surface. Trout get to know them and routinely eat them when
they drift overhead.

The same thing goes for grasshoppers. During hopper season
(in my part of the world it's in July and August) trout become
familiar with them as there are always a few unlucky hoppers
blown onto the water. And they usually float, wiggling luringly,
for a long time before they drown. Trout feeding below the surface will swim up and eat a big fat hopper.

We don't see trout rhythmically sipping on these big critters
on the water's surface like we see trout eating mayflies during a
hatch because their presence is more random. But since trout
know what hoppers look like, we can pound 'em up with flies

Golden stonefly adult.

A Stimulator fly used to imitate a golden stonefly will often attract trout to the surface during the stonefly season.

even though there is no consistent surface feeding. Cast suitable imitations like Elk Hair caddises, Stimulators and Dave's Hoppers in the right type of water and trout will come up. These patterns often work well in rough water and along windblown banks.

You also can pound up opportunistic cutthroats on many small mountain streams even when none are rising and no hoppers or caddisflies are around. Cutts have a fondness for flies like the Elk Hair caddises, Royal Humpies and plain old Adamses. The first two are bushy, easy-to-see, high-floating flies, and cutthroats will usually come up to them even when they are not feeding on the surface.

Pounding up cutthroats in small mountain creeks is the closest you'll come to a sure thing in fly-fishing. Cutts in small creeks are a good combination for novice fly-anglers. A place to take kids. A couple of years ago I promised to take a young fellow, Mike Day, fly-fishing. He was 12 years old and had never fly-fished before. He had never cast a fly rod. He'll forgive me for saying his casting still needed some work at the end of the day. But Mike learned how to get the line out a few feet and landed around a dozen cutthroats that day. Although I helped him cast to some fish—there were some risers that day—most of the cutts Mike landed were solos.

Refusals

Trout will sometimes swim up to a dry fly and turn away at the last second—a refusal. A refusal can look a lot like a real hit that you've simply missed. If it happens a few times, there's a good chance the fish are spooked by something.

Their refusals can be the result of a number of things: a tippet that's too thick; an imperceptible dragging of the fly; the wrong shape, size or color of fly; or a poorly tied fly. Whatever the cause, something's wrong. Refusals are not all bad. At least you are fishing a fly that gets the trouts' attention. And they are looking up. Things could be worse. The trick now is to figure out why the trout are turning away.

Run through the possibilities: Is the tippet too thick? Is the fly dragging? What about the fly? Watch closely. If you are certain the trout are eating the most obvious bugs on the water and yet they don't take your imitation, try a smaller fly. If you have the same fly in a slightly different color, try it. Check the belly side of the surface insects. They are often lighter than the top. Are the trout really rising to the species of fly you are trying to imitate, or are they eating some less-conspicuous species hatching at the same time? Are they eating emergers instead of the more obvious adults? Are they eating the spent spinners on the water that you can't see that well because they lie flat? Observe, change flies and evaluate. Something is bound to work.

Putting trout down

There's a problem worse than refusals. The rising trout you approach and cast to may quit feeding altogether. What's happened is a subtle form of scaring rising trout called putting fish down. A rising trout may be mildly aware that something out of the ordinary is going on. Your casts may be a bit sloppy or perhaps the fish may not accept the fly you're using. So the fish drops to the bottom and waits until things return to normal. After about the time it takes to smoke half a decent cigar, most trout will start feeding again. If a rising trout quits feeding after a few casts, back off and let it rest awhile.

Fish that never go for your fly and quit feeding may be telling you some of the same things as refusals. Check things out and consider changing something—fly, tippet or position—as you would for refusals.

Keeping it up!

Dry flies are normally supposed to float high on the water. Some dry flies float better than others. Floatability depends on the type of construction materials, fly style, the choppiness of the water and whether you are catching fish. It seems some patterns always need tending to keep them afloat and others just keep riding high. I have tied down-wing caddisfly dries with a piece of closed-cell foam for the wing that I've dyed brown with a felt marker. If these flies get dragged under, they literally bob right back up. And then there are waterlogged caddis dry flies that sink halfway down the drift and trout eat them anyway.

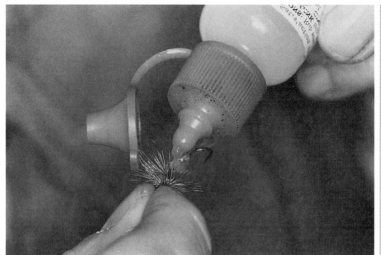

Fly floatant is applied to dry flies to help them float and prevent them from becoming waterlogged.

To keep your dry flies afloat, dry them from time to time by gently squeezing them between your fingers with or without a rag. After gently squeezing the fly, I hold it to my lips and blow hard through the hackles and fibers to remove excess water. You can also remove excess water from dry flies by making several short snappy false casts with only a few feet of line in the air. The snapping action flicks out the water. Just don't get carried away and snap off the fly. Then apply fly floatant or dressing, gently squeeze the fluid through the fibers and remove any excess. Start fishing again.

Strike indicators for dry flies

A perpetual problem of dry-fly anglers everywhere is being able to actually see the fly. On smooth water, with the sun at just the right angle, you can see a #20 midge. And your 6x tippet looks like a towrope as it bends the surface film. But lots of times it is hard to see even large flies. Looking into the sun is obviously a problem, but I find the worst days for seeing small dry flies are overcast days, when the water surface has a bright silvery sheen.

Poly yarn (top) and closed-cell foam (bottom) can be used as strike indicators for dry flies.

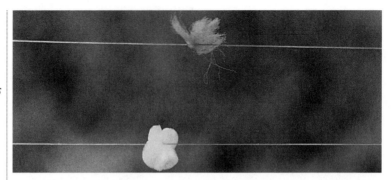

Fly patterns that use white calf-tail hair for the wing are usually easy to see. They are great if you are fishing to nonselective trout—meaning that the trout will eat them. However, if your highly visible pattern is not what the trout are eating, you still have a problem, and an indicator is a great option that most fly-anglers don't use but should.

A small strike indicator is tied to the tippet about 18 to 24 inches from the fly. The indicator helps in a couple of ways. Since you'll be able to see it, you have a general idea of where to look for your fly, and as often as not you'll be able to find it. However, if the fly is very small and the water glare is just so, the fly still may not be visible. So the indicator is watched instead. If rises are few and far between, all you have to do is set the hook when anything rises near the indicator. If many fish are rising, you keep an eye solely on the indicator. If it stops or is jerked slightly you set the hook.

Of course, you can't use brightly colored hard plastic foam indicators. They are great for nymph fishing, but they will spook rising fish.

There are three types of indicators that will not scare fish. I already said you can use a buoyant dry fly as a strike indicator when fishing a subsurface nymph. You can tie a bushy dry fly like a caddisfly or Humpy a couple of feet from the smaller dry fly you are having difficulty seeing. There are a couple of ways to do this, but the simplest is to tie on the bigger fly first and then tie on a short piece of tippet to the bend of the bushy fly. The smaller dry

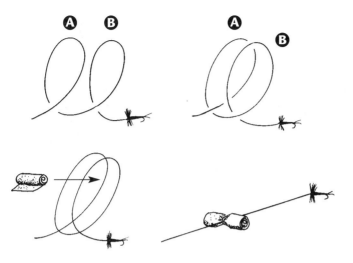

The clove hitch knot is used to attach closed-cell foam to the leader and tippets. Loop A is made first. Loop B is then placed in front of Loop A by sliding it in front (not by flipping it over). The foam roll is inserted and the loops tightened on the foam. Excess foam is trimmed.

fly is then tied to the end of this piece of tippet. Personally, I don't like using a second large buoyant dry fly as an indicator for small flies, but some anglers do. I find that in smoother water the larger dry fly can make unacceptable waves that may spook the trout. I also feel that the larger fly can put spooky fish off their feed. I mean, how would you feel if you hadn't seen a big funny-looking bug all day, and then suddenly one keeps coming by time after time?

Yarn or packing foam can be used to make excellent dry-fly indicators. Some anglers tie on small clumps of synthetic knitting or crocheting yarn. Phentex is a popular and cheap yarn used by fly-tyers and fly-fishers. White Phentex (it's made with something called Olefin) is sometimes used for wings on spent spinner flies or upright wings instead of calf tail. Cut a 1-inch length and attach it to the tippet with a clove hitch. Then trim it down to ½ inch. If you use a clove hitch you'll have to cut the tippet to remove the yarn. Phentex and other indicator yarns are available in specialty fly shops that sell fly-tying materials and fly-fishing supplies. Experiment with yarns in your home, but don't use wool or wool blends for strike indicators because they absorb water and don't float for long.

For small dry flies I prefer to use indicators made of packing foam. You know what it is. It's the flexible closed-cell foam sheeting, usually less than ⅛ inch thick, used to pack electronic equipment. The sheets are usually milky white, although it can be found in shades of pastel blue and pink. The white foam doesn't spook even the wariest trout because it looks like natural foam on the water. Closed-cell foam does not absorb water like other foams.

I cut sheets into small portions about 1 inch square and carry them in a small tin in my vest. Size doesn't matter much since the foam squares are easily trimmed to size with scissors. A small square of closed-cell foam is attached to the tippet, again with a clove-hitch knot. When used as a dry-fly indicator the foam is trimmed down to pea size. To remove the foam, gently but firmly pull on the tippet line from both sides. Usually, the line shears the soft foam. Sometimes the tippet breaks, but worse things happen.

Hookup or long-distance release?

When do you raise the rod and tighten the line on a rising fish? Not too soon and not too late. That's helpful, eh? I don't think any amount of reading or any number of suggestions will help you hook a fish that takes a dry fly. The fish hits, you tighten up and the fish is hooked or not. It's like a shell game—who knows where the right answer lies? If you are too slow the fish will detect a ruse and discard the fly. If you strike too fast the fly will be yanked away from the fish, which simply doesn't get hooked.

There are, however, guidelines that tell us when to tighten up on the line after a trout takes a dry fly—like saying the first line of the Lord's Prayer before striking. But the circumstances of hooking up vary so much there can't be hard and fast rules. If some hooking theories work on occasion, they are confined to a very narrow set of circumstances and therefore of little practical value.

Hooking comes with practice and luck. Of course, you'll hook trout when they hit your flies. Sometimes it will be as much coincidence as technique. Other times your on-stream intuition, honed by observation, will take over and you'll just know when to hook up.

When a trout takes a dry fly, lift the rod. When a fish is seen approaching a fly, there is a tendency to pull the fly away too quickly. Wait a second or two.

I recall one September vacation when I spent a couple of great days on the Crowsnest River. Over two days I had caught a lot of rainbows and was very pleased with it all—some of the best dry-fly fishing I have experienced on the Crowsnest. Warm days, no wind, blue-winged olives and midges hatching, and aggressively feeding rainbows. I was catching them with some regularity. Things don't all come together like that very often. By midafternoon on both days, rainbows moved from deeper runs and pocket water into a shallow riffle to feed on midges and blue-winged olives. (Blue-winged olives normally prefer to hatch on overcast, even rainy, days, but in autumn they often come off on sunny days.)

I have a low satisfaction threshold, and having caught several fish on both days, I was happy as a clam. On day two I actually sat on a large boulder and cast to rising rainbows in the shallow riffles. Pretty slack but quite fun. I was as content as could be. But that afternoon I swear I had two dozen consecutive strikes and never hooked one trout. Hit after hit I failed to hook up. I tried to hit as soon as they took the fly. Nothing. I waited, sometimes on purpose and sometimes because I'm slow to react. Nothing. Too fast? Too slow? Just right? I couldn't hook a fish that afternoon to save my soul.

Then there are days when you hook the majority of trout that rise to your flies. How can anyone claim to have a surefire theory specifying when to strike a trout? Clearly, too fast never hooks a fish, so if you are having difficulty, wait a split second before lifting the rod.

Take it easy when lifting the rod. Just tighten up and the fish will do the rest. If you strike too hard—which will also likely be too fast—you may execute the LDR because it doesn't take a lot of force to snap fine tippets. And sooner or later while fishing a small creek, you'll hammer a 6-inch cutthroat and it will come flying out of the water. Maybe into the bush. Take it easy. Time and practice will help.

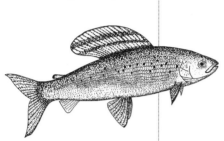

Chapter 7

Nymph and Steamer Fishing

Everyone's first image of fly-fishing is that of casting delicate dry flies ahead of a steadily rising rainbow or brown trout. And then watching as the fly approaches the target and the nose of the silvery rainbow or tawny brown gently grabs the imitation. This is the ultimate in fly-fishing—something all fly-anglers pursue and hope for. The image was promoted by the movie *A River Runs Through It*. Remember young Brad Pitt casting a dry fly to that big rising rainbow and then going for an underwater adventure? A little movie magic with lenses, light and specially colored fly lines helped the artistic effect of fly-fishing. It *was* pretty to watch.

But the reality of fly-fishing is if you want to consistently catch trout under a wide range of weather and water conditions (not to mention fish moods) you need to learn nymph fishing: casting wet flies that travel beneath the surface. Then there's streamer fishing: the use of minnowlike lures made from feathers and fur. Fishing under the surface doesn't have quite the traditional appeal of dry-fly fishing, but it's still fun and it's how many trout—yea, most—are caught on many streams.

Why are we interested in fishing below the surface instead of with classy dry flies? Because trout eat the vast majority of their food under the water.

205

Various experts have estimated that of the total biomass consumed, somewhere around 90 percent is underwater food: the nymphs, larvae and pupae of aquatic insects, and other food animals like small fish and leeches. Ninety percent is not surprising when you consider that insects and fish live under the surface. That fish, especially trout, even come to the surface to eat insects and make life fascinating for fly-anglers is a bonus. I've been known to grouse when trout aren't rising and I think they should be. But I am thankful for the opportunity to fish at all. And when they're not feeding on top, I'm happy to fish with nymphs.

A quick investigation of any trout streamed will reveal that the stones and vegetation are teeming with nymphs, larvae and pupae of countless species of insects. It is not uncommon to find dozens of mayfly and stonefly nymphs under a single plate-sized stone. Scores of cased caddisfly larvae can be seen on a single head-sized stone. There are midge pupae by the thousands. It's a real bug factory down there—and the fish love it!

There is great significance in this for the fly-angler. If the cafeteria is down below, then most of the time that's where we have to fish. Trout, bass, panfish and other freshwater gamefish also eat sunken terrestrial insects like ants, beetles and hoppers. They chase and eat small fish like sculpins, daces, minnows and fry of their own kind. You may not see a lot of action on top and figure the fish aren't eating. But unless they are completely bummed out and not eating because of some high pressure ridge or looming low pressure system, they are a happy lot feeding under the surface. Don't give up and go home because there is no surface activity during your first fly-fishing trips. Try fishing with wet flies under the water.

For as much as several days at a time fish may never rise to the surface because their needs are met exclusively underwater. During the cooler parts of the year trout may continue to feed primarily under the surface for weeks on end—only coming up occasionally to take surface insects during sporadic hatches.

So when no fish are rising, it's too early to head home and you can't "pound 'em up," fish with a nymph or streamer.

Nymphs

Nymphs are what we call the underwater stages of insects. We use artificial flies called nymphs to imitate these insects. So as not to get into trouble with the entomology crowd, we need to acknowledge that not all underwater stages of aquatic insects are correctly called nymphs. The eggs of some insects like caddisflies and midges hatch into larvae which in turn change to pupae before emerging as adults. So technically, the term *nymph* is incorrect for imitations of caddisflies and midges. However, for simplicity, fly-anglers usually refer to the flies they use to imitate the underwater stages of insects as nymphs, whether they are trying to imitate true nymphs, larvae or pupae.

Even fly-anglers who insist on using correct terminology—like pupa instead of nymph—say they're going nymph fishing. You don't hear, "Yup, we're headed to Frenchman's Creek to larva fish."

Traditionally, a wet fly was (and remains today) any fly fished below the water's surface to imitate pupae, nymphs, submerged terrestrial insects and even small minnows. Traditional wet flies often have wings to simulate a drowned adult aquatic insect. Streamers are wet flies that imitate small fish like trout fingerlings, sculpins, daces, leeches and crayfish.

Where to nymph fish

For the novice, nymph fishing can be quite daunting. Catching trout on dry flies gets more glory, but in reality it is usually easier than nymph fishing—especially when the trout are rising. Nymph fishing usually takes a bit more thought. Usually.

You have to read the water and figure out where the trout might be, so you know where to place your nymph fly. And where trout *usually* are is on or near the bottom. They can also be between the bottom and surface, near the surface or near the bank. Although trout *may* be between the bottom and top, unless there are obvious clues like subsurface swirling, you can bet they are near the bottom. So get your nymphs down deep with one or more split shots.

Trout usually are not just anywhere near the bottom in random fashion. As we saw in the trout chapter, they tend to hold at the bottom of deeper runs, behind and in front of boulders, in seams between fast and slow water, and in drop-offs. So that's where you nymph fish. You sort out the boring water from the high-probability water and fish where they are mostly likely to be. "Most likely" being the operative phrase here.

The best way to understand where to nymph fish is to go fishing. The more you fish, the more you gain experience. The more you gain experience, the more fish you catch. But there's one thing you will never accomplish: You will never completely figure the trout out, and just when you think you have they'll do something different.

Nymph fly selection

Before you head out, take time to consider the nymph flies you should have in your fly boxes for the places you're going to fish. Staff at fly-fishing stores can offer advice about waters near their store.

A few of the more popular trout-stream nymphs include: Hare's Ear, Pheasant Tail, Prince Nymph, Zug Bug, San Juan Worm, Blue-winged Olive, Montana and other stonefly nymphs, and sparkle caddis pupa. Many smaller nymphs are now tied with bead heads.

The prominent and accomplished fly-angler I mentioned earlier uses only two types of nymphs: Hare's Ears and Pheasant Tails in several sizes with and without bead heads. That sounds incredibly minimalist considering the multitude of species down there. True. When we dredge the bottom of a trout stream and look closely there are many types and sizes of mayflies, caddisflies and stoneflies. Look again. The majority of mayfly and

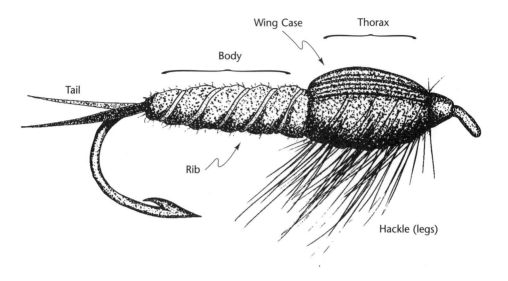

Wing Case   Thorax

Body

Tail

Rib

Hackle (legs)

stonefly nymphs are shades of brown or olive green with a smattering of dark ribbing. Select a few nymphs of what seem like different species in a range of sizes and place them in a tray. Now toss in three or four different sizes of Pheasant Tail and Hare's Ear nymphs. The artificial flies give the strong impression of the shape and color of many of the naturals. It's pretty easy to make fly selection a whole lot more complicated than it needs to be.

    There are dozens of locally popular nymphs in addition to these. Members of my hometown Brooks Fly-Fishing Club have used a club-developed fly we call Black Mink. It's effective in streams, ponds and rivers throughout Southern Alberta, where most of us fish. Two members have used it successfully in Montana. Although it has caught trout throughout the year, it is particularly effective in the late fall, winter and early spring. It's still evolving as a pattern. Last fall I tied a few Black Minks with short strands of pearl sparkle, which seemed to make it even more effective. But early this spring the original pattern version was better. The fly is simply great, but it does have one weakness: mountain whitefish love it, too. But that's life. You can't discard a good trout fly just because less desirable fish like rockies eat it.

A basic nymph fly.

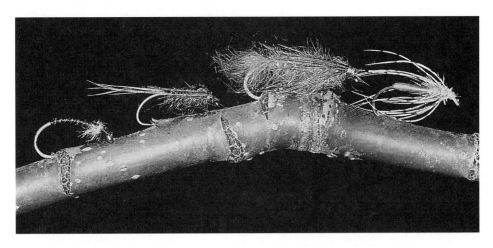

Wet flies, from left to right: midge pupa, small mayfly nymph, Hare's Ear and soft hackle.

Some days, when the trout are off—or I'm off—rockies are quite welcome.

One group of flies underused by many fly-anglers (and I include myself here) are traditional wet flies designed to imitate a wide range of subsurface insects. Two popular general groups of wet flies used today are traditional winged wet flies and soft-hackled wet flies. Traditional winged wet-fly patterns imitate emerging pupae, dead aquatic insect adults or dead terrestrial insects. The wings of soft-hackled wet flies presumably imitate the legs of emerging caddisflies. Both can be cast upstream to rising trout; however, they are more commonly cast across and swung downstream through fish-holding areas.

With time the novice nymph angler will develop more and more knowledge about stream and river insects and will assemble a collection of nymphs and wet flies that works. However, start nymph fishing by buying a basic selection of flies like those above or those recommended at your local fly shop.

The flies you use will change during the year because trout feed on different species of insects as activity changes with the seasons. The fly or flies that caught fish last week or last month may no longer work. That's because different species of insects are active (and thus more available) at different times of the year. For example, in early spring and again in late fall, several species of blue-winged olive mayflies become active and hatch. Small Blue-winged Olive nymphs can catch trout if fished an hour or two before the theoretical starting time of a hatch. In June caddisflies and stoneflies may be active, and the trout will eat the pupae or nymphs that we try to imitate with artificial flies. And just to make fly selection more complicated, different rivers have different species of bugs.

But relax. Don't be put off nymph fishing because all of this is starting to sound too complicated. The few nymph patterns recommended above are tied to give the general impression of aquatic insects, and they'll catch fish under a wide range of conditions and bug activity. You don't need a different fly for every day of the month and a set for every stream.

Rigging with nymphs

Attach the nymph to the end of the 3X or 4X tippet that's attached to the end of your leader. You may want to tie a 10-inch section of tippet to the bend of the main fly and attach a second smaller dropper nymph to this short piece of tippet. A small nymph can also be tied below a buoyant dry fly. The dry fly acts as a strike indicator and also as a lure.

When nymph fishing you'll want to use a strike indicator to help detect strikes. Attach a strike indicator to the line about 6 to 10 feet from the fly. A good rule is to place the indicator twice the distance from the fly as the water is deep. If you have indicators with a hole drilled through, put the indicator on before attaching the nymph. I prefer indicators that are slotted and can be attached and removed at any time by sliding the line into the slot and securing.

If your nymphs are weighted (that is, they have small pieces of lead or other metal tied inside) you might not need split shots. If the nymph is supposed to be near the bottom, then it should be tagging bottom now and then. If not, add one or two split shots to the tippets about 1 foot up from the main fly. Go fish.

Top: A dropper nymph can be tied below another nymph and fished deep.

Bottom: It also can be tied below a buoyant dry fly and fished just below the surface.

Fishing with nymphs

There are many different methods of rigging, different casting techniques and different ways to manage the line to control the drift of nymphs in the water.

The most common nymphing technique is to cast more or less upstream—usually a bit to one side—and let the fly dead-drift downstream. The exact direction of the cast and subsequent drift depend on the relative position of the angler to the water to be fished. Sometimes the cast is almost directly upstream. However, if the run is out and away, the nymph is cast at about a 45° to 70° angle upstream, and then the line, nymph and indicator run downstream parallel to the flow. All of this, of course, depends on the type of water, the opportunity to wade, obstructions, wind and other factors. We can generalize about casting nymphs, but in reality virtually no two sections of water are fished exactly the same.

Nevertheless, there are a couple of common mistakes novice fly-anglers make. They often fail to use enough weight to get the fly near the bottom. Unless trout are clearly chasing nymphs just below the surface, the best place for the fly is near the bottom. When nymph fishing, the fly should be bumping on the stream-bed from time to time, which will be suggested by the strike indi-

Strike indicators for nymph fishing.

cator. This can present a bit of a problem. How do you know if the fly is bouncing or snagging on the bottom, or if it's been eaten by a trout? Usually you don't and you're advised to tighten up whenever the indicator dips. With experience the angler can sometimes tell the difference. Yet even experienced fly-anglers are occasionally surprised when they raise the rod, thinking the fly is snagging, only to find the fly hooked to a trout. And conversely, we all "hit" a sure strike only to feel the fly firmly attached to some fly-eating snag on the riverbed.

Another frequent problem is failure to control the line so the fly drifts freely along. Excessive drag makes the fly travel in an unnatural way. And more importantly, line drag prevents the fly from getting near the bottom.

Wet flies can also be fished downstream on a tight line. The line is cast across the stream or at an angle downstream instead of upstream. The fly then swings downstream and toward the bank, where the angler is standing. This centuries-old method is easy and often very effective. It contradicts previous comments about not letting the line drag. True, but there are times when

Typical nymph-fishing setup with strike indicator at the surface, leader with two split shots and nymph fly.

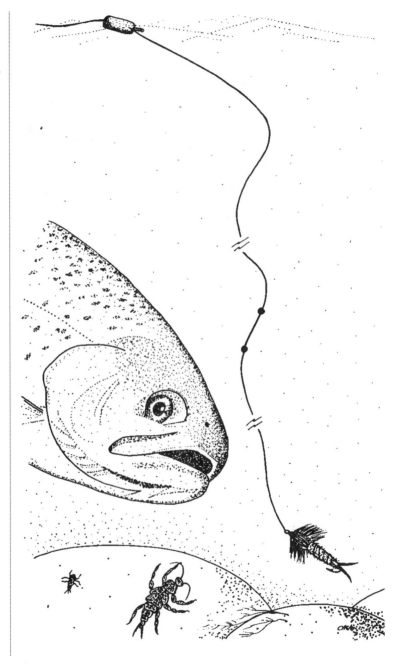

nymphs swim to the surface. A fly on a tight line—because it travels shallower—can give the impression of a nymph swimming toward the surface to emerge. Sometimes this method just seems to work well without making a whole lot of sense. But that's fly-fishing for you.

Line is mended to reduce line drag so the nymph dead-drifts near the bottom.

Covering the water

You'll want to make sure all the fish-holding areas in a stretch of water are adequately covered by your nymphs. It's easy to cover well-defined sections of the stream like narrow runs and drop-offs. Start casting your nymph at the bottom of a narrow run and work your way up until it's been covered. You may have to make two or three casts at each standing station to cover the width of the pool. To work across a drop-off, start at the side

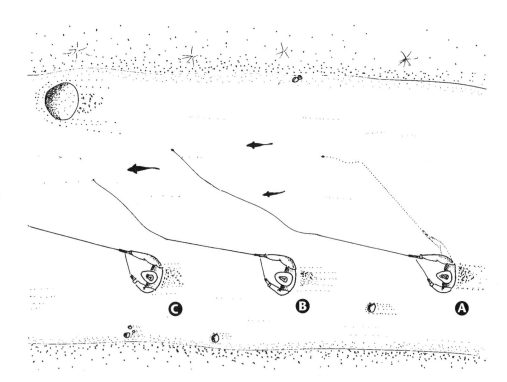

A run is fished
starting at the
downstream
end at position
A. The angler
then moves a
few feet ahead
to B and finally
to C. At each
station several
casts are made
to ensure all
probable fish-
holding areas
are covered.

nearest you and cast in succession across the drop until you're satisfied the nymph has traveled wherever trout might be. It might take three casts to cover a narrow drop or as many as ten casts if it's 20 feet wide. Place the nymph on the shelf above the drop-off so the fly falls into the pocket. The trout are more like-ly to be right below the drop-off than several feet downstream.

But what about large expanses of glides or runs? How do you make sure the water is thoroughly covered? In your mind parti-tion the section to be fished like a chessboard. Perhaps the area is large enough that you can visualize two or three chessboards out in front of you or upstream. Cast your line in sequences that ensure the nymph travels through all squares of the chessboard. You'll start with the row of squares closest to you and then work across. When the board has been covered, move upstream or over to the next game.

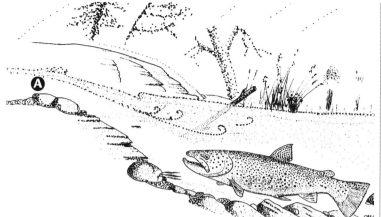

When fishing drop-offs the nymph is cast well up in the shallow water at position A to allow it time to sink to fish level.

When to strike

When nymph fishing with a strike indicator, you raise the rod immediately upon seeing the indicator dip down or hesitate. There is normally slack line between the indicator and the nymph, so by the time the indicator moves, the fish has already been mouthing the fly for some time. No time for waiting any longer. Probably no one has ever verified this, but I'd guess that the vast majority of failed hookups while nymph fishing are because the trout has released the nymph before the angler reacts.

Fishing with streamers

Streamers are effective for catching trout, pike, bass and pan-fish. Streamers are wet flies tied to imitate small baitfish, leeches and nymphs. Some patterns imitate an actual type of baitfish or perhaps a leech; some are tied to give the general impression of something to eat; others can be downright attractors that don't really look like anything at all, but are flashy enough to induce a fish to strike. Many patterns combine impressionism, imitation and attraction. It's not hard to accept that some flies don't imitate anything yet attract fish to bite just because they are flashy if you

Streamers either imitate small fish or are flashy enough to evoke a strike.

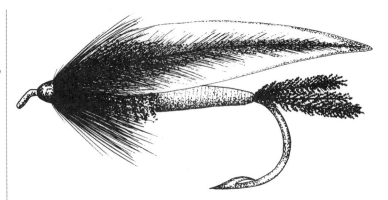

check out some popular pike and bass flies down at the local fly shop. I've never been able to figure out what one of my favorite trout streamers, the Spruce Fly, is supposed to imitate.

Popular streamers include Wooly Buggers in a wide assortment of colors, Muddler Minnows, Spruce flies, Black-nose Daces and other silvery minnows like Zonkers, and marabou leeches.

Streamers tend to attract larger trout because they are a "full-meal deal" compared to aquatic insects. They also can induce aggressive breeding trout to attack. Rainbows and cutthroats breed in the spring and browns and brookies in the fall. All may attack smaller fish (imitated by streamers) to rid their redds (nests) of egg robbers. But one of the main reasons I use streamers is that they are good searching patterns that allow me to cover large areas of runs and glides—often far out sections that I couldn't probe with a nymph.

If you see trout rise when you're casting a streamer, don't reach for your dry-fly box too quickly. Make a cast and maneuver the fly so it swings in front of the rising fish. If it's a large aggressive feeder there's a good chance it will hit the fly. When it hits tighten up. Hopefully you're hooked to a fish.

If there is no surface action and a run looks as if it has a deep fish-holding zone, use a weighted fly with one or more split shots attached about 1 foot up from the hook. To swim the weighted streamer through a deep pocket, mend the line upstream after the cast and let out a little extra line. The weighted streamer will then

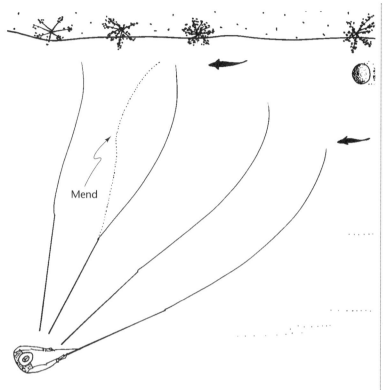

Mend

The down-stream swing. A streamer is cast across the stream and allowed to swing down and around with the current. The line can be mended upstream as shown to allow the streamer to sink deeper. Unlike nymph fishing, a run is worked from the top end downstream to the tail.

sink deep for its swing through the hole. (I like to attach split shot just above the surgeon's knot closest to the fly when streamer fishing so the shot won't slip down. You can also use a sinking-tip line for streamer fishing.)

Streamers are quite easy to fish if you understand where they're supposed to be and how they're supposed to behave. Your streamer should be swimming through the fish-holding area. It should be actin' naturally. We try not to fool too much with dry flies and nymphs, usually letting them drift naturally on top or though the water. But we need to give life to streamers. We are trying to imitate a fleeing fish or perhaps one that is crippled and faltering as it swims. We might be simulating a sculpin or dace leisurely holding behind a rock—swaying back and forth in the current, unaware that a big trout is about to answer the call to dinner.

Streamers are fished on a tight line. They are cast more or less across stream and allowed to be carried downstream by the current. Usually, there is no slack in the line, and you can feel the hit when a trout takes the fly. When downstream casting and swinging, you typically allow the lure is to swing all the way around until it is straight downstream. After stripping the lure toward you the cast is repeated.

Streamers can be fished in winds that are too strong for nymphing. It's pretty hard to cast a weighted nymph into the wind. But you can always move ahead of the trout-holding area, cast with the wind, or slightly across, and work a streamer fly toward the fish. If there is a downside to streamer fishing, it's that the lures are usually cast quite long distances, and you are advised to become a fairly proficient caster before trying them.

The downstream swing

On one of my favorite trout streams a pod of well-educated rainbow trout always feeds on the surface of a hard-fished hole. These rainbows usually have no intention of taking any combination of fur and string we delicately present to them. They've seen it all and they're fussy.

I've been down to this hole dozens of times. It is approached from a high trail, and there's a good view of the upstream riffle and the smooth trout-infested pool. In the pool, rainbows are usually feasting on a surface hatch of miniature bugs or milling around in the film, inhaling heaven knows what species of emergers or tiny midges.

"What's the problem?" you ask. "Feeding rainbows. Isn't that what we are always praying to find? Just match the hatch and catch." Well, these rainbows are damn hard to fool with artificials—at least the standard ones. If they've seen one counterfeit insect on a hook, they've seen a thousand.

What can we do when we've used all the textbook fly-fishing techniques? We've matched the hatch, presented dry bogus bugs in fine form, mended line and drifted drag-free. We've slid emergers through the film. And tumbled stonefly patterns freely along the nether reaches of deep fish-holding pools where the trout surely lie. We've frisked the water head to tail—but nothing. This is how it often goes in this pool.

Early one morning many Septembers ago I tried a different fly and a different casting and retrieve method that worked then and has produced many times since. My brother, Gary, and I arrived at the pool shortly after sunrise, and the rainbows were glorping away at invisible bug dust. I was ready with my imitations of the October caddisflies they had surely snacked on during the moonlit night. (This was the theory we had concocted the previous evening at the riverside campsite, where we watched big caddis flit about the surface. This theory was hatched over too many hot rums. I quit drinking several years ago, but these wild fish theories still emerge.)

We carefully crossed the river downstream and literally crawled upstream to the edge of the gravel bar mere feet away from the surface trout. Sitting on the gravel I accurately false cast my elsewhere successful October caddis imitation over the rising fish. At the right measure I gently let it fall well upstream of the foraging rainbows. Delicate. Light rings. No drag. One cast. Two casts. A dozen. Nothing.

I decided to match the hatch or at least put on something really tiny since I was not certain what microscopic critters the trout were after. I tied on something like a #20 midge pattern, Adams or Blue-winged Olive. I can't remember. There were a couple of refusals, and after several more casts there was nothing. By now I had lost interest in being stealthy. I openly stood on the bank, made the occasional sloppy cast and the rainbows kept feeding on or near the surface.

Now, what I'm telling isn't new. But it was new to me then, and it worked for me that morning. It worked the next day. It worked on another river the next week and into October. It has worked with one particular nymph—the Prince Nymph—and works with other nymph patterns as well. Minnowlike streamers fished the same way also catch trout. The method? Across-stream or downstream casting and swinging.

Gary had caught a few trout using the Prince Nymph in this and another nearby river a few days before. But if these fussy trout wouldn't take the obvious, why would they take this concoction of feathers that looks like no real bug I'd ever seen? I had stood at the edge of this pool for nearly an hour and didn't hook a fish. Frustrated, I tied on a #14 Prince Nymph. And like Gary had instructed earlier, I cast it across the pool and let it swing down and arc across to my side. Bump.

The second cast connected me to a decent rainbow. Cast, mend, swing, bump—hookup. In this stingiest of trout holes I landed eight rainbows in the next hour. This was exceptional for this spot, and since then I've never landed as many fish there in one go. A good morning, especially after the slow start. More importantly, I learned something different.

This method doesn't always work. No method does. But it's always worth a try when other flies and methods aren't getting the job done.

Casting across and swinging a fly downstream is, as I said, not new. Over fifty years ago Roderick Haig-Brown wrote about this technique for steelhead in his treasure of a book *A River Never Sleeps:*

> I started down the pool happily, rolling the fly out into the tumbled water, mending the line upstream to give it a chance to sink well down. . . . The fly came over the loaded place, and I held it there in quiet water at full stretch of the line knowing how it hung, how it looked, how the water plucked at it and gave it life. I moved my left hand up to recover line, and the pull came. . . .

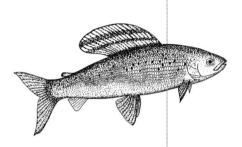

Chapter 8

Fly-Fishing for Pike, Bass, Panfish and Other Fish

Trout are the original quarry of fly-fishing anglers, but many other species of freshwater fish in North America are pursued with fly gear in flowing and stillwater. There are, of course, no rules about what types of fish can and cannot be caught on flies, and just because fly-fishing started with trout doesn't mean we have to stick to tradition.

There are several reasons for the increase in interest in chasing fish other than trout. Many of these other fish are found in lakes and ponds and are often closer to home and therefore more accessible more often. No matter how much many fly-anglers may prefer trout fishing in streams, if they want to fish on a weekday evening or Saturday afternoon, they have the choice of chasing pike, bass or panfish or not go fishing at all. For local fly-anglers in my hometown, trout fishing in streams and rivers is at least a full-day commitment to justify the 3-hour drive. But the nearest pike lake is ten minutes away, and Ken Zorn caught a 43-inch monster this spring on his favorite pike fly. It was easily over 20 pounds. Beats watching TV.

Additionally, many mountain trout streams are not legally open or accessible for fishing in the winter, and spring fishing is often disrupted because waters are muddy from the spring run-off. Around

Author with a nice pike caught in a lake 10 minutes from his home in Southern Alberta and much closer than the nearest trout stream.

my home province, trout-stream closures often coincide with optimum fishing conditions for pike in local ponds.

Another reason fishing for species other than trout is becoming more popular is because some trout streams are losing their charm as more people take up the sport. (I don't know if Cicero, the Roman writer and politician, was a trout fisherman, but he had it right when he said, "Man is his own worst enemy.") While some trout streams are becoming spoiled by their own success—or at least losing charm—many waters containing other gamefish are not as crowded.

I'm primarily a trout fly-fisherman and admit there is a illogical tendency for some fly-anglers to think of trout as more elite than other species. But no one can deny the popularity of pike, bass and their other sunfish kin, and other freshwater gamefish. And anyway, fish are fish. They're all slimy critters; we put all or most of them back; and trout are overrated—or at least no better—for eating than other species. So we fish where we can, when we can, how we can and for what we can.

The "other" fish routinely pursued by fly-anglers in North America include bass, other types of sunfish and pike. Surely, I've missed a favorite or two, but these are the most popular alternatives to trout. I include mountain whitefish because they are closely associated with trout in many western rivers and have prevented more than a few skunks when the trout are off. Arctic grayling are not accessible to most fly-anglers, but they are a great gamefish on the fly rod. If you ever have a chance to travel to the Northwest Territories, take your fly gear and go find some grayling. They are as pretty a fish as you'll ever hook, and you'll catch dozens in scenery that is spectacular in its own way. Enough said.

Northern pike

Northern pike, *Esox lucius,* are native to the Northern Hemisphere and range from the northern United States through Canada to Alaska. They are also native to Europe and Asia. On the Mongolia trip mentioned before, my colleagues and I were staying in the northern town of Darhan about two hour's drive south of the Russian border and just a few hours south of Lake Baikal. One evening we went for a walk and ended up at a one-time sports arena that had been turned into a machinery warehouse. It was full of Russian-built potato harvesters destined for China— but the Mongolians couldn't afford them. We wandered in and soon ended up in the office of the manager, who spoke English. We chatted about this and that to do with our jobs and families, and at one point the conversation drifted to fishing. The Russian manager, who normally didn't fish, had been out fishing the night before with a local and caught many fish. He didn't know what they were, but they had big teeth. I sketched a crude pike and showed him. His eyes lit up and he replied, "Ya!" Pike are everywhere in the northern part of the world.

I fly-fish for pike for a few reasons. Since I live in a prairie town there isn't a lot of trout fly-fishing close by (the Bow River and a couple of local trout ponds excepted) so I frequently head out in the spring and early summer in search of post-spawn pike. They are a blast on a fly rod, especially in May when their metabolism and fighting spirit are tops. The largest pike I've landed on fly gear was 38 inches—about 13 pounds. And let's just say landing it in a float tube was interesting.

Pike spawn in shallow water, and if you look in a few bays—often before the ice has left the main part of the lake—you might see them swirling around creating more pike. I've had limited success wading and casting to pike in shallow water during breeding season. Streamers can be stripped right in front of surface-floating pike, but when they have sex on their pea-sized brains they just aren't interested in them. But if you can find them after the spawn, they are usually hungry. By then they're likely to be in deeper water and not accessible from shore, so you'll need a float tube or small boat to go after them.

A 7- or 8-weight fly outfit is needed for pike. Even if the pike where you fish are not very big, the heavy outfit will help you cast big streamers. A weight-forward floating line will do for most pike fishing, although you'll want to consider buying a bug- or bass-tapered line if you'll be doing lots of big-fly angling. Leave your new 5-weight trout rod at home even if it has a great guarantee. A feisty 12-pound pike will probably shatter your light trout rod, and casting big streamers is difficult on light gear anyway. Pike don't usually make long runs, but when they go, they are unstoppable, even with a heavy rod.

Attach 4 to 8 feet of 15- or 20-pound level mono leader to your fly line with a loop-to-loop connection or nail knot. A tapered leader is not necessary for these big flies. I use about 6 feet of level monofilament leader so I can maneuver the pike in close without the worry of the loop connection hanging up in the top guides, which could happen with a leader much longer than the rod.

The loop-to-loop connection makes for fast leader changes if necessary. Instead of a clinch knot I prefer to tie an overhand loop in the fly end of the leader and use a loop-to-loop connection to connect the mono leader to steel leaders attached to the flies.

Some pike fly-anglers prefer to use up to 30-pound monofil-

Hair fly used for pike that imitates a mouse. A plastic-coated steel leader is attached.

ament leaders and tie flies directly to the leader without steel leaders. Fine. I tried it once and lost a fair-sized pike because it hit from the side and sheared the heavy leader. Since then I've used plastic-coated 30-pound braided steel leaders. They are attached to the flies by threading through the eye and then twisting several loops up about 2 inches. These are then fused together with the flame from a lighter. The twisted loops are heated quickly until they bubble white but not so long that they burn. The splices are stronger than the single strand of leader.

There are not many pieces of fly-fishing equipment that are as mandatory as jaw spreaders and long-nosed forceps when pike fishing. Even when the streamer hook is in the front lip, a pike will usually clamp down hard, making it difficult to remove. Occasionally, they'll take the hook quite deep, and the jaw spreaders and long forceps are a must for hook removal without hurting the fish and you. And a related suggestion: Don't try a lip hold on a pike. I did once. Blood everywhere. My blood. A pike has a mouthful of razor-sharp pointed teeth up to ½ inch long inside its strongly muscled jaw.

There are many published fly patterns for pike, and most fly shops carry a few local designs. Diving deer hair, flash filament and synthetic hair streamers are popular in many places; however, any number of different 3- or 4-inch streamers with a bit of flash will work if the pike are in feeding mode. My two favorite color combinations include brass flash filaments mixed with orange artificial hair, and chartreuse and yellow, again with a few flash filaments. Also popular are streamers that look more like local baitfish: light-colored undersides with dark backs and a few silvery flash filaments.

There is a tendency to use very large streamers up to 8 inches long, and I tried these when I first started fly-fishing for pike. I seemed to be getting far too many false hookups—fish on for a few seconds and then getting off. The pike were presumably getting their teeth temporarily tangled in the long fibers and then pulling free because they were nowhere near the hook at the front. A common solution for this problem is to add a second hook (called a trailer or stinger) to the back end of the fly. However, it is more difficult to release pike with two hooks, and there's a greater chance of unsuccessful release. More pike seem to stay on since I switched to smaller streamers not more than 5 inches in total length with most around 4 inches.

Buy pike streamers tied with artificial fibers that do not hold water when they are lifted from the water. The nonabsorbent artificial fibers drain instantly, unlike some natural tying materials. Although rabbit fur and marabou feathers look great in the water, they absorb lots of water and can be quite difficult to cast because of the added weight. Big flies are not the prettiest or easiest to cast anyway, and you don't want the added bother of trying to chuck a few ounces of water along with the fly.

Weed guards made from thick monofilament or fine guitar string are helpful when fishing through weed beds, especially later in the year.

There's not a whole lot to say about technique. Try various depths and strip speeds until something works. You may have to use a sinking-tip line later in the year when the pike move to deeper cooler water, but most of the time they will be shallow enough to use a floating line. If pike are in more than a few feet of water, adding one or two split shots to the leader will help sink the fly.

There are three general ways to cast to pike from a small boat, kick boat or float tube. First, you can hold more or less in one position and cast toward a likely pike-holding area, covering the water in a fan-shaped pattern. Then you can drift or paddle to the next area. Second, you can paddle slowly in combination with casting and strip retrieves, often casting to the side away from the tube's path. The third is to troll slowly and trail the line behind. In a belly tube this is too slow for effective pike-fly action, so I combine the trolling speed with a slow jerky retrieve. Lots of water is covered this way. If I find an area where the pike action picks up, I'll stick around and drift cast. And if the fish seem localized in a tight spot, I'll try to stay there, which may mean backing into the wind and kicking slightly to hold in one place.

Strip speeds don't have to be fast, but they have to be lively. Sluggish retrieves just don't get pike excited. Short snappy 4-inch strips are usually adequate to stimulate a strike if there are feeding pike in the neighborhood.

So where are pike likely to be? They like to hang out in tall weed cover, on the edge of tall weed beds or suspended over or just inside short weed beds. It's no evolutionary mistake that their color and body patterns are similar to freshwater weeds. They blend in to the weed cover well, which prevents them from being seen and eaten by larger pike when they are small. Pike, like most fish, are light-colored on bottom and dark on top, allowing them to blend into the usually darker lake bottom when viewed from above and into the lighter sky when viewed from below.

Try fly-fishing for chain pickerel, a smaller cousin to pike, if they inhabit lakes where you live.

Bass

Largemouth and smallmouth bass are members of the Centrarchidae family along with the panfish: crappies, bluegills and sunfish. This family is collectively the most sought-after group of gamefish in North America. A friend heard a recent radio report that claimed Americans spend $4 billion each year on bass-fishing equipment alone!

There are a lot of largemouth and smallmouth bass around; there are a lot of folks fishing for them; the bass are aggressive and they eat flies, perhaps taking them more readily than hardware in heavily fished waters. They are a great gamefish and may be closer to home than the nearest stream trout.

At least two features distinguish largemouth from smallmouth bass. First, the end of the upper jaw on a largemouth bass extends beyond the rear of the eye, while the back of the jaw on a smallmouth doesn't. The dorsal fin on both species has two distinct parts. The front lobe is spiny and the rear lobe has softer rays. On a largemouth bass the front and rear lobes of the dorsal fin are separated, and there are two distinct, or nearly distinct, dorsal fins. The two parts of the dorsal fin on a smallmouth, although deeply lobed, are connected in one fin.

Largemouth bass, *Micropterus salmoides,* have many local names including black bass, green bass and even bucketmouth. Today largemouth bass are found in lakes and ponds in almost every state and the southern parts of several Canadian provinces. They like weedy sheltered areas where they have both food and protection. They are warmwater creatures and tend to live and feed in shallow water.

Their original, much smaller range was confined to the Great Lakes region in south-central Canada, down through the Mississippi system to Florida, and in Mexico. Today they are found in most lakes and ponds where water temperatures and aquatic plants will support them and the things they eat: insects, crayfish, frogs and small fish. (I've also heard that they will eat small birds—like pike are reported to do. No doubt the occasional bird gets gobbled up, but if bass are like pike I suspect this is at best an overstatement—small birds are not regular fair. Over a period of several years I spent dozens of hours taking pictures of waterfowl in a camera blind standing in pike-infested shallows. I never once saw a pike take a bird. Yet I saw pike swirling around and

Largemouth bass.

saw lots of small water birds cruising in the same area. Bird feeding happens, but it's likely overrated. It sure sounds macho, especially if you're a pike or bass angler.)

Nonetheless, largemouth bass are aggressive feeders and will eat almost any form of food or bait that looks or acts lifelike—even if it doesn't look very natural to us. Surface poppers are the bass form of dry-fly fishing, and a wide assortment of them and streamers catch largemouth bass. Clearly, some surface bass bugs are imitations of real food items like frogs, but it takes some imagination to mentally match popular patterns with living creatures. Some bass bugs remind me of bar-scene aliens in one of the Star Wars movies—but the bass don't seem to mind. If poppers act lifelike or suggest life and will fit inside a bass's mouth, they are likely to be attacked.

Poppers have blunt or indented heads made of cork, deer hair or plastic. When line is stripped in fast short strokes, the flat front of the head "pops" on the surface, announcing its presence to lurking bass. So in addition to the attractive appearance, poppers make sounds. Good bass flies also have good natural action from materials like rubber legs, marabou feathers and rabbit fur.

Bass-fly colors are a matter of much debate. Favorite colors tend toward bright yellows and reds, and natural olive greens and browns, alone or in combination with white. Some not-so-natural bright colors like blue, orange and chartreuse work at various times, sometimes without making a great deal of sense. Black is the preferred color for night fishing. When in doubt, check at a local tackle shop for the current hot colors.

Bass also attack streamers that imitate small fish, leeches, crayfish and other larger aquatic creatures. Flies like Wooly Buggers, Muddler Minnow variations and leeches—the same ones we use for trout—on #4 or #6 hooks are popular bass lures. But if the bigger flies are not working try hook sizes as small as #12 or so.

The first time I fly-fished for largemouth bass I visited one fly shop and a local sports store near the destination lake. I dropped about thirty bucks on an assortment of wild-looking bass poppers. It turned out to be windy and rough on the water, and I couldn't picture the bass coming up for surface flies in such choppy water. So I tied on a weighted #8 Wooly Bugger with a few strands of sparkle flash—just like the ones I use for trout—and immediately got into an assortment of bass and panfish.

Retrieve bass flies in a way that gives the fly some lifelike action, perhaps suggesting a crippled creature vulnerable to attack. For subsurface flies, start with a standard 4- to 6-inch jerky strip retrieve. Try retrieving a popper in 1-foot strips and then letting it rest. If that doesn't work try more constant stripping. You may have to vary retrieves until you find one that works—sometimes fast and jerky works and sometimes slow and cautious works. As always, check at the local fly shop or sports store to see what retrieves are popular with the local bass.

To cast larger flies you'll want either a standard weight-for-ward line, or a bass or bug-taper line. For those times when the bass have moved to deeper water, you may need a sinking line, but for most largemouth bass fishing, a floating line will do since you'll only need to get the fly down a few feet.

If the bass are in tree-infested water or heavy weed cover use a 7½-foot tapered leader with a heavy butt section and about 10- to 15-pound tip. For most makes of tapered leaders that would be a 1x or 0x. Lighter 2x or 3x leaders will suffice for smaller bass in less cluttered water. Add up to 2 feet of tippet to save the tapered leader when you change flies. The advantage of the tapered leader is that you can change to smaller flies by adding a short section of, say, 2x or 3x tippet.

Bigger flies cast quite well on a short section of straight monofilament leader, but you'll have to change to a tapered leader if your buddy is catching bass on smaller flies.

An 8½- or 9-foot rod made for a 6- or 7-weight line is suitable for most largemouth bass fishing. As with fly-fishing for pike, it's not so much the size of the fish that dictates the type of rig as the size of the flies and the conditions where the fish. If you plan to hook some real hawgs (bass speak) in heavy cover, you may need an 8- or even a 9-weight rig. You can get by with the medium-action rod you use for trout, but if you are going to buy a fly rod just for bass fishing then get a stiff fast-action rod that will help you chuck the bigger flies and have some authority in underwater tree-stump forests and weed beds. I've caught some big fish in weedy water with a soft 7-weight, but my newer fast-action 8-weight levers larger fish out of the cabbage.

Smallmouth bass, *Micropterus dolomieu*, are conceivably the most important freshwater gamefish species in North America. They thrive in water too warm for trout and too cold for large-mouth bass, but can live in water that supports both; therefore, their range is wide. They have been introduced into a few lakes in my home province of Alberta, and there is evidence they even reproduced in one lake a few years ago, which shows they are a hardier lot than largemouth bass, which don't survive our winters.

In addition to being readily available to millions of anglers, smallmouth bass are prized for their fighting and acrobatic ability. And, although their average size is considerably smaller than largemouth, they are considered *the* trophy species of the basses.

Unlike largemouth bass that prefer stillwater and avoid all but the slowest of flowing water, smallmouth bass live in quite lively rivers. Also, unlike their larger cousins, they prefer rocky areas in lakes and streams, and can be found over subsurface gravel bars, reefs and rock shelves. They also tend to hold in deeper water than their big cousins. Smallmouth bass eat aquatic insect larvae and pupae, crayfish and small fish.

Smallmouths—bronzebacks—feed actively in the morning and evening and will take surface flies at night, although casting can be tricky in the dark. Because they feed on a wide range of aquatic insects just like trout, they will eat appropriate nymph and dry-fly patterns. High-floating Wulff-style dry flies and Humpies will catch smallmouths during insect hatches that encourage surface feeding. Their taste for a wide range of subsurface critters makes them susceptible to streamers like Muddler Minnows, leeches, crayfish and Wooly Bugger-type patterns.

Because of their smaller size and tendency to live in snag-free areas, lighter 6-weight rigs can be used. Floating or sinking-tip lines are used for river fishing for bronzebacks. However, because they tend to hold and feed in deeper water in lakes, you'll need a sinking line for the times they are well under the surface.

Panfish

Panfish is a general term for a number of smaller members of the sunfish family including crappies, bluegills, rock bass and other small sunfish species. Bluegills and crappies are the primary panfish sought by anglers. They are a food fish, and bag limits are usually quite liberal because they tend to be prolific breeders. The various warmwater panfish species range from south-central Canada through most of the Midwest and eastern parts of the lower forty-eight states. Panfish live in a wide range of streams, natural lakes, reservoirs and artificial ponds in cities, and on farms. Yellow perch are usually grouped in with panfish, although they belong to the closely related (get this) perch family. Perch are a coldwater panfish, which originally ranged in Canada up to the 60th parallel (where the sunfishes could not survive) from Alberta to Nova Scotia and down through the central and eastern parts of the United States. Most panfish species get full marks for catchability, their cute looks and taste.

Panfish are most likely to be found hanging around weed beds where there is protection and food. They also will seek protection around submerged trees, logs and piers, and will school around rocky points and ledges. Most species are most active when the water temperature approaches 65°F (16°C), and they become especially keen to attack flies when they are spawning in the spring or early summer. Small streamers, nymphs and sponge-bodied poppers are likely to be attacked if they are cast near spawning beds. During midday, in the warmer parts of the summer, slowly strip streamers through deeper water or shady areas using a long leader with fine tippet on a floating or sinking-tip line. Fish in the shallows with streamers or nymphs on summer mornings and evenings.

Panfish aggressively feed on a wide range of foods including aquatic insects, small fish, terrestrials like hoppers and spiders, and, of course, artificial flies that imitate any of these. When I was a kid, Ken Marshall and I hitchhiked out of the city to camp at a local perch pond. For reasons I don't recall (we were either out of worms or just being naturally inquisitive) we picked some small red berries in the bush one evening and used them to catch no end of small perch off a short pier. They'd eat anything. A few years ago yellow perch got into our local trout pond and would readily attack small dark nymphs that were intended for trout.

A wide selection of small trout nymphs and streamers that imitate natural foods will catch panfish. Muddler Minnows, Wooly Buggers, Hare's Ears, Zug Bugs and other streamers and nymphs that imitate the food species of the lake you are fishing

Young anglers can learn about fly-fishing by catching panfish in small farm ponds.

should be tried. Patterns with peacock herl and bead heads or dumbbell eyes give the streamers flash and diving action in the water. Floating foam-bodied and rubber-legged panfish bugs are popular with panfish fly-anglers.

Although panfish eat a wide range of food items they can be selective and have preferences that may have to be matched with the appropriate fly. Studies have shown that the preferred foods of panfish vary with time of year and that males and females may even eat different food items. Ask at local fishing shops for advice about fly patterns and techniques for the particular panfish and water you plan to fish.

A common sunfish, one of many panfish species in the sunfish family.

Yellow perch is one of the northern panfish.

Gear for panfish should be light enough to allow these small critters to show off a bit. An 8-inch panfish will barely put a bend in a medium-action 6- or 7-weight trout rod, but will dance around on a light 3- or 4-weight rod. A floating line with a 7½- or 9-foot 3x or 4x tapered leader is fine for most panfish angling. Tie on a couple of feet of 4x or 5x tippet to the leader. Use leader and tippet sizes to match the size of flies used. A sinking line may be required for occasional deepwater fishing.

Arctic grayling

I have a soft spot for arctic grayling, *Thymallus arcticus,* the only species of grayling in North America. Arctic grayling also live in the western part of Russia and are closely related to the European grayling. They are members of the trout (Salmonidae) family and have the essential fleshy adipose fin on the back near the tail. Grayling have an outstanding sail-like dorsal fin that is long, tall and flecked with shades of sky blue and red or pink. The fin on an adult male is about one quarter of the entire body length and is about as tall as the body is deep.

In North America grayling are common in Alaska, Yukon, the Northwest Territories, and northern parts of British Columbia, Alberta, Saskatchewan and Manitoba. There are small populations in Montana, Utah and Wyoming.

I was fortunate to fish for grayling on two separate trips to the Northwest Territories a few years ago. If you have the opportunity to travel to northern regions that have high populations of arctic grayling, you are in for a real treat. It's not a matter of whether you'll catch grayling, but how many. If they are in within casting range, you will catch one after another.

During both years that my brother and I fished for grayling we were staying at Mackay Lake Lodge, a fly-in camp about an hour north of Yellowknife in the Northwest Territories. Mackay Lake is long and narrow, and there are many side rivers entering it. The lay of the moss-covered rocky land, with its countless

lakes and networks of connecting streams and waterways, is quite *Arctic graying* different from southern waters. Smaller flowing "lakes" become *taken in* narrow, widen again and narrow into rivers before finally enter- *Canada's* ing into the main part of larger lakes. All of this widening and *Northwest* narrowing—at least where we were situated—creates many ideal *Territories.* grayling-holding waters, since they prefer to hold in fast oxy- genated water. They hold where water exits a lake, in narrows between lakes and in faster water as it enters a lake. Up north it is not always clear—and not important anyway—whether you are actually fishing a river or just a fast part of a lake.

    Other grayling rivers, like those in the northern part of Alber- ta, are more like rivers in the south and more like trout streams.

    One of the big thrills on my two grayling fishing trips were the caribou. We visited the same lodge during the same week of two consecutive years. In the middle of both weeks the barren ground caribou showed up on the southward-bound leg of their annual migration. It was possible to wade in the rough-and-tumble of a narrows and watch hundreds of caribou walk through shallows or swim deeper parts of the narrows, sometimes mere yards away.

Although arctic grayling are easy to catch, on our two trips we caught them on dry flies one year and nymphs the next. On the first trip they came up to Elk Hair caddisflies and other bushy dry flies like Humpies, and it didn't matter that they were not rising and that there were no surface insects. Clearly, these fish have to be strongly opportunistic to survive in such a harsh climate with short summers. When they rarely, if ever, get fished, they are not too fussy about patterns. But it seems they have some discrimination or at least mood swings known only to them. Exactly one year later to the week, they wouldn't look at a dry fly. After several unsuccessful casts with the same dry flies that had worked the year before, we resorted to swinging bead-head nymphs through the rapid waters. Immediate success. It was usual to have several "taps" on each swing and hook grayling every two or three casts.

The grayling in northern Alberta come up for standard dry flies like Adams, Humpy and caddisfly patterns. And just like way up north, if they won't come up for the dries, bead-head nymphs on #12 hooks will work.

Mountain whitefish

Mountain whitefish, *Prosopium williamsoni,* also incorrectly called Rocky Mountain whitefish, or simply rockies, are common to many trout drainages in western Canada and the United States. Like arctic grayling they have the telltale adipose fin common to all members of the trout and salmon family. Most trout fly-anglers don't usually fish for whitefish, but some catch them for the smoker. In many of Alberta's streams whitefish can be

kept for the pan all year long, whereas there are seasonal closures for trout. Limits in some American states are generous. For example, they're 50 per day in Idaho.

Mountain whitefish are both a curse and a blessing for trout anglers. Usually, rockies are caught as a side attraction while trout fishing, and aren't considered in the same class as trout, which is a snooty way of looking at native fish that have more right to be in the water than we do. If the trout are *off,* catching rockies is acceptable, and we appreciate them despite our mild contempt for them when the trout are *on.*

There would potentially be more trout if the rockies didn't eat trout eggs. And perhaps in some rivers we'd be up to our wader tops in suckers if the whitefish also didn't eat sucker eggs.

Mountain whitefish caught on a Black Mink.

It's a fine balance that's existed for decades, and since in many waters the whitefish are native and the trout are not, we shouldn't be questioning the big scheme of things too much. They are a part of a western trout angler's life and must be tolerated if not actually praised as a gamefish.

Rockies fight fairly well, and during the winter, when there is ice in the water, they usually scrap with more vigor than rainbows. That makes sense because they are native and rainbows are not, at least where I fish in southern Alberta. Early and late in the season it's common to catch a few rockies early in the day when the water is cooler and they are feeding. Then, after a couple of troutless hours and the water has warmed, we'll catch rainbows and no more whitefish. And that's okay.

There's not much to say about fly-fishing gear for mountain whitefish. Rockies are caught with trout gear, although you'll never hear, "Yup. I had this guy up in Calgary make the sweetest little 4-weight mountain whitefish bamboo rod."

Mountain whitefish will come up to dry flies, but of the many dozens I've caught in the past decade only a handful were caught on dries. Rockies frustrate large numbers of fly-anglers when they rise along with trout during a solid insect hatch. It happened to me a few years ago on the Missouri River at Craig, Montana. Their rises tend to be quite splashy, but at first they pretty much look like, well . . . trout rising. It takes awhile to catch on to the differences, and frankly there sometimes is precious little difference between a rockie's rise form and a trout's. A few years ago, during a midge hatch in March, I cast to one quiet sipping fish on the Crowsnest River. It was going to be the first rainbow of the year on a dry fly. I missed it a couple of times and let it rest until it started feeding again. I finally hooked it and sure enough it was a whitefish. Any number of "experts" would have sworn it was a rainbow.

The vast majority of rockies I've hooked over the years were caught while fishing for rainbows with small nymphs like our local favorite, the Black Mink, which they love. They also eat small San Juan worms, midge pupae patterns and Hare's Ears.

Just like trout. Although they are clearly a secondary prey of fly-anglers there are times when I give up on uncooperative rainbows and try to catch rockies. We don't drive two hundred miles to catch mountain whitefish, but we try to salvage the occasional trout trip when the trout are in a funk and we can't figure them out.

Chapter 9

Fly-Fishing in Lakes and Ponds

The main subject of this book has been fly-fishing for trout in flowing water. But fly-anglers across North America spend countless hours fly-fishing in man-made ponds and natural lakes for trout, pike, bass and panfish.

The lakes and ponds you'll come across vary as much or more than the fish and the techniques used to catch them. There are warm southern low-elevation lakes that are teeming biological factories producing all kinds of aquatic life including big fish. In contrast, high-altitude lakes in the western mountains of North America are less productive. They may be 6, 8 or 10 thousand feet or more in elevation. Depending on latitude and altitude they can be cold and infertile, and the fish-growing season can be short. Most stillwaters are somewhere in between these extremes.

A few years ago the local irrigation district flooded a new reservoir near my hometown, which was stocked with hatchery trout. A few large rainbows got in from the Bow River that fed the reservoir via a canal. The flooded prairie spiked the reservoir water with nutrients and within two years there were all sorts of rainbows over 10 pounds being caught. The largest documented was over 19 pounds, and I photographed my brother with a 13-pound rainbow.

He didn't catch it, but the opportunity to take a picture of such a large rainbow couldn't be missed. This hawg factory slowed down after that, the trout were not replaced and it's now emerging as a decent and stable walleye fishery.

Small high-plains and mountain ponds offer great fishing for trout and breathtaking scenery.

In contrast, some of the small high lakes in Alberta are so infertile, according to fish biologist Jim Stelfox, that they have the capacity to produce only a few pounds of fish per year in an entire lake. In 1994 I fished 6,000-foot Moat Lake in majestic Tonquin Valley in Jasper National Park. My wife, Willie, and I were staying at a rustic lodge on Amethyst Lake we had ridden to on horseback. A couple of other guests and I decided to walk a mile over to Moat Lake to fly-fish from shore. There didn't seem to be a lot of fish in the lake, but a bead-head nymph cast near the random sporadic rises usually resulted in a strike. These fish were hungry and looking for food in the clear cold water. Their bodies were lean, and their heads were slightly too big for the rest of the body, a sure sign there isn't much to eat. To give a sense of the short season in high-country lakes, the ice doesn't come off up there until June. And when we rode out over a 7,000-foot pass there was fresh snow. It was mid-August.

I've fly-fished in lakes over one hundred miles long and in farm ponds you could cast across. I've caught my share of 10-pound pike, many 10-inch trout and smaller panfish. Sometimes the quarry has been hatchery trout that were too stupid to know what an insect was, yet they would eat a pea-sized brown fly that resembled a food pellet. Something not to be particularly proud of, but you have to adjust technique to the situation. A couple of years ago I landed and released two big brown trout that lived in a beaver pond. There were only four browns in the entire pond. Mind you, the pond was smaller than a tennis court and they were easy to see. Let's say it was an interesting lesson in fish sight.

It would seem the only thing these types of fly-fishing have in common is the still water. But surprisingly, they have a lot in common when it comes to fly-fishing. The types of lake and pond fishing I have done have varied very little in technique. I've caught rainbow, brown and brook trout, and pike, bass and panfish all with a floating line, one or two split shots and some type of wet fly—all stripped in with about the same technique. After all, fish are fish and water is water. About the only variables you have to deal with are where the fish are, how deep they are and what they are eating. That sounds overly simple and it is. But, of course, it still doesn't mean you'll catch fish. There are never any guarantees.

Sometimes you can figure out how to fish stillwater in no more time than it takes to decide on the best way to carry your float tube from your 4x4 to the water. There's a trail and you walk down it. There are fish in the lake and you catch them. It's that simple. Perhaps you've fished in this lake before or you talked to the folks down at the local fly shop and they told you how to go about it. Or maybe the fish are just easy. Then there are finicky lakes containing fussy fish that move around the lake and change depth and feeding habits with the rising and falling of the sun in Tibet—or so it seems.

Locating fish in a lake that is new to you may prove difficult.

There may be no clues, and to make things worse the fish may be off when you arrive. If other fly-fishers are bobbing around in float tubes, watch them for a while and then drift over and talk to them. Immediately paddling over and joining the watery flock may prove nothing. Anglers are notorious for flocking together for no good reason. Watch first.

Whether the fish are easy or tough to figure out there are many places in stillwaters where the probability of catching fish is higher than others.

Where to fish

Lakes and ponds can be easy or difficult to read depending on the clarity of the water, the surrounding topography and the structures in and around them. It's not difficult to figure out where to fish when you can actually see them swimming around or when they are rising. That doesn't mean you'll catch them, but at least you know where they are. Often, however, there are no obvious signs of fish: no visible cruisers, risers or swirls. You have to find them. Fortunately, they tend to prefer certain locations.

The importance of weed beds, no matter where they occur in a lake, cannot be underestimated. Recall the three factors that define a prime lie in a stream: ease of holding against the current, protection from predators and availability of food. Weed beds in a lake offer all three. Protection from current is not normally an issue, but weed beds stabilize wave action in shallow water. Weed beds near outlets or inlets offer protection from the current. They also hide gamefish from the view of predatory birds like osprey, pelicans and cormorants. Most importantly, weed beds are underwater barnyards of activity teeming with microorganisms, insects and small fish.

Toward nightfall it's amazing how close trout will actually come to shore in search of dinner in the shoreline weeds. One night a few years ago Art Kruger and I were casting caddis dry flies to randomly rising rainbows at the local pond. We were in

Anatomy of a lake and where fish typically can be found.

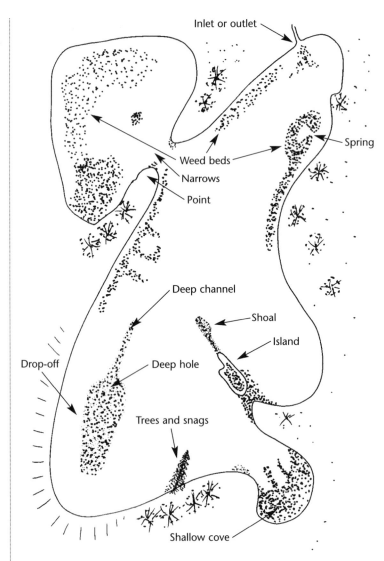

hip-deep water about 30 feet from shore, casting outward as you'd expect. A rainbow swirled between Art and the shore so he cast his caddis to shore (knowing Art you can bet it was a #14 tan caddis) and hooked a nice rainbow in knee-deep water on the edge of the shoreline weeds.

Fish along the edges of weed beds or cast flies into bays and pockets in the beds. If you are floating, retrieve wet flies over the top of submerged weed beds.

Weed beds are popular holding places for most gamefish.

Any sort of natural or man-made inlet or outlet can attract fish. Fish are often drawn to inlets because of higher oxygen levels, an inflow of food organisms and possibly more comfortable temperatures. Also, wild trout in lakes must have access to flowing water to breed and maintain populations. Rainbows and cutthroats will move into inlets in the spring, and browns and brookies in the fall.

Underwater springs also will attract fish because the water flowing from a spring is likely to be cooler in summer and warmer in the spring and fall. In clear water a spring may show up as an area of either increased or reduced vegetation.

Underwater structural variations can attract fish. Sharp dropoffs allow fish to move to preferred temperature zones with little horizontal movement and expenditure of energy. Surrounding landforms may offer clues to underwater structures. If the shore of a pond rises slowly there's a good chance the adjacent underwater is also shallow. If the water is clear you may be able to confirm it. If a steep hill crashes into a lake there's a good chance it carries on downward.

Deep holes and channels in an otherwise boring lake bottom may be a cool water haven for trout and other species when Sirius the Dog Star rises and sets with the sun—the dog days of summer.

Islands and shallow reefs or shoals provide conditions similar to shorelines. The nearby water is likely to support weed beds that hold food and gamefish. They have the added benefit of not being accessible to shore anglers, so the fish may not be as bothered. Points of land jutting into a lake provide the same structural variations as islands.

Shallow bays are the first parts of a lake to be free of ice in the spring, and they warm up faster, promoting early insect and fish activity. But by late spring or early summer, shallows may be too warm for most gamefish.

Narrows have been the subject of fishing writing for years. But serious consideration has to be given to narrow channels of water between two shores as places to fly-fish. As fish move from one part of a lake to another they may have to swim through a narrow portion of lake.

In clear shallow lakes, drop-offs and other structural variations can easily be seen. But in murky or deep lakes you'll need a fish finder/depth finder to find drop-offs, deep pockets or shoals.

Many man-made reservoirs are damnably monotonous. True, some are contoured around surrounding land and have bays, shallows, deep holes and even islands. But my local trout pond is as mundane as a hole in the ground can get. It was made with earthmovers and created as a "borrow" pit for a huge nearby earth-filled canal. It has squarish sides and a bottom planed level by the big machines. According to the guys who fly-fish in tubes equipped with fish finders it gets uniformly deeper out to about 75 yards and then levels out to a uniformly flat plain. There are two fingers jutting into it and occasional weed beds out from shore. But the rest of the floor is covered with a shallow uniform mat of weeds. There are not a lot of trout left in the pond now, but in its heyday the rainbows were randomly scattered. They just cruised and ate everywhere because one part was about the same as another. Your local pond may be similar.

Lake temperatures and fish

The depth fish are found in a lake is affected by temperature and oxygen, which vary considerably with the seasons. Fish depth in summer is complicated by the presence or absence of temperature layers. Whether a lake forms temperature zones is related to depth, wind speeds and shoreline cover, and there is no magic lake depth where layering will happen for sure in summer. Where I live on the open plains, the wind can howl, and I'm told that lakes of 25 feet or less will not layer because the wind mixes the water. Although distinct temperature zones do not form in shallow lakes, the water temperature will still vary by depth, and fish will seek the level where the combination of temperature, oxygen and food is optimal. In a shallow lake, say, less than 25 feet or so, trout are likely to be at or near the bottom in summer. Even warmwater species like bass will drift into deeper water when the temperature rises above their comfort zone elsewhere.

Deep lakes in summer are another matter. Early in spring the water temperature in deep lakes is quite uniform. However, as summer approaches, the surface water warms up and becomes less dense, and at a certain point it will no longer mix with the cold dense water below. The warm oxygenated top layer varies from a few feet down to about 50 feet. Rooted plants, algae and insects thrive at various depths in the upper layer.

At the lake's bottom is a cold stagnant layer that does not have direct contact with the surface, and the oxygen declines there in summer. Little light penetrates the deeper layer and plant growth is minimal. Fish avoid the cold, dark lower depths

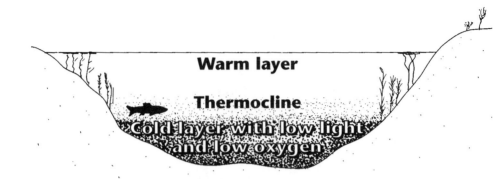

Summer temperature layering in a deep lake.

of deep lakes during the summer months, which is just as well because attaching a fly line to a downrigger sort of defeats the purpose, doesn't it? You will be hard pressed to get a fly down past 30 feet or so even with the heaviest sinking line. (Sure, you could add a bunch of weights, but well . . . you might as well get out your spinning outfit.)

Just below the warm surface layer is a zone of rapid temperature change called the thermocline. Fish, particularly trout, move into the thermocline in summer. Within a short depth range they can find a comfortable temperature, the proper oxygen level and enough light to look for dinner. This doesn't mean fish stay in the thermocline all the time. Most gamefish are notorious for heading to shallow water in the evening to chase small food fish. This may happen because water temperatures in shallow water may become more tolerable toward evening, and they are less likely to be snatched up by an osprey in the low light. The layers in a deep lake mix together in the late fall and are more uniform in chemistry and temperature until the next spring.

The significance of all of this lake–environment stuff can get lost if we don't know what the preferred temperature comfort levels are for fish. Trout are most active and comfortable between 50°F and 68°F (10°C and 20°C). In deep lakes they're likely to be down near the thermocline, which may be 10 or 15 feet in early summer and as deep as 20 or 30 feet or more during the dog days. In early spring and late fall they'll seek warmer shallows.

Warmwater species like bass and their sunfish kin prefer temperatures between about 65°F and 75°F (16°C and 23°C). Until water temperatures in the spring rise to 55°F or 60°F (12°C or 14°C) bass are in a funk, and it will take many warm days to get them moving. But as their metabolism increases they head to the warmest shallows even when water temperatures are still below their preferred range. They'll stay in relatively shallow water during the spring spawn and remain there until it gets too hot. Then during the day they'll head down to where it's more comfortable, moving back to shallows to feed in the evening.

The preference for a certain temperature range is overridden by things like availability of food. You may not like the cold of winter or the searing heat of summer, but you'll go out to the local pizza shop to get a meal if you have to. Same with fish.

Boats and floats

You've determined where the fish might be located according to underwater structure and water temperature. Now you have to get to them. There are two ways to do this. You can either wade from shore or use some sort of watercraft. Wading can be successful and a lot of fun. In some ponds or lakes wading may be the only option because it's not possible to get your watercraft near the water's edge or local laws may prohibit its use.

But if you are serious about fly-fishing in stillwater it is worthwhile to invest in a one-person doughnut-shaped float tube, U-tube or pontoon boat (also called a kick boat). They range in price something like fair to high-quality rods, say, $100 to $500. My new kick boat cost just a few dollars more than either of my two best reels. All three types are propelled with flippers attached to wader boots. However, many anglers add oar locks to small pontoon floats, and some larger kick boats come with oar locks and oars. If you are thinking of buying a pontoon boat and also plan to use it on rivers, you'll need to spend more money for a larger kick boat. Small models are not recommended for flow-

Farm ponds don't have to be big to hold fish.

ing water or at least nothing more than slow gentle rivers. Large pontoon boats are too big for easy carrying, so you'll have to judge which size of kick boat is best suited to the type of lake fishing you plan to do.

Personal floats are not high-performance watercraft, and there are a few safety and maintenance concerns. Top speed in a flipper-propelled tube or kick boat is less than one mile per hour. Where I live on the plains, the wind can pick up with no warning, and I'd hate to be far from shore when one of these howlers comes up from the wrong direction. And then there is lightening to worry about. Whenever and wherever you use floats common sense and caution are essential.

On the positive side, float tubes and kick boats are almost impossible to tip even in the roughest water. Float tubes usually have an additional float bladder that doubles as a backrest. In Alberta the authorities consider this to be a suitable backup safety float or personal floatation device. Check the regulations

Fishing a high-plains lake from kick boats. The trout seem to swim around and feed in a random fashion similar to the cattle grazing on the surrounding prairie.

regarding float tubes and personal floatation devices where you'll be fishing. Kick boats are another matter. Most jurisdictions require you to wear a personal floatation device or at least have one on board. No matter what the local law dictates, carry one anyway.

Another essential safety and maintenance precaution is to never exceed the manufacturer's recommended maximum pressure. You'll have to keep an eye on the tube pressure because the combination of rapid temperature and elevation change affects pressure and might result in a rupture. One day this summer I drove from about 4,000 feet in elevation, where I had used my kick boat for trout fishing in some high lakes, down to 2,000 feet to fish for bass. When I arrived at the lower site the tubes were flabby, and I figured they were leaking, but it was just the change in air pressure. Before heading back to camp later in the day, I let out air until they were flabby again. Halfway home I stopped for gas and let more air out. By the time I arrived back at 4,000 feet, the tubes were fairly tight again.

If you already own a cartop boat you can fly-fish from it, but there are some advantages to personal floats compared with boats. Floats are more portable and they can be packed to a pond not accessible by car. My float tube and kick boat are stored in the garage all summer and always ready to load in the truck, whereas the cartop boat takes more time to get ready. And no matter how well I get organized in the boat, I never seem to be able to prevent snagging the fly line on something in the boat. The line is forever wrapping around an oar lock or battery terminal, or I'm stepping on it. These are not problems in either a float tube or kick boat. Maybe it's just me.

Tackle for lakes and ponds

The weight of rig and type of rod you choose to fish with on lakes will depend on what you are fishing for and where. Your 6-weight rig will do for most types of pond and lake fishing for trout, bass and panfish. But there are exceptions. Big pike and bass in rough cover demand something like a 7- or 8-weight outfit. If you are looking a rig specifically for big pike or bass, buy a stiff fast-action rod. It will cast bigger flies better and handle bigger fish in weeds with more authority. You'll want nothing shorter than a 9-foot rod for fishing from a traditional float tube because you sit so low in the water.

Of course, you'll use a floating line for dry flies and poppers. I also use a floating line most of the time with nymphs so I can quickly change to dry flies if the need arises. I read somewhere that you cannot get a nymph down more than 3 or 4 feet with a floating line. However, a nymph tied to a 12-foot leader with a couple of small split shots will easily sink down to 10 or 15 feet and stay there most of the trip back to the tube provided the retrieve is fairly slow.

I don't do a lot of fly-fishing in deep lakes and own only one sinking line that I resort to if necessary. But if the majority of your fly-fishing will be in stillwater where the fish are liable to be deep,

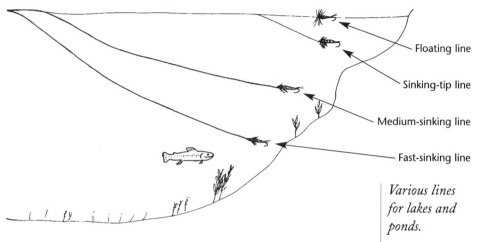

Floating line

Sinking-tip line

Medium-sinking line

Fast-sinking line

Various lines for lakes and ponds.

you must consider buying at least one sinking line or perhaps two. They have different densities and therefore sink at different rates. High-density fast-sinking lines stay down deeper when slow trolling than medium-density lines. When you fly-fish with wet flies in a lake, take along a floating line and a medium- or fast-sinking line unless information about the lake is different.

On calm water you'll have to use long light leaders to prevent spooking rising trout. The leader and tippet should normally be around 12 feet and the tippet no heavier than 4X or even 5X. Shorter leaders and thicker tippets, however, are usually satisfactory on rougher water and when fishing with nymphs. You'll need heavier 2X and 3X tippets when fishing in rough cover for big trout or bass.

Stillwater flies for trout

When stillwater trout are feeding they swim around, gorging on damselflies, dragonflies, midge pupae, freshwater shrimp (scuds), water boatmen, mayflies, minnows and leeches. Most of the feeding is subsurface, but you'll need an assortment of dry flies as well as wet flies. You usually can't go wrong with a standard assortment of caddis and mayfly dry-fly patterns. Just as in

*Chunky pond
rainbow caught
with the aid of
a sinking line.*

streams, trout in stillwater eat emergers and can fool you into thinking they are eating adults on the surface. Emerger flies or the appropriate nymph fished just below the surface might be the answer. And just as in streams, trout in lakes might be eating bugs off the surface, but not the most obvious bug. If your big matching-the-hatch mayfly pattern doesn't work, have a close look at what the rising fish are actually eating.

More often than not you'll fish below the surface for trout in lakes and ponds. In the trout ponds I've fished on the plains and in the foothills, I've had best luck with Black Mink, marabou damselflies, caddisfly pupae with bead heads and leech patterns. Freshwater shrimp, or more correctly scuds, are also common to many lakes and ponds, and these should be tried if they are in the water. In some lakes trout eat huge numbers of midge pupae.

If you are uncertain what fly to use on the lake trout you are after, you can't go wrong with a #6 or #8 black or olive Wooly Bugger, a #6 marabou leech or a #6 marabou damselfly. If the trout are feeding, unless they are very fussy, these flies are as likely as any to work. Try using two wet flies, say, a #6 Wooly Bugger followed by a smaller bead-head nymph.

Match the surface dry flies and experiment with nymphs. If you've seen adult damselflies in the reeds, there's a chance a damselfly nymph might work. Pay attention. Ask other fly-fish-

Gills

Wing pad

Lakes and ponds usually teem with food like this damselfly nymph.

ing folks on the water. Most anglers will tell you what fly is working for them. Maybe they'll give you one. And as always, if you plan to fish in a lake or pond, ask at a local fly shop about flies have proved successful.

General techniques

You are going to fish on the surface with dry flies or somewhere down below with wet flies on either floating or sinking lines. These combinations have a couple of things in common. First, rarely will you fish with slack line in the water. This doesn't mean you will always be stripping in dry flies or wet flies, but you never want slack line on the water that will prevent you from detecting or striking a fish that takes your fly. Because you don't want slack, fishing with dry flies on a lake is no time to have memory coils in your fly line. The line will coil up on the surface and pull the fly toward you. Before heading out straighten the line as described in the equipment chapter.

Second, always fish with your rod tip held low to the water. This gives you complete control of the line and allows you to simply lift the rod when a fish strikes. Imagine a rod held high: the fly line will sag toward you and line control will become impossible.

The rod tip is kept low when fishing in still-water, and the line is usually kept tight while nymph and streamer fishing. Slack is taken out of the line when dry-fly fishing.

Dry-fly techniques

Trout rising in flowing water tend to hold more or less in one spot, but in stillwater they're prone to cruise around in a somewhat random fashion. If there are several fish rising within casting distance and none appears to be holding in one spot, cast your dry fly into the fray and keep an eye on it. If slack forms in the line, gently strip it in so you are in contact with the fly.

The trick with a single riser is to figure what direction it is traveling, assuming it is moving. It may be apparent—perhaps you saw it arc out of the water heading somewhere. But often you won't be able to tell for sure, so you have three choices. Cast 10 or 15 feet to the left, the same distance to the right or exactly where the fish rose. I'd recommend one side or the other. You then have a fifty-fifty chance of picking the right direction. If left or right doesn't work, place your fly right where the rise was. The trout could still be there.

On other occasions a cruising trout will rise several times in a row, and it is obvious where it is headed. If you're within casting distance, aim the fly well ahead of the last rise. That way the splash rings will have dissipated by the time Walter arrives. But more importantly, the fly has to land ahead of the fast-swimming trout.

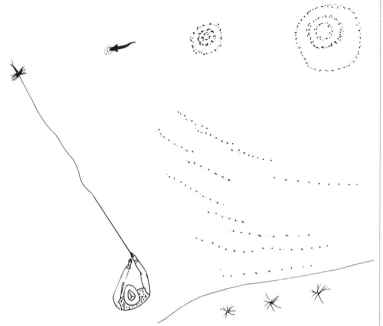

A fly is cast well ahead of a fish that rises several times in a row.

When using large dry flies on lakes, try tying a small dropper midge or caddis pupa on a short section of tippet tied to the bend of the dry fly. The wet fly will hang suspended a few inches below your dry fly and may attract a subsurface feeder that isn't interested in the insects on top.

Normally, dry flies are fished drag free on stillwater just as in streams. On stillwater this means you leave them alone and let them sit. Retrieve slack line that drifts toward you, but other than that let the fly remain in one spot until it has drifted too close and you choose to cast it again.

Another popular method of fishing on some lakes is to skitter dry flies across the surface or give them twitches now and then. Skittering can induce strikes when big caddisflies are on the water. These critters emerge at the surface and skitter toward shore like little motorboats out of control. Twitching dry flies can be deadly. My youngest son, Mike, and I were fishing a farm pond late one evening many years ago. Trout were rising but wouldn't take our stationary caddisfly dries at first. Twitching them was the ticket. Just one or two quick 6-inch tugs were all it took to induce a strike. We caught several fish before it was too dark and we had to head home. (Stream fishing for difficult trout and catching the occasional one is mighty satisfying. But going to a farm pond stocked with fat hatchery fish with a kid and catching a whole bunch has its own pleasures. And if one is hooked badly you don't feel guilty about knocking it on the head, cleaning it and dropping it off at the farmhouse on the way out. Provided, of course, that taking one or two fish has first been cleared with the owner.)

Wet-fly techniques

The wet flies used on lakes imitate a host of insects and other critters that are moving all the time. Some nymphs take rest breaks and hold suspended from time to time as they wiggle along, and, of course, stillwater aquatic insects and other animals stay still when attached to vegetation. But generally, they are a mobile lot, and therefore most of the time when we fly-fish below the surface in stillwater we retrieve the flies. Most of the time.

Assuming you know what fly to use there are two things you will vary while fishing with wet flies in lakes: the depth the fly travels and the retrieve.

Use a floating line, perhaps with split shot, or a sinking line that takes your fly down to where the fish are. After casting let the fly sink for varying lengths of time or countdowns until you start hooking fish. If you've been told the fish are near the bottom or you suspect they are, count how long it takes for the fly to snag on the bottom weeds. Then, on subsequent casts start retrieving a second or two sooner, so your fly travels just above the weeds.

Three things need to be varied in the retrieve: the speed of each strip, the distance the fly travels each time and the interval between strips. That's a lot of combinations and these can be further embellished with twitches of the rod tip or small twitches

Small farm ponds offer pleasant evening recreation for fly-anglers of all ages.

with your rod-hand finger that is controlling the line. If you are not sure what retrieve method to use, start with something simple and change from there. I've had the most success retrieving wet flies in short 4- to 6-inch strips at about 1- to 1½-second intervals. This retrieve has worked with marabou damselfly imitations, Black Minks, leeches, Wooly Buggers and pike flies. I've caught trout, pike, bass and panfish with this retrieve. Sure, other methods work, but this is a good place to start if you don't have different information.

If this retrieve doesn't work, try some variations if there are no other anglers around to ask or imitate. Try bringing the fly in slowly using short steady pulls on the line. Then try stripping faster and increase the length of each strip. Perhaps let the fly sit or sink for a few seconds between strips. Scuds are reported to shoot ahead and then suspend for a few seconds. Try a similar retrieve to imitate the action of the natural bugs. It's worth a try, although the ones I've watched in an aquarium and in local ponds

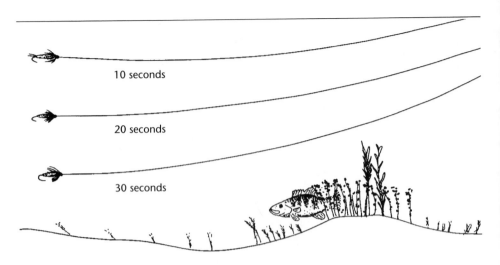

10 seconds

20 seconds

30 seconds

never seem to stop moving. If there are caddisflies emerging, try fast stripping a sparkle caddis pupa to simulate a speeding adult heading for the surface. Damselflies swim by undulating their bodies sideways in a willowy manner. Leeches swim fairly fast by undulating their bodies up and down. Again, try to simulate the willowy action of the naturals with your retrieve.

If you're nymph fishing and trout start rising, don't change to a dry fly right away, especially if you've had some luck with the nymph you have on. If you can figure out which direction a riser is moving, cast 10 or so feet ahead of the rise and retrieve the same as before—assuming that worked. If the trout is not locked on to some food type on the surface, it may eat your wet fly even though it was taking dry flies at the moment. Naturally, this works better with a floating line than a sinking line.

In addition to keeping the fly moving by casting and retrieving, you also can troll a fly or troll and retrieve. These are good ways to cover the water. If you hook a fish make mental note while bringing it in of where you hooked it, especially if the wind blows you some distance while landing it. Then go back and fish the same spot again. The fish you caught could have been a random cruiser, but you also may have found a popular hangout.

You also can drift-fish. Start wherever you want the breeze to

take you and cast and retrieve as you drift along. Again, if you *Fly-fishing for* pick up a fish or two, paddle back to the active area and try again. *rainbow trout* If you catch more fish on the second pass, change your tactic *in a prairie* from drifting to staying in one spot. *reservoir.*

Most of the time you will keep your wet flies moving in lakes by stripping in line or trolling. But wet flies like midge pupae can be cast and allowed to sink with no retrieve. I fished this way in a high lake years ago near Kamloops, British Columbia. My brother-in-law Bill and I visited an acquaintance of his one night, and we got to talking about fishing. Not a surprise. Before the evening was over it was settled. He had given me some chirono-mid (midge) flies, and I was to borrow his cartop boat the next day and head to a high mountain lake near the city. I never did catch any of the large Kamloops rainbows that live in that lake, but then again neither did any of the three or four locals on the water who seemed to know what they were doing. At least they were fishing like I had been told to. Since then, fishing nymphs on stillwater like this has worked for me a few times in ponds. However, I've used a small strike indicator to keep the nymph just above the lake or pond bottom. The floating indicator is also handy to detect strikes.

The cast-sit-and-wait method is simple. A small pupa or other wet fly is tied to the leader on a floating line, cast and left to sink. It is then left sitting still for several minutes. The line is watched closely, and any tugs are responded to by lifting the rod and tightening the line. This may be an interesting technique, and the trout may be damn big, but for me it's a tad boring. Given my druthers, if I'm not going to catch fish I'd rather not catch them while wading a stream or at least casting around from a float tube.

Maybe I'm being unfair because the fishing was slow that day. Clearly, a 5-pound rainbow would have changed my mind on the matter. This long-leader midge pupa method works well for hundreds of anglers in some high mountain lakes. Try it sometime.

The most excitement that day came from shore when a bear wandered through a cattle camp. There was lots of shouting and dog barking. While loading the boat on the top of my station wagon—parked in a bushy isolated trail—it occurred to me that I didn't know where the bear had gone.

Glossary

Following are explanations, descriptions or definitions of words and phrases common to fly-fishing.

Action (or rod action) The flexibility or stiffness of the rod. Most graphite fly rods are classed as having actions like extra-fast, fast, medium-fast, medium or slow. Fast rods are quite stiff and slow rods are quite flexible or willowy. A medium-fast or medium rod is a good starting action for most types of fly-fishing. Fast-action rods are desirable for casting heavy pike and bass flies.

Aquatic insects Insects having two or three distinct stages in their life cycle, one or two of which occur in water. Mayflies, caddisflies, stoneflies and midges are common aquatic insects of interest to fly-anglers. Adults live on or around land vegetation, and after mating they lay eggs in water. The eggs hatch on the streambed or lake bottom into larvae or nymphs depending on the species of insect. The adult flying insects emerge out of nymphal or pupal shucks either on the water's surface or along the stream bank.

Anadromous Any fish that migrates from saltwater to freshwater to spawn. Some coastal populations of cutthroat, rainbow (steelhead), brook and brown trout are anadromous.

Attractor flies Brightly colored or flashy flies—like Royal Coachman, Royal Trude or Royal Humpy—that attract fish presumably because of color or brightness. They have little obvious similarity to natural insects or other natural food.

Back cast That part of the fly cast where the rod and line are lifted up and backward so the fly line travels straight behind the caster.

Backing Braided nylon or Dacron line wound onto a fly reel before the fly line. Between 25 and 50 yards of backing are added for trout fishing. This nearly doubles or triples the overall line length on a fly reel. Backing serves two purposes. It bulks up the reel spool so that the fly line is wound in a larger diameter, which makes for faster line retrieval and helps ensure that the fly line is less likely to form bothersome coils. Backing also provides extra line needed from time to time when a large trout makes a long run and hauls out more than the 30-yard fly line.

Bass (or bug) taper A weight-forward fly line with the thick belly of the line more concentrated near the front than a regular weight-forward line. It is used to cast heavy bass and pike flies.

Belly The thickest section of a tapered fly line.

Blank The shaft of a fly rod usually made of graphite. Blanks are adorned with handles, reels seats and line guides to create working fly rods.

Butt The thick end of a tapered leader connected to the fly line. Also the lower section of a fly rod.

Caddisfly An aquatic insect belonging to the order Trichoptera. It has two underwater stages, larvae and pupae, that we imitate with artificial nymphs. It hatches into a mothlike adult with tent-shaped wings that are usually mottled shades of light brown or gray.

Dead-drift The unrestricted travel of an artificial fly through or on the water. The purpose of dead-drifting a fly is to simulate a natural nymph that has been washed from streambed rock or vegetation and is drifting uncontrollably in the water. Most are poor swimmers. Dry flies are normally dead-drifted on the water's surface, but this is more commonly called drag-free drift.

Double-tapered fly line Fly lines vary in thickness along their length to enhance casting distance, casting ease and fly presentation. A double-tapered fly line is thickest in the middle (belly) and tapers uniformly toward the front and back. The thinnest part of the line is at both ends.

Downstream swing Streamers, some nymphs and traditional wet flies are cast across the stream and allowed to swing downstream usually on a tight line. This action imitates a minnow, an insect swimming downstream with the current or a drowned insect drifting downstream.

Drag (and drag free) When the current between the angler and a dry fly is faster than where the fly is, the fly line is pulled ahead of the fly, and subsequently the fly is dragged along the surface. This is not desirable because most natural mayflies drift along at exactly the same speed as the water surface—drag free. Normally, dry flies are fished drag-free. If necessary, the fly line is mended upstream to relieve the line tension and stop the drag, thus simulating the drift of natural insects.

Drag (reel) Internal mechanisms that restrict line flow from a reel. Drag can also be applied with the palm or fingers of the hand.

Dressing *See line dressing.*

Dropper fly A second wet fly tied on the tippet leader or on a piece of tippet knotted to the bend of another fly. A popular way of tying on two nymphs is to tie a large one at the end of the tippet and then to tie approximately 10 inches of tippet to the bend of the first hook. The second fly is tied to the trailing piece of tippet.

Dry fly An artificial fly that floats on the water's surface. The combination of stiff hackle, floatant and light hook prevents the fly from sinking. Dry flies are intended to simulate natural aquatic or land insects that float on the water's surface.

Drying patch A patch of sheep's wool and hide, about 2 x 3 inches, attached to a fly vest. Water-soaked flies are removed from the leader and hooked to the patch to dry. They are returned to the appropriate fly box when dry. This prevents the individual fly and others in the fly box from rusting.

Dubbing The natural hair or artificial fibers used to form the body of many flies (noun). It also is the process of attaching dubbing material to the tying thread and hook when tying flies (verb).

Dun The first of two adult mayfly stages. A mayfly nymph travels to the water's surface, and the adult dun emerges from the nymphal shuck. The dun later molts into the second spinner stage. Mayfly duns are usually quite dull, at least compared to the spinners, which have shiny wings. Dictionaries describe *dun* as a "dull grayish brown color." However, colors of mayfly duns and spinners vary, and many species are nowhere near brown. Dun-colored hackle capes (feathered chicken skins used for fly tying) are light or dark gray with no hint of brown.

Eddy (or back eddy) A pocket of water in a stream, usually in a bank indentation, that swirls in a circle. Half the stream flow in an eddy is opposite that of the main flow in the stream. Surface insects often get caught in the endlessly swirling water. A popular hangout for trout.

Emerger An aquatic insect just prior to emerging from the pupal or nymphal shuck. Midges, mayflies and some caddisflies emerge at the water's surface. The nymphs or pupae swim to the surface, get stuck in the surface film and the new adult insect literally crawls out of the nymph exoskeleton on the surface. Trout like to eat emergers at this stage. Emerger flies, or just emergers, imitate emerging insects.

Exoskeleton The hard (or hardish) external shell, similar to that of a lobster, on the outside of an aquatic insect nymph or pupa. Insect nymphs shed this shell several times during their underwater stay. At the moment of emergence adult mayflies crawl out of their exoskeleton on the water's surface. The empty shell is called a shuck.

False cast Back and forward casts that allow the angler to lengthen the amount of line being cast before the line is allowed to drop to the water. False casts help the angler change the direction of casting. A few snappy false casts also help remove excess water from dry flies. False casting also is used to measure the distance of the cast relative to a rising fish. Many new fly-anglers false cast too much. That is, they cast back and forth in the same direction and do not let line out—they just flail away with no real purpose.

Film The water's surface and a thin layer of water just below it. Emergers and other nymphs are often fished in the film when they are emerging.

Flat A smooth shallow section of a stream.

Floatant Paste or liquid applied to dry flies to increase floatability. Floatants waterproof flies and prevent water from getting into the tying materials.

Floating line A fly line that floats along its entire length. For most types of stream and river fishing a floating line works fine. It is used for dry flies and also can be used for fishing weighted nymphs and streamers.

Float tube (belly boat, belly tube) Doughnut or U-shaped tubes housed in a nylon or other synthetic fabric harness in which an angler sits. Normally, waders are worn to stay warm and dry. The float is moved with flippers attached to the wader boots.

Forceps Fine, long needle-nose pliers with scissorlike handles. Forceps are used mainly for removing hooks from fish mouths, pinching down hook barbs and squeezing split shots onto leaders.

Forward cast The delivery portion of the fly cast. The forward cast starts when the line has straightened out behind.

Freestone stream A stream fed primarily with surface run-off that usually flows over loose rock, boulders and bedrock. In contrast are spring creeks (or chalk streams and limestone creeks) that are spring fed and therefore alkaline.

Glide A section of slow smooth water. Most are a few feet deep, but some are quite shallow and smooth because of the slow water speed and smooth streambed. Glides can be very difficult to dry-fly fish and often require long and light leaders.

Hackle A long slender feather from the neck or back of a chicken. One hackle feather (sometimes two) is wound at the front of a dry fly to simulate legs and to assist with floating. Stiff hackles are used on dry flies to support the fly on the water. Softer hackles, usually from hen chickens, are used to simulate legs on wet flies and nymphs. Hackle also refers to the part of the fly tied with a hackle feather.

Hatch The popular term for the emergence of adult aquatic insects from their underwater nymphal or pupal form. For example, mayflies hatch on the water's surface and drift downstream on the surface for a few seconds to a minute or two depending on species and weather conditions. Hatch is also the collective emergence of many insects at one time, as in, caddisfly or mayfly hatch. (It is more correct to say that aquatic insect eggs hatch into pupae or larvae—like chickens hatch from eggs—but we anglers use the term differently and in a scientifically incorrect manner.)

Haul, hauling and single hauling A power casting technique in which a sharp pull is given to the fly line with the left hand (assuming a right-hand casting arm) when the rod is powered backward or forward during the back and/or forward cast. This increases the line speed and casting distance and is frequently used when casting large streamers. If the extra tug is performed once, then it is called a single haul. A double haul cast includes both the back cast tug and the forward tug.

Head (of pool) The upstream end of any significant type of water such as the head of a pool, riffle, run or glide. The head of a pool is usually just below a shallower run or riffle and often drops off quickly from the riffle or run just above. The head of a pool is often a good holding spot for trout. At the front of the pool, trout are protected from the faster water above and are supplied with food washing down from the faster upstream water.

Hook keeper A small wire loop wrapped on the fly rod shaft just ahead of the handle. A fly is hooked into this loop to prevent it from catching on streamside vegetation when the angler is on the move.

Imitative fly A fly that imitates a specific natural insect. It is supposed to actually look like a real insect. Mayfly patterns like the Pale Morning Dun and many caddis dry flies are imitative.

Impressionistic fly A dry fly, wet fly or nymph that gives the general impression of an living insect while not actually imitating one single insect species. Life may be suggested by shape, color or action in the water. The Adams dry fly and Hare's Ear nymph are examples of impressionistic flies.

Kick boat A one-person watercraft with pontoons and propelled with flippers. Kick (or pontoon) boats have an above-water seat and usually a storage platform for carrying supplies. They are normally used for stillwater fishing; however, larger models are equipped with oars and are used for floating on rivers.

Larva (or larvae) The first underwater stage of some aquatic insects like midges and caddisflies. Soft-bodied larvae hatch from the eggs laid by the adult insect. These change into pupae that later emerge as adult insects on the water's surface.

Leader Tapered or level monofilament line tied at the end of the thick fly line. Most commercial leaders are 7½- to 9-feet long. Level tippet leaders are usually tied at the end of tapered leaders, increasing overall leader length to about 9 to 14 feet. Knotless tapered leaders can be purchased, or tapered leaders can be made by tying several pieces of increasingly thinner monofilament together. Tapered leaders are required so light flies can "turn over" properly. Level monofilament leaders can be used for heavy streamers and nymphs.

Level fly line A fly line that is the same diameter over the entire length. Although inexpensive they are not recommended for fly casting. Fly lines for casting are tapered to enhance casting distance and fly presentation.

Line clippers Nail clippers or speciality clippers used to remove tag ends after a knot has been tied. Also used to cut flies from knots.

Line dressing Liquid compounds applied to fly lines to keep them supple and clean and to maintain their floatability. Fly lines should be treated with line dressing several times each season.

Lining a fish The undesirable placement of a fly line over a fish—especially a rising fish—when an upstream cast travels too far and the thick fly line lands on top or ahead of the fish. Long leaders and tippet sections are attached to fly lines so flies can be placed near a rising trout without the thick fly line spooking the fish.

Loading a rod During the back cast the speed and weight of the fly line causes the rod to bend backward. This force "loads" the rod, which provides power to help propel the line ahead on the forward cast. The process is analogous to loading a bow by pulling back on the bowstring.

Loops (line loops or tight loops) The U-shape formed in the fly line during the back and forward casts before the line straightens out at the end of both. Normally, narrow loops are desired because they reduce wind friction and result in longer casts. Wide loops are not desirable except when casting large heavy flies. Loop depth is controlled by the angle of the power stroke and arm speed.

Loop-to-loop connection A fast method for connecting a leader to a fly line. Both lines must have a loop tied or attached at the end.

Marabou A fine, dense downy under feather from turkeys that becomes streamlined and undulates in the water when wet. Dyed in may colors, marabou is a popular material for imitating undulating leeches. (Marabou also is a type of stork.)

Mayfly An aquatic insect belonging to the order Ephemeroptera.

The adult mayfly has upright wings, two or three thin tails and lay eggs on the water. The eggs hatch into nymphs that spend one year in the water before emerging as adults.

Measuring a cast Checking the distance of a cast with one or more false casts in the direction of a rising fish. Once in a while a rising trout is in a tricky position or perhaps in very spooky water. The fly-angler cannot afford to make a mistake by shooting out too much line and lining the fish. A few false casts are made directly over the fish or off to the side to make certain that the right length of line is out.

Memory Coils formed in fly lines and leaders because they are wound onto the reel. The coils in some lines fall free and straighten out while coils in other lines are quite persistent, especially in cold weather. Memory coils re-form after casting as the line is stripped in. When free line is needed for lengthening the next cast it becomes tangled. Coiled line also can be a problem when a fish is hooked and line is being wound to the reel.

Mend, mending line or line mending The adjustment of the fly line position as it floats downstream. While dry-fly or nymph fishing, a bow can form in the fly line between the fly and angler. The bow, which pulls on the fly and causes unnatural drift or drag, is removed by flipping the fly line usually upstream. Line is also mended to allow a streamer to sink deeper for a run through a deep hole and to speed up or slow down a streamer.

Midge A small aquatic insect belonging to the insect order Diptera, meaning "two-winged flies." Mosquitoes are a type of Diptera. Adult midges, or chironomids, lay eggs in the water. These hatch into larvae, which change into pupae. The pupae emerge at the water's surface into adult midges. Most stream and river midges range from less than ¼ to ⅓ inch (4 mm to 8 mm) in length, but some species are much smaller and some are as long as ⅝ inch (15 mm) or more. Midges are likely the most abundant of all aquatic insects. Trout eat enormous numbers of midge larvae and adults.

Native Fish that have lived in a particular water since before man. In other words they were not moved into a particular piece of water from elsewhere. Brook trout are native to many eastern waters, and rainbow trout are native to parts of the West. *See wild.*

Nymph The underwater stage of aquatic insects like mayflies and stoneflies. Adult mayflies drop eggs into the water, which hatch into nymphs that live in mud or around and under rocks for one or more years before swimming to the surface and emerging as adult winged insects. Also an artificial fly used to imitate a natural underwater insect.

Palmered hackle A hackle feather wound from the back (bend) of the hook along the length of the fly body. Palmered hackle gives dry flies extra buoyancy and also gives the impression of the segmented bodies of insects like caddisflies and stoneflies. Palmered hackle is used on dry flies like Elk Hair caddises, and on some streamers like Wooly Buggers.

Palming a reel Controlling the speed of the spool on a fly reel when a large fish runs out line by applying pressure to the outer rim of the spool with the palm of the hand. This is a precise method of controlling line.

Palming spool A reel spool exposed outside of the reel frame that can be palmed or braked with the palm. Some spools are housed inside the reel frame and cannot be palmed.

Panfish Small members of the sunfish family including crappies, bluegills and sunfish. Perch are also considered panfish.

Parachute hackle A hackle wound horizontally on a "wing post" at the top of a dry fly. Parachute dry flies float low in the water.

Pocket water Quiet pockets of water behind boulders where trout hold in faster rough-and-tumble water.

Point fly The main fly tied at the end of the leader when two or more wet flies or nymphs are used together.

Pool A deep section of a stream or river. Trout tend to hold in pools during hot weather and in the winter. Pools are considered favorite haunts for large trout.

Popper (or popper fly) Floating flies made with deer hair, foam or cork with large blunt heads that "pop" when stripped sharply. Used for bass and panfish.

Presentation The way in which a fly is cast onto the water or to a specific fish. Presentation includes the angle of the cast, line or fly noise as it lands on the water, and line and fly position as the fly lands.

Prime lie Any place that offers protection, food and a slow-moving current. Fish will often sacrifice one of the three benefits to take advantage of another. Trout will let their guard down and move into open water where they can be seen by predators if there is a good insect hatch and the feeding is easy.

Pupa (or pupae) The second underwater stage of aquatic insects like midges and caddisflies. Larva transform into pupae, which in turn emerge as adult insects.

Putting fish down The spooking of rising trout usually caused by sloppy casting. There's a difference between putting fish down and outright horrifying them. It's generally believed that a fish that's put down will start feeding again after it has been rested.

Quartering (upstream or downstream) Casting at an angle other than straight up or downstream. A quartering upstream cast would be in an upstream direction but at an angle of, say, 30°.

Reading water Examining the water in a river or lake to determine the most likely places where the fish might be holding. Reading water requires understanding what the underwater structure looks like, where the currents and quiet holding places are and where food is likely to be. Understanding this is especially important to successful nymph fishing.

Refusal Occurs when trout swim up to look at a dry fly and turn away at the last moment. The angler will see a swirl near the fly. The trout could have refused to take the fly for any one of a number of reasons: the fly may be poorly tied or may be the wrong shape, size or color, or the tippet may be visible.

Resting water Leaving water alone for a short period. Fish that quit feeding after they have been cast to are prone to start feeding again after a few minutes. But they quit for a reason, and the angler has to assess what caused them to quit and change the fly or tippet, or cast differently.

Riffle A choppy, fast, shallow oxygenated section of flowing water. Some insects like blue-winged olives tend to emerge in riffles or in pools below riffles. Rough riffley water hides the fish from overhead birds of prey. Riffles tend to be noisy, and because the surface is broken an angler can often approach quite close to the fish.

Rise (or rising) A fish eating an insect on or near the surface.

Roll cast A cast used to flip line forward when obstructions prevent back casting.

Run A general term for deeper flowing river water that is not a pool, riffle or glide. Runs tend to be deeper and less choppy than riffles and yet faster and shallower than pools. The bottoms of runs are favorite holding places for trout.

Seam The transition zone between two or more types of water: fast and slow, deep and shallow, choppy and smooth. A seam may be long and narrow, or it may be a somewhat snarly shape as conflicting types of water come at each other from different angles. There's always a seam where a side channel enters and collides with the main stream channel. Many fast runs are bordered on at least one side by slower water. The seam or transition zone between is a popular hangout for trout because they are often prime lies (not to be confused with other fishing lies). Trout hold easily in the slower seam water while waiting for food to drift by in the fast-water cafeteria. They also are protected from view from above because the water surface is usually not smooth.

Shock tippet A heavy section of monofilament or metal leader tied ahead of the fly to prevent sharp fish teeth from cutting the line. Wire or heavy leaders are essential when fishing for pike.

Shuck The empty skin or exoskeleton of an emerged pupa (midge) or nymph (mayfly or stonefly). When insects emerge at the water's surface, the exoskeleton remains attached to the emerging adult for a brief period. A trailing shuck is often imitated with emerger fly patterns. After the adult has emerged, the shuck remains floating on the water.

Sinking fly lines Fly lines that sink along the entire length. There are different sinking rates from slow to very fast. Sinking fly lines are usually not required for fishing most streams and rivers. They are used extensively for lake fishing and are used to fish weighted nymphs and streamers in deep river pools.

Sinking-tip fly lines Fly lines that float along most of their length except for the first few feet, which sink. They are used in lakes and for fishing nymphs in deep river pools.

Slack-line cast A type of downstream cast in which extra line is allowed to fall onto the water. The extra, or slack line, then straightens out, allowing for longer drag-free drifts.

Slick A smooth slow section of a river or stream. These can be very tricky to fish because of the smooth surface and lack of natural water noise. The smooth slow water allows the fish to get a clear and close look at the fly. Tippets also show up very well. Refusals are not uncommon. Quiet wading is critical. *(See glide.)*

Slot limit To maintain breeding populations of trout, fishing regulations sometimes require that all fish between an upper and lower length be released. For example, a 12- to 18-inch slot limit would require that all fish between these two lengths be released.

Soft hackle A flexible feather hackle tied on some wet flies and nymphs to imitate legs. Also a wet fly or nymph that has been tied with a soft hackle, as in soft-hackle fly.

Spent spinner A dead or dying spinner mayfly that has dropped onto the water's surface. Its transparent wings spread out and lie flat on the surface. Trout often eat spent spinners because they are easy prey.

Spinner The second and last adult land stage of a mayfly. Spinners molt from the adult duns in vegetation near the water. Spinners breed shortly after molting, and females drop eggs onto the water's surface. Spinners have shiny wings and prior to mating "spin" up and down in the air close to the water's edge.

Spring creek Productive streams fed solely or primarily from underground springs with alkaline water. They run clear most of the time, even after rains. They have more constant water temperatures and often stay open throughout the winter. Also called limestone or chalk streams.

Steelhead A type of rainbow trout that is born in freshwater, migrates to saltwater and then returns to freshwater to spawn. *(See anadromous.)*

Stonefly An aquatic insect belonging to the order Plecoptera that lives in stony fast-moving water. Stoneflies vary widely in size with some species being very large—up to 2 inches (50 mm) or more in length. They have one underwater stage fly-fishers imitate with nymphs. Most hatch into adults by crawling underwater to shore. Trout eat adults that accidentally fall onto the water from bank bushes and dying females that fall to the water after laying eggs.

Strike indicator A small white or colored float made from cork, plastic or yarn. Also a dry fly attached to the leader when nymph fishing. The indicator helps show when a fish has taken a nymph.

Streamer A wet fly imitating a small fish or leech. Streamers are usually quite large and normally cast across and downstream.

Structure Underwater stuff like rock ledges, deep pockets, boulders, gravel bars, sunken logs and trees. If the bottom of a lake or river is anything but dead flat, then it has structure. In a stream, structure is important to trout because it provides holding and hiding places.

Surgeon's knot Knot used to tie tippets to leaders and tippet sections together.

Tapered leader A clear monofilament leader tied at the end of the fly line. It tapers from the thick butt end, which is attached to the fly line, to the thin end where the fly or tippet leader is attached.

Tail (of pool, etc) The downstream end of any significant type of water, such as the tail of a pool, riffle, run or glide.

Terrestrial (or land) insects Insects that spend their entire life on land or in the air—except when they fall onto the water. Terrestrial insects include ants, grasshoppers, beetles, flies, bees and leafhoppers or jassids. Although none of their life stages actually live in water, they are found along rivers and streams and are commonly eaten by fish.

Thermocline A zone of rapid temperature change between the cold bottom layer and warmer surface water of a deep lake in summer. Many fish live in the thermocline in summer because they prefer the cooler water. Oxygen levels in the thermocline are adequate to support insects, plants and fish.

Thorax The midsection of a nymph between the head and the abdomen. Insect legs are attached to the thorax.

Thorax pattern A dry fly with the flotation hackles tied around the middle instead of near the head or eye of the hook.

Tippet (or tippet leader) Sections of level monofilament fishing line tied to the end of a tapered leader. Usually, 1 to 3 feet of tippet are tied to the leader. Manufacturers have developed specialty tippet lines that are much thinner for their strength than standard spinning monofilament. Tippet line is sold in 25- to 30-meter spools.

Tip-top The uppermost line guide on a fly rod.

Turn over The orderly straightening out of the leader and fly at the end of the cast. Tapered leaders are used so the leader and dry fly continue moving forward and completely straighten out. If a fly and leader does not turn over, it piles up.

Weight (of lines and rods) Fly lines are classed by the weight of the first 30 feet of the fly line. Weight classes range from 1 to 13 (or 15 depending on which reference you read). Lines are normally matched to rods with similar numbers. The heavier the line, the higher the weight-code number.

Weighted fly Some nymphs, streamers and wet flies have lead or other metal weight wound around the hook shank when the fly is tied. The extra weight helps get the fly to the bottom. Flies also can also be weighted with one or more split shots attached to the leader or tippet.

Weight-forward fly line A tapered fly line with the heaviest part (belly) near the front of the line. It tapers to a narrow diameter toward the front and back from the thickest section. Special weight-forward tapered lines (bass or bug tapers) have the heavy section more concentrated near the front and are used to cast heavy pike and bass flies.

Wet fly Any fly fished below the water's surface that imitates pupae, nymphs, submerged terrestrial insects or small minnows. Traditionally, wet flies were usually tied to imitate sunken terrestrial insects or dead adult aquatic insects like sunken bees or dead mayflies. More specific terms (nymph, pupa, streamer) are used for most wet flies, which are tied to represent the living underwater stages of insects and animals.

Wild fish Fish that breed naturally, hatch and grow in the water where they live. Brook trout first transplanted decades ago in western waters now maintain themselves naturally and are called wild. Trout can be wild if not native. *(See native.)*

Wind knot An unwanted knot that forms in the leader during casting. A complete loop forms in the leader and the fly passes through. Wind knots tend to form when wind blows the leader off course, but may also be a sign of poor casting technique.

Further Reading and Viewing

While many fine fly-fishing books and videos are available, the following have proved especially helpful for me on many occasions.

Books

Cordes, Ron and Gary LaFontaine. *Pocket Guide to Fly Fishing the Lakes.* Troutbeck and Greycliff, 1993.

Hafele, Rick and Dave Hughes. *The Complete Book of Western Hatches.* Portland: Frank Amato Publications, 1981.

Hughes, Dave. *Handbook of Hatches.* Harrisburg: Stackpole, 1987.

McClane, A. J. *McClane's Standard Fishing Encyclopedia and International Fishing Guide.* New York: Holt, Rinehart and Winston, 1965.

Murray, Harry. *Fly Fishing for Smallmouth Bass.* New York: Lyons and Burford, 1989.

Pobst, Dick. *Trout Stream Insects.* New York: Lyons and Burford, Publishers, 1990.

Scammell, Bob. *The Phenological Fly.* Red Deer: Johnson Gorman, 1996.

Whitlock, Dave. *Guide to Aquatic Trout Food.* New York: Lyons and Burford, 1982.

Waterman, Charlie. *Black Bass and the Fly Rod.* Harrisburg: Stackpole, 1993.

Videos

Basic Fly Casting. With Doug Swisher. Mastery Learning Systems, n.d.

Fly Tying Basics. With Jack Dennis. The Jack Dennis Fly Fishing Video Library, 1987.

Fly Fishing for Trout. With Gary Borger. Sportsman's Video Collection, n.d.

Flyfishing for Pike. With Larry Dahlberg. In-Fisherman Communications, 1989.

Formula for Success: Trout. With Doug Swisher, Gary Borger and Rick Hafele. Field and Stream/Leisure Time Products, n.d.

Jack Dennis' Learning to Fly Fish for Trout. With Jack Dennis, Gary LaFontaine, Mike Lawson and Dan Abrams. The Jack Dennis Fly Fishing Video Library, 1987.

Nymphing. With Gary Borger. Borger Films, 1982.

Tying Trout Flies. With Gary Borger. Mastery Video Series, 1992.

Index